Cross-Cultural Communication and Aging in the United States

LEA'S COMMUNICATION SERIES
Jennings Bryant/Dolf Zillmann, General Editors

Selected titles in Intercultural and Interpersonal Communication (W. Barnett Pearce and John Daly, Advisory Editors) include:

Noor Al-Deen • *Cross-Cultural Communication and Aging in the United States*

Berger • *Planning Strategic Interaction: Attaining Goals Through Communicative Action*

Casmir • *Communication in Eastern Europe: The Role of History, Culture, and Media in Contemporary Conflicts*

Daly/Wiemann • *Strategic Interpersonal Communication*

Leeds-Hurwitz • *Semiotics and Communication: Signs, Codes, Cultures*

Segerstrale/Molnar • *Nonverbal Communication: Where Nature Meets Culture*

For a complete list of other titles in LEA's Communication Series, please contact Lawrence Erlbaum Associates, Publishers.

Cross-Cultural Communication and Aging in the United States

Edited by

Hana S. Noor Al-Deen
University of North Carolina at Wilmington

Foreword by
Jennings Bryant
University of Alabama

LEA **LAWRENCE ERLBAUM ASSOCIATES, PUBLISHERS**
1997   Mahwah, New Jersey   London

Lawrence Erlbaum Associates, Inc., Publishers
10 Industrial Avenue
Mahwah, New Jersey 07430

Library of Congress Cataloging-in-Publication-Data

Cross-cultural communication & aging in the United States / edited by Hana S.
   Noor Al-Deen ; foreword by Jennings Bryant.
          p.   cm.
   Includes bibliographical references and index.
   ISBN 0-8058-2294-1 (c : alk. paper). —ISBN 0-8058-2295-X (p : alk. paper)
   1. Aged—Communication—United States. 2. Minority aged—United States.
3. Intercultural communication—United States. 4. Intergenerational relations—
United States. 5. Aged in popular culture—United States. 6. Pluralism (Social
sciences)—United States. I. Noor Al-Deen, Hana S.
   HQ1064.U5C77 1997
   305.26'0973—dc21   97-6306
                                                                  CIP

Books published by Lawrence Erlbaum Associates are printed on
acid-free paper, and their bindings are chosen for strength and durability.

Printed in the United States of America
10 9 8 7 6 5 4 3 2 1

*In memory of my parents who taught me respect for elders.
To my brothers, Ghazi and Kenan, and to my sister, Wajeda,
for their love. To my husband, Omar, and to my yorkshire, Fafy,
who have nurtured me with unconditional love and support.*

Contents

Preface

The 'graying of America' has been progressing rapidly. This dramatic increase in the age of the U.S. population can be underscored by the fact that in 1996 the first of the baby boomers crossed into their 50s and the rest of them will follow within the next two decades. According to *Aging America: Trends and Projections* (1991),[1] about 22% of the U.S. population will be age 65+ by 2030. This shift in populace will draw greater attention during the following decades due to this group's economic, social, and political clout.

The communication discipline has devoted increasing energy toward the study of aging in recent years, yet most communication scholarship has insufficiently addressed a crucial factor in communicative relationships—culture. Other disciplines in the social sciences have included culture, but not communication, in their study of aging. Hence, this book has opted for combining three powerful elements (communication, aging, and culture) that have an increasingly profound impact on this multicultural society.

The book focuses on older Americans in various communicative contexts within the framework of their cultures. It is composed of original research by contributors who are experts in their fields. The greatest significance of this work stems from the fact that much of the older population in the United States has been negatively viewed and treated. This stands in stark contrast to most of the world, which holds elders in high esteem. We can definitely take a page from them and provide our elders with the opportunity to live the autumn of their lives with dignity and respect. This research may ultimately serve such a purpose and enhance the quality of life for upcoming generations of elders.

---

[1] U.S. Department of Health and Human Services. (1991). *Aging America: Trends and Projections* (DHHS Publication No. 91-28001). Washington, DC: Author.

In this volume, the term *cross-cultural communication* is used inter-
changeably with the term *intercultural communication* because both deal
with people from different cultural backgrounds. Co-culture is employed
in lieu of subculture, thereby giving equal weight to all cultures within the
United States, regardless of size or power of the group. After all, the U.S.
Constitution states, "We the People of the United States."

This book is designed as a reader for college students in communication,
gerontology, anthropology, sociology, and any related fields. It can also be
used by professionals in gerontological service areas, by libraries, and as a
personal reference.

The chapters are grouped into four parts, with each part presenting a
sample of related topics. Part I deals with some perspectives in cross-cultural communication and aging. Chapter 1 presents a cross-cultural communication perspective for research about elders in American society.
Chapter 2 examines age-related female coping strategies as reflected by
women's interview responses about their aging concerns. Chapter 3 explores the opportunities and problems associated with the use of infotainment technologies by older adults.

Part II presents cross-generational communication and aging. Chapter 4
explores how cross-generational continuity is promoted through the use of
Hawaiian Creole English. Chapter 5 assesses the quality of communication
that younger Arab Americans offer their elders. Chapter 6 presents an
examination of mentoring relationships among elders, their children, and
grandchildren in a Mormon community.

Part III demonstrates cross-cultural communication and aging within an
organizational setting. Chapter 7 describes societal and organizational
values that have contributed to views of elders. Chapter 8 reports a field
study of the nursing home and retirement community from a cross-cultural
communication perspective. Chapter 9 explores the impact of changing
sociocultural perspectives and the public health care system of Indian
Health Service (IHS) on aging Native American women's roles.

Finally, Part IV incorporates popular culture and aging. Chapter 10
examines commonly constituted images of older men, women, and magical
beings in a wide variety of folk and fairy tales. Chapter 11 analyzes cultural
models of aging contained in various contemporary self-help works that
treat aging. Chapter 12 examines the prevalence and role of older people in
daytime television soap operas across ethnic lines. Chapter 13 assesses the
portrayal of aging in daytime television commercials to determine whether
recognition of the new gray market has visibly improved the treatment of
an aging population in commercials.

ACKNOWLEDGMENTS

This project is the outcome of efforts by many individuals whom I wish to thank sincerely. My deepest gratitude is extended to the contributing authors of this book. Their hard work and efficiency made the task easier.

To Jennings Bryant, I am profoundly indebted for his insightful advice, geniune encouragement, and totally professional demeanor. Without his considerable help, this project would not have been viable. I am also grateful to him for writing the Foreword for this book.

My sincere thanks are conveyed to Lawrence Erlbaum Associates for giving me the opportunity to publish this book. I would like to extend my deepest appreciation to Marcy B. Pruiksma, Book Production Editor, for her diligence, proficiency, and pleasantness. Also, I would like to thank Kathleen M. O'Malley, Acquisitions Editor, Sara T. Scudder, Editorial Assistant, Sharon Levy, Promotion Director, and all of the other individuals who were directly involved in this project for their zealousness.

A final note of thanks goes to the College of Arts and Sciences at the University of North Carolina at Wilmington for providing essential financial support for this project.

—Hana S. Noor Al-Deen

Foreword

Jennings Bryant
The University of Alabama

A sampling of excerpts from the popular press highlights the timeliness and importance of *Cross-Cultural Communication and Aging in the United States.* Two dimensions—aging and diversity—are emphasized in these quotations. The beauty of the present volume is that it focuses on the union of these two critical dimensions and does so from a communication perspective.

Aging

• "In simple terms, the baby boomers are getting old, a phenomenon many experts call the 'age wave'. In fact, the fastest-growing minority in the United States is the 'very old' (the 85-and-older population), a group that is projected to expand from 3.1 million in 1990 to approximately 17.7 million by the year 2050" (Nieman, 1994, p. 16).

• "When baby boomers start to hit 65 in 2011 the impact on society will be 'the equivalent of the waves of immigrants who came to the country, or the urbanization and industrialization of the country'" (Sweet, 1996, p. 3).

• "Been to Florida lately? You may not realize it, but you have seen the future—America's future, about two decades from now. The gray wave of senior citizens that fills the state's streets, beaches, parks, hotels, shopping malls, hospitals, Social Security offices, and senior centers is, of course, an anomaly created by our long tradition of retiring to Florida. Nearly one in five Floridians is over sixty-five. But early in the next century a figure like that won't be exceptional. By 2025 at the latest the proportion of all Americans who are elderly will be the same as the proportion in Florida today. America, in effect, will become a nation of Floridas—and then keep aging" (Peterson, 1996, p. 55).

• "Centenarians—those who have celebrated 100 or more birth-days—are the fastest-growing segment of American society" (Centenarians get head start, 1996, p. 10).

Diversity

• "By 2020, a new group will assume majority status in California: Latinos. Anglo Americans will weigh in at around one-third of the popula-tion. Asian- and African-Americans combined will make up no more than 15% of the state. Like all major demographic shifts, this one sorely tests the very assumptions of our society . .... The unrecognized genius of America has always been the essentially unfinished nature of its cultural identity. Despite the many attempts to link 'Americanness' to a single racial group, America's promise still lies in its liberation from Old World notions that political and ethnic identities are one and the same. The advent of the post-minority era forces us to re-explore what it is to be American" (Hayes-Bautista & Rodriguez, 1995, p. 1).

• "Estimates run from four million to nearly six million Muslims living in the United States—more Muslims than Episcopalians—nearly as many Muslims as Jews" (Islam surpasses Episcopalianism in U.S. membership, 1996, p. 2).

• "The key group is the Hispanics, whose numbers are now just about equal to the blacks. They are assimilating into the American mainstream, though more slowly, for all sorts of reasons, than immigrant groups in the past. Most Latin American immigrants have had little connection with Latin American culture, about which they know nothing—in this respect, they resemble the Italian immigrants of yesteryear" (Kristol, 1995, p. 73).

• "As for the fastest growing minority in the United States, the Asians, they are succeeding economically while disappearing as a racial-ethnic group at the same time—and at a rate unprecedented in American history" (Kristol, 1995, p. 73).

• "I am delighted at the presence of Jewish feminists who wish to partici-pate, on a more equal basis, in rituals and observances, and who study Hebrew and the Talmud . . . but I simply do not know how to cope with a learned, observant, lesbian rabbi. It is all very confusing" (Kristol, 1995, p. 73).

Aging Plus Diversity

• "In 2030 only about 15 percent of the over-sixty-five population will be nonwhite. But about 25 percent of younger Americans will be nonwhite. This will create a potentially explosive situation in which largely white senior Boomers will be increasingly reliant on overtaxed minority workers" (Peterson, 1996, p. 55).

• "When we consider the great demographic shifts [aging and diversity] that will shape our national future over the next fifty years, we are speaking not of a mere transition but of a genuine transformation" (Peterson, 1996, p. 55).

As if the conjunction of these two major social and demographic trends was not enough, the milieu in which these dramatic shifts are taking place is a social system unlike any other in history—an advanced information society. Dramatic changes in the nature of communication and our technological information infrastructure are also causing us to rethink civilization as we have known it. "Civilization now stands at one of those great historic junctures that arise only a few times in a millennium. The central organizing forces of society are being reshaped by powerful new technologies of light and silicon. But in what ways, and to what end" (Burstein & Kline, 1995, p. 1)?

Many of the most important questions and issues that emerge from the juxtaposition of these powerful social trajectories are communication questions and issues. And those are just what *Cross-Cultural Communication and Aging in the United States* is designed to address. Considerable intellectual energy has been consumed in the preparation of these chapters, and sound theoretical insights are frequently offered.

Moreover, many of the issues dealt with in this book have practical as well as theoretical implications. A recent book designed to provide insights regarding the practical effects of aging, diversity, and informationalization—*Future in Sight: 100 of the Most Important Trends, Implications and Predictions for the New Millennium* (Minkin, 1996)—indicates that among the handful of industries that will be most affected by these changes in the next millennium are media and entertainment, home computers and information, and advertising and marketing services. A number of the chapters in this volume are extremely useful in addressing the future of these practical communication enterprises.

It is rare for a book to feature sufficient vision to struggle with all of these diverse tributaries in an integrated fashion. Hana Noor Al-Deen is to be congratulated on the quality of her vision and the contributors on the quality of their execution.

REFERENCES

Burstein, D., & Kline, D. (1995). *Road warriors: Dreams and nightmares along the information highway.* New York: Dutton.

Centenarians get head start. (1996, March 8). *Chicago Sun-Times*, p. 10.

Hayes-Bautista, D. E., & Rodgriguez, G. (1995, October 22). America's changing face. *Milwaukee Journal Sentinel*, p. 1.

Islam surpasses Episcopalianism in U.S. membership. (1995, December 18). *Cable News Network Transcript #220–14, 1–4.*

Kristol, I. (1995, November). Ethnic fragmentation and social conditions. *American Jewish Committee Commentary, 100,* 73.

Minkin, B. H. (1996). *Future in sight: 100 of the most important trends, implications and predictions for the new millennium.* New York: Macmillan.

Nieman, D. C. (1994, November). It's never too late . . . to change lifestyle habits. *Vibrant Life, 10,* 16.

Peterson, P. G. (1996, May). Will America grow up before it grows old? *The Atlantic Monthly, 277*(5), 55–63.

Sweet, L. (1996, May 21). Study cites challenge as baby boomers age. *Chicago Sun-Times,* p. 3.

About the Contributors

Arlyn T. Anderson   (BA, University of Colorado, Colorado Springs, 1994) is a graduate assistant in the Department of Communication and Mass Media at the University of Wyoming, Laramie, Wyoming. His research interests include family communication, personal relationships, and cultural communication.

Winifred Brownell   (PhD, Communication, SUNY at Buffalo, 1973) is a professor of communication studies and associate dean of the College of Arts and Sciences at the University of Rhode Island. Her research interests include aging and communication, acceptance of new information technologies, media use among the elderly, and analysis of media images. Dr. Brownell has published a variety of articles and chapters and is currently directing the John Hazen White Honors Colloquium Series at the University of Rhode Island on "Mortal Questions."

Jennings Bryant   (PhD, Mass Communication, Indiana University, 1974) is a professor of communication, holder of the Reagan Endowed Chair of Broadcasting, and Director of the Institute for Communication Research at the University of Alabama. Author or editor of a dozen scholarly books, more than 40 book chapters, and approximately 75 journal articles, Dr. Bryant's research interests are in media effects, entertainment theory, and new electronic media.

Mary Cassata   (PhD, Indiana University, 1967) is associate professor of mass communication at the State University of New York at Buffalo. She is Director of Project Daytime, which carries out studies on daytime television soap operas. In addition to soap operas, her research interests concern television's portrayal of the elderly and television violence.

William R. Cupach   (PhD, University of Southern California, 1981) is a professor in the Department of Communication at Illinois State University. His current research explores the management of awkward and challenging interpersonal relationships. Among his recent publications are *The Dark Side of Interpersonal Communication* (coedited with Brian Spitzberg) and *Facework* (coauthored with Sandra Metts). He currently serves as Associate Editor for the Communication section of the *Journal of Social and Personal Relationships*.

Thomas J. Darwin   (PhD, University of Texas at Austin, 1993) is an assistant professor in the Department of Communication at the University of Memphis. His research areas include the rhetoric of science and medicine and the rhetoric of popular culture. His work has appeared in *Argumentation, Philosophy and Rhetoric, and Text and Performance Quarterly*, among other places.

Daniel A. DeJoy   (PhD, Northwestern University, 1975) is an associate professor in the Department of Communication at North Carolina State University. His specialty is in speech pathology. He is Director of the Communication Disorders Concentration at NCSU.

Christi L. Grooters   (BA, Trinity University, 1993) is Program Supervisor, Winslow Court Retirement Community, Leisure Care Incorporated, Colorado Springs, CO. As an undergraduate volunteer at local nursing homes in San Antonio, TX, she developed her interests in intergenerational communication with emphasis on the elder coculture and its symbolism. Subsequently, her professional work has enabled the further development and application of the cross-cultural communication perspective in the education and training contexts.

Wendy J. Hajjar   (PhD, Purdue University, 1993) is an assistant professor in the Department of Drama and Communication at the University of New Orleans, Louisiana. She has completed an ethnography entitled, *Media Consumption in the Nursing Home*, and is currently conducting interviews for a project entitled, *Family Values: Parenting With Television*.

L. Brooks Hill   (PhD, University of Illinois, 1968) is a professor and Chair, Department of Speech and Drama, Trinity University, San Antonio, TX. His areas of specialization are public and intercultural communication. His research addresses the communication problems of American cocultures, with recent attention to intercultural ethics, contracting, and negotiation for a Japanese book on *Intercultural Understanding and Communication*. He currently serves on the editorial board for *Intercultural Communication Studies* of the Institute for Cross-Cultural Research.

Barbara J. Irwin   (PhD, State University of New York at Buffalo, 1990) is an assistant professor of communication studies at Canisius College in Buffalo, New York, where she specializes in teaching courses in mass communication and advertising. She is also Associate Director of SUNY at Buffalo's Project Daytime. Her principle research interests, in addition to soap operas, are the social and cognitive effects of the media.

Akbar Javidi   (PhD, University of Oklahoma, 1986) is an associate professor in the Department of Speech and Theatre, University of Nebraska, Kearney. His specialties include aging and cross-cultural communication.

Manoocher N. Javidi (PhD, University of Oklahoma, 1987) is an associate professor in the Department of Communication at North Carolina State University. His specialty is in organizational development and cross-cultural communication.

Pamela J. Kalbfleisch (PhD, Michigan State University, 1985) is an associate professor at the University of Wyoming in Laramie, Wyoming. Her research focuses on elements of trust and distrust in interpersonal relationships. She is the editor of *Interpersonal Communication: Evolving Interpersonal Relationships* (1993, Lawrence Erlbaum Associates), coeditor with Michael J. Cody of *Gender, Power and Communication in Human Relationships* (1995, Lawrence Erlbaum Associates), author of *The Persuasion Handbook* (1989, Kendall Hunt), and author of *Mentoring Relationships as Personal Relationships* (in Press, Guilford).

Diane M. Kimoto (PhD, University of Southern California, 1993) is a Volunteer Coordinator at the American Red Cross. Her research focuses on rich topic areas within the field (involving culture—Afrocentric and Hispanic identity, sexual intimacy—negotiation of safer sex, aging—cultural continuity, and deception—social accountability), trying, in these domains, to better understand how personal and interpersonal processes relate to one another.

Larry W. Long (PhD, University of Oklahoma, 1979) is a professor in the Department of Communication at North Carolina State University. His areas of emphasis include public and applied communication, with special concern for problems of elders. Recognition of his extensive scholarship includes the outstanding research award from the Commission on Communication and Aging of the Speech Communication Association. He has held the positions of Program Planner, Vice-Chair, and Chair of this Commission.

Penelope N. Long (PhD, Illinois State University, 1987) is Coordinator of Advising, Department of Communication, North Carolina State University. Beyond administration, she also teaches interpersonal and small group communication and maintains a research emphasis on intergenerational interpersonal communication. Author or editor of several articles, chapters, and books, she received an outstanding research award from the Commission on Communication and Aging of the Speech Communication Association.

Norbert Mundorf (PhD, Indiana State University, 1987) is an associate professor of communication studies at the University of Rhode Island. Dr. Mundorf was a visiting professor at the University of Mainz in 1994. His research interests include acceptance of new information technologies, media use among the elderly, multimedia and health promotion, and international telecommunications. He has published in a variety of domestic and international journals and is coeditor of "New Infotainment Technologies in the Home" (Lawrence Erlbaum Associates, 1996).

Hana S. Noor Al-Deen (PhD, State University of New York at Buffalo, 1988) is an associate professor at the University of North Carolina at Wilmington. Her teaching and research specialties are mass communication, intercultural communication, and aging studies. Dr. Noor Al-Deen's work has appeared in books, journals, and conventions. She served as an elected officer for a number of divisions in the Southern States Communication Association. She is a member of the American Humane Association, American Society for the Prevention of Cruelty to Animals, and People for the Ethical Treatment of Animals.

Enid J. Portnoy (EdD, West Virginia University, 1986) is an assistant professor of communication studies at West Virginia University and former national Chair of the Commission on Communication and Aging for the Speech Communication Association of America. She teaches courses on communication and aging, gender and communication, nonverbal communication, business and professional communication, and issues in gerontology. Her research area is reminiscence. Dr. Portnoy is a skilled dramatic reader, public speaker, and workshop presenter who frequently creates and presents programs for senior citizens.

Lynda Dixon Shaver (PhD, University of Oklahoma, 1990) is an associate professor at Bowling Green State University. As an Oklahoma Cherokee, her research focuses on women's health issues and diversity in health care settings, with projects at university schools of medicine in Indiana and New Mexico and at Yale. As a consultant and researcher, she has worked in business, governmental agencies, and educational organizations. Some of her recent publications include the following: coauthor of *Strategic Communication in Business and the Professions*, coauthor with Paul M. Shaver of a chapter on HIV patients, and coeditor/author of *Women Prisoners: A Forgotten Population*.

Carole E. Tallant (PhD, Louisiana State University, 1980) is a professor of communication studies at the University of North Carolina at Wilmington. She specializes in performance studies including storytelling, and children's literature. Her publications have appeared in *Theatre Journal*, *Southern Speech Communication Journal*, *Tar Heel Journal of Storytelling*, *Literature in Performance*, and *Text and Performance Quarterly*.

I

PERSPECTIVES IN CROSS-CULTURAL COMMUNICATION AND AGING

INTRODUCTION

Part I reviews some general perspectives in cross-cultural communication and aging research. These perspectives demonstrate various issues that greatly affect the lives of our elders. Chapter 1 argues for the need for a cross-cultural communication perspective in communication research on aging. It deals with challenges derived from questionable assumptions about elders and challenges due to the inadequate consideration of culture in communication and aging research. Chapter 2 discusses the perceptions of older women under the lens of culture to discover the framed lines that define them and the challenges that face them in their coping strategies with old age. Chapter 3 advocates that greater accessibility of older people to entertainment and information (infotainment) technology has the potential to reduce their isolation, facilitate friendships across geographical distances, and provide information on a variety of concerns. The challenges of using infotainment technology may improve their quality of life.

The three chapters suggest some of the ways to improve the status of our elders, and the theme of this section is to address some of the challenges that our elders encounter in American society. Although they do not provide a panacea, the ideas presented in this section do provide hope for greater awareness of such challenges.

1

Aging and the Elders From a Cross-Cultural Communication Perspective

L. Brooks Hill
Trinity University

Larry W. Long
North Carolina State University

William R. Cupach
Illinois State University

The aging of American society is no longer an anticipated projection but is instead a daily reality for our families, our society, and our political processes. The increasing longevity of life now frequently entails that families spend approximately as many years tending to their elderly parents as their parents spent tending to them as children. The net effect of this situation is that ever-increasing numbers of American families have an elder parent living at home with them or have responsibility for the care of one or more of those parents elsewhere. Whether desired or not, economic realities are forcing more of our elders into dependency patterns with their children that they may have wanted to avoid. The social impact of these changes is compelling this fast-paced, youthful society to reassess the treatment of our elders and the entire process of aging more than preceding generations have done. Whether the families or the broader society are caring for these aging citizens, no one can escape the political impact of the aging of America. Current debates on Social Security, Medicare, and Medicaid keep everyone at least partially engaged in the economic and political dimensions of this reality.

As members of the "baby boom" generation reach their 50s, an increased emphasis on understanding the aging process and its social implications has become apparent in both popular and scholarly literature. Even a brief trip

5

to the local bookstore will reveal numerous treatments of the topics involved. Self-help books popularize the natural process of growing older, glamorize the golden years, and generally try to correct the abusive myths about the aging process so widespread in the youth culture of obsessive independence in American society. Beyond the self-help genre are numerous books about the social, economic, and political issues involved. Propelled of late by the balanced-budgeting frenzy, we are forced to consider programs designed to care for the elders, especially whether we as a nation can afford the programs. Obviously, politicians argue, we must either raise taxes or curtail benefits, and either option causes intense reactions by ever-shifting alliances of political groupings; all of these positions are variously expressed in the increasing flood of popular literature.

Reflecting values generally held by American society, the popular literature tends to stereotype the aging process and elders. Because of the relatively new efforts to create integrated paradigms in the scholarly literature, many popular authors have been forced to rely on pretheoretic and unintegrated research when providing recommendations for elders and their families. In this fashion, the popular literature tends to exhibit a microscopic approach and an emphasis on overcoming dysfunctions. For example, Seymour's (1995) book, *Aging Without Apology: Living the Senior Years with Integrity and Faith*, reflects the value that "new and modern" is perceived to be better than "old and traditional" and that perceptions held about elders by younger and middle-aged persons can be altered if the elder will consciously modify his or her behavior and exhibit a positive outlook on life. The work of Beers and Urice (1992) provided similar advice for elders and instructions for younger family members to assist the elder in adjusting to changes in biological aging processes.

Paralleling popular work, the scholarly literature in this subject area is also growing, but the productivity is slowed by the rigorous demands of scholarship and is certainly not commensurate with the rapid rate at which the elder population has grown. Currently, several scholarly works are in press, and some of this work will probably address a paradigm by which to synthesize disparate pockets of knowledge and will provide a more comprehensive understanding of aging. Despite the need in public discourse for stronger substantive foundations, the scholarly literature on elders and the aging process is comparatively weaker than in numerous other areas of human studies. We seem to know a great deal about specific aspects of the aging process, biologically, psychologically, and socially, but we have neglected some important features and especially a containing framework for our chunks of specific information.

Even though opportunities to integrate research about aging across disciplines and contexts have existed, several pressures have collectively constrained this development. Perhaps most prominent among these restraining pressures is the strong dependence on medical and psychological paradigms. This is understandable, however, because any study of aging has its roots in these bodies of knowledge, and a wealth of scholarship is available therein. Despite this wealth, these two areas tend to narrow the focus and restrict more comprehensive consideration of the total situation of the elders. As a probable influence of the medical and psychological research, pressures to publish at probability levels with narrow applications have directed much of the researchers' time. We need to balance these incremental efforts with more expansive essays that question paradigmatic efficacy and, perhaps, provide additional insights from a broader, more comprehensive perspective. Of all the areas of social concern, none urges a comprehensive synthesis of what we know more than the treatment of our elders and the aging process because this is not simply a biological or psychological or social phenomena. This is, instead, a very complicated combination of all three scientific areas, further compounded by economic and political circumstances.

Regardless of the complications involved, everyone, especially scholars, should be seeking a framework that can render what we know into more usable form for public discourse on the social issues that confront us. If scholars defer, then once again, we demonstrate our excessively cautious unwillingness to assist in the resolution of social issues at a time when we are collectively under pressure to provide useful translations of our research for the broader population. Because of its expansiveness and practicality, communication scholarship can provide one possible framework within which to synthesize our knowledge in usable form, and for the past 15 years, scholars in communication have struggled to realize this potential. Unfortunately, their efforts toward understanding how communicative relationships change and social pressures evolve as societies grow older fall short of their potential. Despite the impressive work in the anthropology of aging, medical and psychological research has diverted attention of communication scholars away from cultural variables. Perhaps the missing link in realizing this potential is the expansion of the communicative perspective to include cultural variables in a broader framework.

No one really questions whether culture influences the process of aging and communication. In fact, anthropologists regularly contribute detailed and revealing ethnographies of elder-care facilities (Henderson & Vesperi, 1995), cross-cultural comparisons of the aging processes and treatments of the elderly (Holmes & Holmes, 1995; Keith & Members of Project A.G.E., 1994), and other cultural perspectives. However, these studies lack the integrative and practical advantages of a communication orientation. Despite the contributions of this growing body of communication research, the role of culture in aging and consequent social problems have been insufficiently explored, and with few exceptions, no one has ventured to integrate the cultural and communication perspectives.

Thus, the purpose of this chapter is to describe how a cross-cultural communication approach to aging can provide useful guidelines for such a framework of scholarly inquiry and directions for solutions to many of the social issues involved. Our goal is to identify relevant constructs and articulate issues of theory and research that deserve priority. The first section supports the need for a cultural perspective. The second section describes and considers implications inherent to this approach. The final section presents a set of commitments that identify some of the potential contributions of a cross-cultural communication approach.

THE NEED FOR A CULTURAL PERSPECTIVE

In his foreword to *Human Communication and the Aging Process* (Carmichael, Botan, & Hawkins, 1988), Robert Butler, Pulitzer Prize-winning physician and founding director of the National Institute of Aging, acknowledged the importance of communication and, simultaneously, the importance of culture:

> The study of aging in America has made important strides over the past two decades. One of the significant characteristics of this period has been the emergence of gerontology as an interdisciplinary field rather than a unified discipline with a particular focus. As knowledge in the field increased, it became apparent that the aging process touches the entire human condition and that all disciplines potentially have valuable contributions to make. ...the communication systems of our culture may be part of the social problems of aging, they may also hold the solutions to those very problems of aging—a positive message indeed. (p. vii)

Although he was emphasizing communication behaviors, Butler's reference to culture underscored an important component missing in communication and aging theory and research by highlighting the fact that communication systems are a component of culture and may hold answers to several social problems.

Micro- to Macro-Analyses

As an offspring of gerontology, communication and aging research adopted the inherent orientation of its parent, aiming toward the communication features of the physical and psychological aging of humans. Until 1978, human interaction was viewed primarily as an artifact of biological and mental aging processes. An inherent tendency in this research was to identify strategies for stabilizing dysfunctional aspects of communication behavior experienced by elders in American society. Thus emerged a significant body of literature by communication scholars, primarily emphasizing sociopsychological and communication correlates of the biological aging process.

In their review of the communication and aging literature, Nussbaum, Thompson, and Robinson (1989) also emphasized the importance of understanding the functional, pragmatic nature of communication behaviors at the relational level. They indicated, "...for us, the elderly individual is not seen as a personality inventory ... but as an active participant in a system of relationships, who is constantly adapting and attempting to maintain relational equilibrium" (p. 2). Extending their position, attaining and maintaining relational equilibrium is influenced by social roles, norms, and values emanating from a society with a particular worldview, that is, a cultural context.

Rather than expand the increasing number of microanalytic analyses, research should embrace a consideration of more macroscopic social concerns that emphasize people and their relations with each other. Such macroscopic studies require consideration of culture that dominates the form and content of social roles, norms, and rules for communicative interface in relationships (Montgomery, 1992). Limitations in communication and aging literature suggest that a cultural–social focus is a relatively new, positive contribution. Two of the more prominent limitations deserve expansion.

Limitation One: Neglect of Culture

New treatments of communication and aging are currently in press; whether, and to what degree, they address cultural variables is yet to be seen. However, the two most prominent state-of-the-art books on communication and aging were examined for their consideration of the cultural perspective on the aging process. In one of them, Nussbaum, Thompson, and Robinson (1989) did not address the concept of culture, reflecting a lack of emphasis among communication scholars on this perspective. Another state-of-the-art book by Carmichael, Botan, and Hawkins (1988) mentioned culture as a piece of the foundation for examining communication and aging. However, the discussion was limited to a single paragraph preceded by an "Organizational-Cultural" subheading. Later in their book, within a chapter entitled "Communication and Aging in Organizational Contexts," references to culture were used as a point of departure to describe how organizations as microcultures communicatively isolate elders who are members of the company. Among the examples were limited training opportunities and age bias (Botan, 1988). Carmichael's (1988) treatment of "Intercultural Perspectives of Aging" in a separate anthology about intercultural communication identified the value and potential topics involved in a cross-cultural communication perspective, but he focused primarily on building a case for the consideration of the elders as a distinctive subculture within the study of intercultural communication.

An inherent intracultural bias exists in the communication and aging literature. As Robert Butler (cited in Carmichael, Botan, & Hawkins, 1988) implied, albeit probably unintended, theory development in this country has been culture bound, that is, notably selecting Americans as the "units" of analysis and thereby perpetuating a western worldview among those who study the elderly and aging process. Further, Carmichael's (1988) evaluation of the *International Handbook on Aging* found that the articles therein reported work by researchers within their own culture, with little cross-cultural comparison. Even the cross-cultural examinations that did exist were based upon analyses of demographic characteristics such as membership size within age categories.

Although the need to study the social implications associated with communication and aging has been emphasized for nearly two decades, intercultural communication variables are largely missing in reported research. Similarly, little mention of aging and communication exists in anthologies representing diverse cultures and is rarely mentioned in work outside of communication. In his review of the *International Handbook on Aging*, Carmichael (1988) observed that communication research was not represented.

Limitation Two: Questionable Assumptions

A sizeable portion of communication and aging research has evolved on questionable assumptions, focusing on dysfunctional aspects of communication by elders and perpetuating the stereotype that getting older may be a concomitant of communication ineffectiveness. Studies suggesting that elders are similar to non-elders are infrequently published because significant statistical differences are often an expectation for journal inclusion. Consequently, research reports discovering differences are valued more than those that may question culturally imposed stereotypes. Although specific researchers doubtless argue against these stereotypes, their motivation for publication and consequent research agendas continue to advance microanalytic orientations and value the discovery of differences.

Increasingly, authors now argue that one of the biggest problems faced by elders is a set of stereotypes perpetuated by our culture and reinforced by research orientations and applications. Some recent work directly indicts these stereotypes about the elders as untrue (Feezel & Hawkins, 1988), yet research projects are often designed to determine prescriptive techniques for effective management of elders based upon the assumption that they will progressively become socially dysfunctional. Clearly, the focus on population, such as elders, instead of on process, such as communication, has perpetuated these counterproductive stereotypes. Unfortunately, the integration of elders into society has not been a primary goal of our culture, and the scholarly literature reflects this position.

CONCEPTUALIZATION AND IMPLICATIONS OF A CULTURAL APPROACH

Numerous perspectives about culture are available from scholars in various academic fields. Among these are two complementary conceptualizations. Building on the work of anthropologists (Goodenough, 1964), we generally think of culture involving three primary dimensions. Culture consists of (a) whatever a person must say or do in order to be accepted by members of that culture—the behavioral dimension; (b) a cognitive and/or semantic framework that can manage the information, attitudes, beliefs, and values that govern the thought processes and behaviors—the cognitive dimension; and (c) the social system that facilitates the maintenance and transference of these behavioral and cognitive components in order to perpetuate the culture—the social/historical dimension. At this broad level, our cultural perspective encourages us to examine the behavior, semantic framework, maintenance structures, and their interrelations to understand the aging processes and elders.

The other conceptualization of culture directs our attention to the concomitant communication aspects of intercultural relations. Here, we have used a symbolic interactionist view of culture that assumes individuals reciprocally transform themselves and their social world through communication (Maines, 1984). Following Collier and Thomas (1988), culture may be broadly defined as a "historically transmitted system of symbols and meanings, and norms" (p. 102). Thus, culture provides a contextual framework in which groups of people share meanings. Within this point of view comes our focus on language and interaction as the primary source of our data and the practical strategies and tactics for addressing the social problems involved.

A more static or structural view of culture may tend to view individuals as members of a single culture. Our position deviates from this view in two important ways. First, individuals simultaneously belong to multiple, overlapping cultures. Specifically, "culture can refer to ethnicity, gender, profession, or any other symbol system that is bounded and salient to individuals" (Collier & Thomas, 1988, p. 103). Some might prefer to call these subcultures or co-cultures. The choice of label reveals whether the emphasis is on the size of the group and its relative power or the more politically sensitive concern for equal treatment and relative level of respect. Regardless of the word chosen, elders in America constitute such a co-culture or subculture (Rose, 1965), and we will use co-culture with all of its political implications. However, any particular elder also fits within other cultures, and the interpenetration and salience of an individual's cultures have implications for the aging processes.

Second, within any culture, meanings among members are shared and overlap, but they are not isomorphic. Within any group are many individual differences about how symbols and norms are interpreted. Thus, two people may both identify with the cultural group of older men in the United States. Although this may promote similarities, especially among outgroup perceptions of them, each person will derive a unique understanding of what it means to be an elder. Anyone who reads the letters to the editor in *Modern Maturity*, the primary magazine of the American Association of Retired Persons (AARP), can readily confirm the individual differences about what it means to be older and/or retired.

Implication One: Aging is a Social and Interpersonal Process

This view of culture has at least three major implications for understanding communication and aging. The first accentuates aging as a social and interpersonal process and departs from more traditional thinking about elders as a population with unique social and personal problems. Accordingly, we urge a focus on the developmental, relational, and social dynamics associated with aging. As McPherson (1983) argued, "There is a need to study the aging biological and psychological organism within the social context; scientists know less about the social and cultural aspects of aging than about the biological and psychological processes" (p. 10). When viewed as a social process, the study of aging directly addresses the vital role of culture rather than merely assumes it. Biological and psychological aging tend to be relatively similar across cultures and co-cultures, whereas the processes of social aging exhibit considerable variation within and between cultures (McPherson). Thus, this cultural approach brings into focus the neglected social and interpersonal dynamics of aging. At the societal level, it compels us to investigate how social changes, such as the economic and political, influence the personal experience of growing older. At the interpersonal level, it directs us to examine how aging is shaped by and reflected in the social and personal relationships of the elders. These foci can offer a more complete understanding of aging.

The changes experienced across one's life span are very personal as well as cultural. For example, the meaning of aging is bound up in one's self-identity that concerns the question "Who am I?" Answers to this central question derive from interacting with others and are shaped by culture and society. As Tajfel and Turner (1979) observed, social identity refers to "aspects of an individual's self-image that derive from the social categories to which he [or she] perceives himself [or herself] as belonging" (p. 40). Aspects of one's social identity thus derive from avowed or ascribed membership in occupational groups, gender classification, age categories, and so forth. In this sense, culture and identity are certainly two sides of the same coin for the individual (Wallace, 1961).

Growing older entails a number of changes in lifestyle and life opportunities. These changes, in turn, can trigger transformation and reconfiguration of identity. The continuities and changes in personal identities are integral to the individual experience of aging and discernment of its meaning. Brown (1990) suggested that there are at least two fundamental issues regarding the connection between identity and aging: (a) the extent to which established, lifelong identities are maintained into old age, and (b) the extent to which individuals take on new age-related identities. Age-related identity, a specific case of social identity, reflects the extent to which an individual identifies with a chronological age group.

Implication Two: Cultural Variability Accentuates
the Meanings of Aging

Perhaps the most central focus in our cultural approach to communication
and aging is represented in the global question, "What meanings are
associated with aging?" Meaning is intrinsic to culture, which provides a
common framework by which individuals make sense of their world and
share that sense with each other. Culture thus derives from and resides in
shared meanings that are worthy of attention in their own right as phenomena central to human existence. Moreover, meanings are important because
they exert direct and profound influence on human behavior. As Fry (1988)
indicated, "It is culture and the meaningful, symbolic structuring of time,
maturation, and the courses of life that inform us about age and shape the
experience of aging" (p. 471).

We assume that the meanings associated with aging are complex and
multilayered, exhibiting variations on both the cultural and individual
levels. "It is because of this interaction of individual and cross-cultural
differences that the aging process is relatively difficult to understand"
(McPherson, 1983, p. 14). Apprehending the various layers of meaning is
integral to understanding aging. One aspect of this complexity originates in
how individuals of a particular chronological age differ in what aging means
to them. This can owe, in part, to personality differences and variations in
life experiences. For that matter, biological aging does not simply occur
uniformly with chronological age. Further, differential participation in
social groups, that is, identification with various co-cultures, also contributes to differences in meaning within an age group (McPherson). Being
poor and female, for instance, leads to a different sense of what aging means
compared to being wealthy and male.

Aside from differences among persons of the same chronological age
within the same culture, changes in meaning also develop across time.
Clearly, notions of aging for an individual change across the life span as
perceptions of aging become more diverse and differentiated when one
moves from young adult to middle age and from middle age to being an
elder. Elders are less likely than younger adults to endorse age-related
stereotypes as typical because the experiences of aging produce more
complex cognitive schema about growing older (Heckhausen, Dixon, &
Baltes, 1989; Hummert, Garstka, Shaner, & Strahm, 1994, 1995).

Individual and developmental, or life course, differences account for
only some of the complexity associated with meanings attached to aging.
Our cultural perspective suggests at least three additional layers of meaning.

First, meanings of aging differ for different age groups, above and beyond individual and developmental differences. Each age cohort is exposed to a unique bundle of experiences tied to economic and political exigencies that correspond to that group's unique history. Thus, 30-year olds and 70-year olds differ in their views of aging not only because they differ in age (developmental difference) but also because they grew up in a different age or era. Second, meanings for aging vary across cultures and co-cultures, a fact documented by comparative research (Cowgill, 1981; Fry, 1980; Gutman, 1977; Palmore, 1980). Being Hispanic, African-American, or Asian-American may thus produce a significantly different meaning of aging from that of the White co-culture (Wieland, Benton, & Kramer, 1994). Third, because culture evolves over time, meanings regarding aging within a culture change over the course of history (Hendricks & Hendricks, 1981). With economic cycles and changing political environments in American society, the changes in perception of aging and elders may produce a bewildering array of possibilities during only one person's lifetime.

Implication Three: Symbolic Activities are Integral to Aging Experiences

This cultural approach leads us to consider how symbolic activities reflect and shape the aging process. These activities can be observed at the individual and the societal levels, whereas comparative research can be used to observe differences among societies. At the individual level, identity is composed of *meanings regarding the self.* Mirroring our conception of culture, identity also entails several categorizations and layers, reflected in questions raised by different authors: How do aging individuals cope with physical and biological changes; how are self-evaluation and self-care adapted to such changes? (Hennessy, 1992). What strategies do aging individuals employ to maintain established and entrenched aspects of their identity? Some evidence indicates that elders choose to interact with other individuals who will confirm and support their established identities (George, 1980). This is consistent with the development of age-related co-cultures (Rose, 1965), wherein aging individuals intentionally select persons for interaction who are similar in age. What factors determine the timing and extent to which aging individuals develop age-related identities; how do these identities function to insulate elders from societal stereotypes?

Other questions emerge at the social level and reflect genuine concerns about the effects of stereotyping: How do social institutions and cultural practices create stereotypes about aging and the aged? How do behaviors of younger, middle, and elder persons undermine or reinforce such stereo-types? How do stereotypes about aging and the aged influence the ways in which elders are treated by other age groups? How do such stereotypes influence how elders behave toward one another? How do stereotypes affect how elders behave toward younger individuals, particularly nonkin? What stereotypes are similar or different across cultures? How do they affect relational equilibrium? As these personal and social questions suggest, this intercultural perspective addresses the semantics of aging. More specifi-cally, the processes of labeling, of developing metaphors, and of forming myths comprise crucial elements of stereotyping.

COMMITMENTS OF A CROSS-CULTURAL COMMUNICATION PERSPECTIVE

The prior sections underscore the insufficient emphasis in the communica-tion and aging literature on cultural processes in the development and maintenance of relational equilibrium. Assumption of a cross-cultural com-munication perspective with a focus on symbolic processes provides a means to expand the breadth and generalizability of current knowledge and a strategy for overcoming the limited conceptualizations of communication and aging processes, constrained research goals, and restricted units of analysis. The following five commitments are not impossible to achieve outside of a cross-cultural communication perspective, but they are indi-vidually and collectively easier to accomplish within this perspective.

Commitment One: Emphasis on Social Stereotyping

Of the many concepts included in the study of intercultural communication, few approach the essence of the area as well as "stereotype". Just as intercultural relations essentially concern how humans treat real and/or imagined differences between people based on group identity, Walter Lippman's (1922) metaphor of stereotype, as applied to human behavior, captured prominent aspects of how people develop these labels, the conse-quences of these categorizations for interactions, and how we might over-come these obstacles to achieve more effective interaction (Triandis, 1972). The study of intercultural communication, therefore, is essentially focused on stereotyping, its origins, manifestations, and resolution of consequences. From a symbolic orientation, this entails how perceptions lead to labeling people, how we manifest the consequences of using the labels in our interactions with those people, and how, through monitoring and modifying communication behavior, we might overcome the negative consequences of these labels and perceptions.

Within this perspective is an assumption that the human need to communicate and maintain relations does not decrease with age but that it is probably altered because of social stereotyping. Sometime during the teenage years, youth in American society develop negative stereotypes of elders as withdrawn, reclusive, and passive. Cross-cultural communication scholars have noted that this state of affairs may result from a cultural set of beliefs or psychologically induced states of illness and self-fulfilling prophecy. Even though this is not a necessary condition, changes will only occur through a widespread approach at several social levels. As we know from cross-cultural comparisons with Asian cultures, alternatives are available; we can certainly learn from the Confucian belief of giving respect to elders and allowing them to grow old with dignity. However, this belief, we should also observe, is deeply rooted in language, social customs, and legal policy (Palmore, 1975). A cultural approach encourages an examination of institutional practices that create and perpetuate stereotypes about aging and elders as well as consequences of such stereotypes for the interpersonal relationships of elders. Such an approach is valuable insofar as it reveals governmental and organizational policies that may adversely disrupt the relational networks of elders. Whatever we can do to help elders sustain their communicative relationships with other people in their social network will help them retain their humanity and more positively engage their situation.

Commitment Two: The Centrality of People

What usually distinguishes communication research from other work in the social sciences is its focus on the development, expression, and adaptation of messages. Whether we like or dislike the wide spread of concerns, this emphasis requires students of communication to investigate the social–psychological origins of language and ideas, the technical and artistic aspects of the expression of messages, and the social understandings necessary for effective adaptation of those messages. No matter how strong the pressures to behave scientifically and to generalize the results of our research, all three of these message foci force us to address the unique and idiosyncratic aspects of individual behavior. We are, therefore, unable to escape the centrality of the individual. To wrestle with this problem of peculiarity is to be at odds with our scientific preferences for commonality, yet this is precisely the sort of scientific quandary the hard sciences are now confronting, with notions of patterned irregularity, random predictability, and the fuzziness of more and more concepts.

The cross-cultural communication perspective places people in the most central position of their relationships. Just as the study of culture and communication is at its core humanistic, we must consider our elders subjectively as well as objectively, with emphasis on their humane individuality. Whereas initial consideration may focus on concerns common to all participants (that is, the need to maintain social–relational equilibrium), attention must then turn to consideration of how messages and meanings may differ as a result of personal characteristics. Consequently, persons and personal relations become more prominent for interpreting the consequences of the communicative act. Ultimately, we seek generalizations about relational maintenance and change through communication, but the realities of this cultural perspective compel us to study the individual as a first priority and any patterns that might emerge as a secondary concern.

Commitment Three: Assumption of Flexibility

With its focus on cultural variables and on people, the cross-cultural communication perspective must presume flexibility, adaptability, and accommodation to constantly changing circumstances. The natural situation imposes a permanent awareness of accommodation and adaptation to overcome the almost nonconscious level of prejudice operating. Unfortunately, our culture has tended to ignore many of the normal communication needs of elders (Carmichael, 1988). The implicit myths of dysfunction have restricted efforts to understand our elders' strategies and tactics for accommodation and adaptation. As a result, the United States has one of the worst records among all cultures for integrating our elders into the mainstream (Carmichael). We seem unable, if not unwilling, to displace our myths, to challenge the beliefs and attitudes underlying these myths, and to see the distinctiveness of elders who, when unfettered by these myths, evolve some very interesting variations on strategies and tactics for communication effectiveness. The principles of uncertainty and anxiety reduction underscore the continued adaptation necessary by elders who are forced to deal with the increasing strangeness of people they once knew in different ways (Gudykunst & Kim, 1992).

Commitment Four: Pragmatic Orientation

This commitment grows out of the preceding commitments. Cross-cultural communication studies provide a more pragmatic slant on research and tend to make the participant both a subject and a researcher. The study of ethnomethodology serves to frame this research perspective (Garfinkel, 1967; Wieder, Kennan, & Hill, 1983). Current research, which cannot engage the relational aspects of communication, is limited in its ability to foster a productive pattern of theory, research, and application in addressing social issues associated with aging. In work with the aging processes and with elders, no one can simply theorize, research, or apply the results of the research and theory without becoming personally involved with the individuals and issues. Cross-cultural perspectives underscore the pragmatic concern for how elders can achieve symbolic congruence and synchrony with society. One cannot focus on people in their natural situation without developing a repertory of skills to help cope with real problems; whether they use these skills wisely is another matter. These same practical skills can also enrich approaches to research and theory.

Commitment Five: Ethical and Humane Considerations of Human Nature

As with the previous commitment, this also grows out of the preceding ones. Ethics basically concerns the various rules and norms a society evolves to help its members deal with each other rightfully and conscientiously. Culture spawns its ethical practices that ultimately become the set of standards for evaluating the rightness and wrongness of actions by people who are members of that culture. One of the more interesting aspects of cross-cultural study is the discovery of different ethical standards and the contradictory nature of standards within a culture. Any serious student of aging and the social problems of elders in America must inevitably confront the ethical contradictions of our treatment of these people. Perhaps even more frightening is the possibility that the sometimes inhumane treatment of our elders may not be a contradiction but is instead a very reasonable extension of our throwaway standards of planned obsolescence. Regardless of what we might ultimately discover, the cross-cultural communication perspective forces one to confront the basically ethical and humane nature of human interaction that, in turn, requires consideration of elders' need to maintain relationships at a reasonable level of quality, no matter in what environment they find themselves. As we can learn from the great Christian theologian Paul Tillich, the ethic of a society directly reflects the relations of any two of its members (Rayburn, 1969). Perhaps a cross-cultural communication perspective can ultimately compel us to address the ethical dimensions of dealing with elders in America.

CONCLUSION

The purpose of this chapter was to present a cross-cultural communication perspective for research about elders in American society. An initial overview revealed a significant gap in the understanding and conceptualization of existing research. Two areas of significant limitation were identified: Despite its relevance, culture is inadequately considered, and communication research on aging builds on questionable assumptions about elders. The central argument of this chapter was that a cross-cultural communication perspective could help fill this major gap. Two complementary conceptions of culture that emphasize symbolic activity provided a point of departure, and three major implications of this conceptualization were presented: Aging is a social and interpersonal process, cultural variability accentuates the meanings of aging, and symbolic activities are integrally associated with aging experiences. The remainder of the chapter identified several commitments that this position entails: The cross-cultural communication perspective focuses attention on social stereotyping, a major source of counterproductive attitudes and behavior regarding the elders' need to communicate and maintain relations; situates the person humanistically in a central position among their relationships; presumes flexibility, adaptability, and accommodation to constantly changing circumstances; generates a pragmatic slant that makes the participants in research both subjects and researchers; and forces one to confront the basically ethical and humane nature of intercultural interdependence.

This cross-cultural communication perspective is fundamentally interpersonal, with emphasis on the relationships between and among people as the dominant feature of culture. The study of communication behavior is the entry point for this consideration of co-cultural relations in American society, and just as it is with any co-cultural relations one cannot isolate the co-cultures involved so simply. Instead, everyone, regardless of co-cultural identity, is a member of multiple co-cultures with varied relations with each other and with the overarching culture. To study this complex web of varied codes, dialects, and patterns of meaning assignment requires sensitivity to the behavioral, semantic, and social/historical dimensions that constitute our culture. Through the use of communication as the primary source of data, we are well positioned to identify not only the co-culture but also the diverse individual relationships within these co-cultures. Despite this apparently confusing array of data, we are, in fact, confronted with the realities of aging and elders. Within this framework reside the realistic daily patterns by which we can better understand the problems of elders and possibly arrive at solutions for them. The solutions will come from a better under-standing of the labeling and myth-making activities that accompany the aging processes and societal reactions to our elders. This chapter established a philosophical position on which to approach these realities.

REFERENCES

Beers, M., & Urice, S. (1992). *Aging and good health: A complete essential medical guide for men and women over 50 and their families*. New York: Pocket Books.

Botan, C. (1988). Communication and aging in organizational contexts. In C. Carmichael, C. Botan, & R. Hawkins (Eds.), *Human communication and the aging process* (pp. 141–154). Prospect Heights, IL: Waveland Press.

Brown, A. (1990). *The social processes of aging and old age*. Englewood Cliffs, NJ: Prentice-Hall.

Carmichael, C. (1988). Intercultural perspectives of aging. In L. Samovar & R. Porter (Eds.), *Intercultural communication: A reader* (5th ed.) (pp. 139–147). Belmont, CA: Wadsworth.

Carmichael, C., Botan, C., & Hawkins, R. (Eds.). (1988). *Human communication and the aging process*. Prospect Heights, IL: Waveland Press.

Collier, M., & Thomas, M. (1988). Cultural identity: An interpretive perspective. In Y. Kim & W. Gudykunst (Eds.), *Theories in intercultural communication* (pp. 99–120). Newbury Park, CA: Sage.

Cowgill, D. (1981). Aging in comparative cultural perspective. *Mid-American Review of Sociology, 7,* 1–28.

Feezel, J., & Hawkins, R. (1988). Myths and stereotypes: Communication breakdowns. In C. Carmichael, C. Botan, & R. Hawkins (Eds.), *Human communication and the aging process* (pp. 81–94). Prospect Heights, IL: Waveland Press.

Fry, C. (Ed.). (1980). *Aging in culture and society: Comparative viewpoints and strategies*. Brooklyn, NY: Bergen.

Fry, C. (1988). Theories of age and culture. In J. Birren & V. Bengston (Eds.), *Emergent theories of aging* (pp. 447-481). New York: Springer.

Garfinkel, H. (1967). *Studies in ethnomethodology*. Englewood Cliffs, NJ: Prentice-Hall.

George, L. (1980). *Role transitions in later life*. Monterey, CA: Brooks/Cole.

Goodenough, W. (1964). Cultural anthropology and linguistics. In D. Hymes (Ed.), *Language in culture and society* (pp. 36–40). New York: Harper & Row.

Gudykunst, W., & Kim, Y. (1992). *Communicating with strangers: An approach to intercultural communication* (2nd ed.). New York: McGraw-Hill.

Gutman, D. (1977). The cross-cultural perspective: Notes toward a comparative psychology of aging. In J. Birren & K. Schaie (Eds.), *Handbook of the psychology of aging* (pp. 302–326). New York: Van Nostrand Reinhold.

Heckhausen, J., Dixon, R., & Baltes, P. (1989). Losses in development throughout adulthood as perceived by different age groups. *Developmental Psychology, 25,* 109–121.

Henderson J., & Vesperi, M. (Eds.). (1995). *The culture of long term care: Nursing home ethnography*. Westport, CT: Greenwood.

Hendricks, J., & Hendricks, C. (1981). *Aging in mass society: Myths and realities* (2nd ed.). Cambridge, MA: Winthrop.

Hennessy, C. (1992). Culture in the use, care, and control of the aging body. In J. Gubrium & K. Charmaz (Eds.), *Aging, self, and community: A collection of readings* (pp. 83-98). Greenwich, CT: JAI.

Holmes, E., & Holmes, L. (1995). *Other cultures, elder years: An Introduction to cultural gerontology* (2nd ed.). Thousand Oaks, CA: Sage.

Hummert, M., Garstka, T., Shaner, J., & Strahm, S. (1994). Stereotypes of the elderly held by young, middle-aged, and elderly adults. *Journal of Gerontology: Psychological Sciences, 49,* 240–249.

Hummert, M., Garstka, T., Shaner, J., & Strahm, S. (1995). Judgments about stereotypes of the elderly: Attitudes, age associations, and typicality ratings of young, middle-aged, and elderly adults. *Research on Aging, 17,* 168–189.

Keith, J., & Members of Project A. G. E. (1994). *The aging experience: Diversity and commonality across cultures.* Thousand Oaks, CA: Sage.

Lippmann, W. (1922). *Public opinion.* Toronto, Canada: Collier-Macmillan.

Maines, D. (1984). Suggestions for a symbolic interactionist conception of culture. *Communication and Cognition, 17,* 205–217.

McPherson, B. (1983). *Aging as a social process: An introduction to individual and population aging.* Toronto, Canada: Butterworth.

Montgomery, B. (1992). Communication as the interface between couples and culture. In S. Deetz (Ed.), *Communication yearbook 15* (pp. 475-507). Newbury Park, CA: Sage.

Nussbaum, J., Thompson, T., & Robinson, J. (1989). *Communication and aging.* New York: Harper & Row.

Palmore, E. (1975). *The honorable elders.* Durham, NC: Duke University.

Palmore, E. (Ed.). (1980). *International handbook on aging: Contemporary developments and research.* Westport, CT: Greenwood.

Rayburn, G. (1969). *Paul Tillich's philosophy of communication.* Unpublished doctoral dissertation, University of Oklahoma, Norman.

Rose, A. (1965). The subculture of aging: A topic for sociological research. In A. Rose & W. Peterson (Eds.), *Older people and their social world* (pp. 3-16). Philadelphia: Davis.

Seymour, R. (1995). *Aging without apology: Living the senior years with integrity and faith.* Valley Forge, PA: Judson.

Tajfel, H., & Turner, J. (1979). An integrative theory of intergroup conflict. In W. Austin & S. Worchel (Eds.), *The social psychology of intergroup relations* (pp. 33–47). Monterey, CA: Brooks/Cole.

Triandis, H. (1972). *The analysis of subjective culture.* New York: Wiley.

Wallace, A. (1961). *Culture and personality.* New York: Random House.

Wieder, L., Kennan, W., & Hill, L. (1983, November). *Ethnomethodology and intercultural communication research.* Paper presented at the annual convention of the Speech Communication Association, Washington, D. C.

Wieland, D., Benton, D., & Kramer, J. (1994). *Cultural diversity and geriatric care: Challenges to the health care professions.* Binghamton, NY: Haworth.

2

Older Women As Cultural Figures in Aging

Enid J. Portnoy
West Virginia University

The cultural frame that focuses on gender is constantly shaping the meaning of how we communicate with each other in society. A gendered culture can be thought of as a mosaic or multicolored quilt with its individual squares reflecting the different adjustments people make within the stages of their lifespan. Gender is socially constructed, and its meaning in a culture is reinforced by interactant partners. The feminine personality is perceived as nurturing, affiliative, and emotionally expressive in its communication responses to others, whereas the masculine personality is perceived as dominant, independent, and emotionally restrained (Wood, 1994).

Although age is another distinctive variable affecting culture, it does not change basic gender characteristics in any extreme manner. Gender identity remains a stable characteristic for most of a person's life within the confines of society's display rules. Such display rules, many of which have never been recorded, affect our attitudes toward each gender.

Reconstructing the self culturally can be accomplished through language and discourse (Levine, 1992). Wood (1994) suggested that women's subordinate position in society encourages them to become sensitive to the need for matching their responsiveness to others. Women have always used "talk" as a channel of reflective communication to draw others into mutual disclosure (Wood).

Old age may be the right time in a woman's life to give expression to feelings about the life course (Nussbaum, Thompson, & Robinson, 1989). Talking about the self can be therapeutic. It permits a woman to evaluate society's negative judgments that often become part of an attitude about herself and others. Thus, recalling the past can increase self-esteem (Baker, 1985).

Because communication and the oral shaping of personal values, ideas, and feelings are identified strongly with women, the sense of bonded "community" that results is strongly based on an implicit understanding of female-to-female experiences. Without the opportunity to demonstrate empathy and caring for another, women often feel unfulfilled. When they reminisce together, query each other, or celebrate or complain together, they display an acceptance of their intertwined gendered and cultural foundations.

Women in the American culture have traditionally used verbal communication to bond with others. The more personal and disclosive details are often exchanged between women of all ages to produce a supportive relationship (Wood, 1994). The purpose of this chapter is to examine older women's perceptions about aging and reminiscence within a culture.

AGEISM

In 1979, Robert Butler identified ageism as stereotyping and discrimination against older people and aging, which tends to isolate the older person from the rest of society. Ageism joins a host of other "isms" that objectify individuals because of some visible markers, in this case, grey hair and wrinkled skin. If women view themselves as mirrored reflections of society's attitude toward them, then aging becomes a trap they cannot escape.

The double standard of aging as related to gender is nowhere more pronounced than in the language and its labels that separate older women, described as "decrepit," from older men, described as "distinguished"(Sontag, 1972). The double standard also refers to the fact that society treats women more harshly than men. Think of all the adjectives that are disrespectful of female members of society. Many terms, such as pathetic, powerless, passive, complaining, weak, and demanding, are part of the ageist stereotypes of old women. Exceptions to this negative labelling are represented by images of either the wise old woman or the benign grandmother, whose advice is beneficial and supportive without being overbearing.

Older women walk a fine line between quiet acceptance of age discrimination and expressions of assertiveness, which are part of what many older women see as their right to freely voice their feelings. It is time for older women to begin to trust themselves and seek a speedy resolution of their anxieties. Recognizing the opportunities before them will be a major task for all older women in the next century and beyond.

PERSPECTIVES ON AGING

Erik Erikson's (1978) theory of the eight developmental stages of life suggested that moving into the older years, an older person must adjust to the swinging continuum between ego integrity and despair. Bolstering self-esteem and feeling confident about life and one's adjustment to it is only one side of the continuum. The opposite end of the continuum, despair, presents an opportunity to question the purpose of life through perceived meager accomplishments and prospects of a bleak future. An older woman's coping mechanisms seem to be more positive when ego integrity is chosen.

In terms of coping strategies, McCrae (1982) suggested that age brings a decrease in six particular coping patterns: hostile reactions, escapist fantasies, sedation, assessing blame, wishful thinking, and indecisiveness. Faith is the only coping strategy that seems to increase with age (McCrae,1982; McCrae & Costa, 1986). Therefore, any reinforcement of ego integrity can be related to the success of an older women's coping strategies. Reminiscence or simple recall of the past can remind women how well they have coped with changes in their past, which may stimulate them to apply such strategies to the present.

Attributing certain qualities to female cultural groups with which we have little contact stereotypes individuals on the limited basis of gender or age. Wood (1994) cautioned against accepting the essentializing phenomena wherein one older female becomes the prototype for all older females. The American cultural bias toward youthful achievements and tangible success seems to exclude older women. Many older women are forced to negotiate their own adaptation to their aging role in the culture.

The choice of coping strategies may be related to role changes to which older women must adjust (retiree, grandmother, widow), to a social network accessibility, or to changes in tasks (caregiving, household moving, baby-sitting, working) and health status. Many older women have seldom been in a position to choose their own roles. It is interesting to remember that only one third of the oldest generation of present-day women even learned to drive (Thorson, 1995). Any career aspirations were narrowly defined when they were growing up. Now, in their older years, women find themselves having to get used to a new set of cultural expectations, including how to relate to their own children and grandchildren.

Riley, Johnson, and Foner (1972) suggested that role changes are related to age changes. As women add to their years, behavioral responses and activities change accordingly. Older women are expected to dress appropriately, engage in tightly prescribed house and garden activities, do volunteer work to help aging cohorts, and invite family and friends to encircle them in a supportive network. They are also more likely to have a partner older than themselves (Mercer & Garner, 1989). If married to an older spouse, women may lean on women their own age or younger to feel younger and more vigorous than if they limit themselves to an aging partner. A constant female friendship among older women often makes it easier for women to retain self-confidence, particularly at the time when they face the loss of a male partner. Spouse loss has been found to be a woman's greatest life crisis (DuLude, 1987). In the United States, the mean age of widows has been reported as age 56 (Atchley, 1994; Hooyman & Kiyak, 1987). In 1990, more than half of the older women over 65 were widows (U.S. Bureau of the Census, 1992).

Unfortunately, when widows join their female friends, unless they are all single, there may be some perceived stress on both sides of the relationship. The widow may feel like an intruder moving in on the privacy shared between other couples, and they may look upon her as someone in search of another partner or the unwilling recipient of their "charitable sociability".

Anxiety and uncertainty often mark a process of adapting to differences between cultural groups. Such adaptation can be learned and predicted by the type of interpersonal network an older woman has. According to Kim (1988), preparing for change into a new life cultural stage must include openness and resilience, which are necessary to embrace a new culture.

METHOD

In order to examine gendered perceptions about aging and reminiscence within a culture, older women between the ages of 55 and 85 were inter- viewed by college students taking a course on Communication and Aging (see Appendix). The participant sample for this study consisted of 80 older women who were West Virginia natives. West Virginia ranks fourth in the United States with a large proportion of senior citizens. As of 1993, 15.6% of the West Virginia population were over age 65.

Participants were either selected by the students from previous acquain- tances or matched from a list of interested older women. During one semester, 50 older women were interviewed, most of them for at least five separate interviews approximately one hour in length. Their responses formed the basis for an elaborated mini share-a-life paper. This was a final project students wrote and shared with their senior partner. In another semester, 30 older women (ages 57–82) were interviewed about their responses to reminiscence and its association with their aging satisfaction.

The first group of 50 women were between the ages of 55–80 and were interviewed five times during the semester. The second group of 30 older women (aged 57–82) explained their concerns during a series of three oral interviews conducted about their perceptions of "your aging years." Mean age of both groups was 66.

Students heard lectures on interviewing older persons, with suggested question categories on aging concerns, perceived roles, pleasures and regrets, personality themes, reminiscence, education, and caregiving to help initiate open-end responses. They were encouraged to initially interview one other elder to practice class communication techniques. Personal interview experiences were then shared with the class.

ANALYSIS OF INTERVIEWS

Forty-three percent of the total participants ($n = 80$) lived in independent housing, 31% of the women resided with other family members, and 26% lived in semi-independent group housing facilities for senior citizens. All of them had spent at least 7 years of their lives in this community. In the sample, 64% of the women admitted that their personal narratives about their past were either "worth sharing" or "very worth sharing," and 15% reported they felt their personal narratives were "not worth sharing." The remaining 21% stated they did not care whether their narratives were shared. Within the total group, 100% of the participants expressed pleasure and satisfaction in having participated in the interview process even though some negative affect surfaced as a result of the recall of personal memories.

When asked if they would participate in similar student interviews in the future, 93% of the older women responded "yes" or "definitely yes." Of the 7% who did not respond in a positive manner, several suggested they did not think they could devote the time to interviews as they were either too busy or would like to try a different activity other than the interview. Interviewing is a method of spotlighting a specific group to analyze connection and separation within their own and the larger culture. How older women view themselves and their cultural position can become an imitative model for younger people within the culture.

Aging Concerns

When asked to rank order their concerns at this time in their lives, older women in these studies listed five: generational communication—keeping the lines open so that they can "read" others, especially family members;

preserving their health so that they can remain independent; finding productive ways to use their free time; preserving their position in microsocieties, referred to as their neighborhood, community, or organizational membership groups; and last, retaining the affection and support of family and friends (Portnoy, 1994).

Over half (56%) of the participants were engaged in some kind of volunteer work or organizational membership that they reported as contributing to their sense of "giving back" to their community. When asked with whom they preferred to share their reminiscences of the past, 87% of the women selected family members.

Communication with family members is reported in the literature as highly valued by older people as a source of comfort and satisfaction in old age (Atchley, 1994; Nussbaum et al., 1989; Portnoy, 1994). With the growth of the older population and the learned role of women as nurturers and caregivers for others, preserving closeness through conversation seems to be a significant element in the lives of many older women (Wood, 1994).

Intercultural communication enables individuals to create new networks and strengthen existing ones. When communicating with older women as a different co-culture within the American culture, age becomes the intervening variable. By analyzing any cultural group's network, it is possible to understand their social relationship processes and how these relationships have developed (Gudykunst & Kim, 1984).

Perceived Roles

Often, interviewees reported that family members, with the best of intentions, decided for an older woman how she SHOULD spend her time. The four top choices proposed for the older women's role were as baby-sitter, family hostess, pet keeper, and community service volunteer. Although more choices exist today for older women, Mercer and Garner (1989) found that women provide almost 100% of the volunteer work worldwide. In 1986, the rate of poverty for older women was as great as it was for older men (Ries & Stone, 1992). However, a new term, "the feminization of poverty," has entered our vocabulary to describe the new financial status of women.

With only a small percentage of older women today who have a sufficient work history, role choices are very significant when considering a comfortable and secure retirement. Over half of the total participants in these studies reported feeling "empty", as one woman explained, due to the lack of a clear mandate as to what an older woman's role function might be.

Caregiving

Many of the choices that older women self-selected or that have been made for them revolve around caregiving. Those who had been married discussed their feelings about caregiving. Of the total group, 47% expressed discomfort with their caregiving roles. Those never married or childless women are often without their own built-in family caregiver for their aging years.

A woman can expect to spend 18 years of her life taking care of her children and an additional 17 more, on average, taking care of elders. When a woman has her own family and children to care for and must also care for older relatives, she begins to understand the meaning of the term "sandwich generation" as applied to her situation. On each side of her "bread" are good reasons and people that demand her care. In addition, with the empty nest being refilled by adult children and grandchildren as well, caregiving becomes a major role for older women. The average age of the female caregiver is 57 (Wood, 1993).

Caregiving concerns do not end even when an older person is moved into institutional housing. When nursing home residents were asked what they looked forward to most in the institutional environment, the majority of them answered "a visit from my family" (Portnoy, 1993).

Educational Opportunities

More than half (64%) of the women interviewed earned no more than an eighth-grade education. Their interest in returning to school or taking courses or workshops under a number of auspices is high, although several women (20%) expressed a reluctance to be among others who had much more formal education than they. Many more participants might have felt the same type of apprehension but declined to share their specific feelings with their interviewer.

The advantages of education that were mentioned included meeting interesting people and being involved with others who had different interests than their own. One of the women emphasized that her purpose in attending different educational activities was to give herself more ideas "to keep me company, when I'm by myself."

When older women today display behavioral changes, they are often the direct result of their having more opportunities. Bateson (1995) stated: "The ideal way to be human is to accept ambiguity and to embrace the possibilities of learning through a lifetime"(p.134). Perhaps a follow-up discussion of her statement should involve trying to find answers to the variety of cultural messages that older women need to learn.

Personality Themes and Continuity

Several themes that reflect the perceived status of these older women emerged from the interview sessions. Not surprising is the influence of personality on their responses. Only 3% of those interviewed from both groups suggested that personality was not an important variable in their reported responses.

In response to statements about their participation in a recall of their past, the majority of respondents (74%) answered positively. Sample responses include:

Thinking of the past makes me feel young again.

I feel my family around me again.

Negative responses were reported by 20% of the participants. Some typical responses are included:

Looking back makes me sad.

I'd rather not remember what was. Let it alone; it's done.

The remaining 6% reported they either did not have time to reminisce or were not aware of having engaged in recalling the past.

The continuity theory of aging suggests that well-ingrained thoughts and behaviors of an individual will be expanded on in old age. We become more like our former selves, therefore, some writers refer to this theory as the "moreso theory" (Atchley, 1994). We grow more like ourselves in our past, only moreso. Time displays our habits as we live out our years predictably.

Pleasures and Regrets

When queried as to what has given them the greatest pleasure at this time of their life, the three most frequently mentioned response categories were *family members, religion, and working* to improve the lives of others. When asked about past regrets, the majority of respondents (80%) mentioned a desire to travel. Respondents suggested that travel would contribute to a broadening of the memories that could be called upon in the future (i.e.,"I want something of real interest to think about in my rocker"). This suggests memories as moveable entertainment images that elicit pleasure for older people when recalled.

Few respondents (15%) had travelled outside West Virginia or its border states, and those who had, did so only for family visitations. Many expressed a desire to be able to travel to see and to communicate with family members more frequently. Most of these older women had to wait until relatives visited them.

No one in this sample expressed the desire to travel to meet people they did not know, as on a scheduled tour or vacation. Rather, they wanted to travel to give themselves a well-deserved gift, one which would outlast any material item they could purchase with the same money. A sample response from one of the participants: "I think I owe it to myself before I pass on to see a little bit of the world."

Travel was considered a self-gratification issue and a reward for a life focused on satisfying the desires of family members first. As one woman put it: "I never would have dreamed of going anywhere just to go. It was too much to ask of my family to be without me, or so I thought."

About 63% of the women interviewed still owned and drove their own cars, though, admittedly, many participants expressed discomfort at driving to other-than-familiar, nearby locations. The older the participant's age, the more frequently they reported hesitations about driving. Fewer than 10% of these older women attempted to drive at night. For older people generally, driving and attendance at functions decrease in the evening due to poor vision and the fear of increased fatigue.

Peer Reliance

Relying upon one's peers rather than family members was strongly empha-sized. Because our society tends to be age-segregated, most participants (52%) mentioned that friendships shared with neighbors and friends close to their own age provided more comfort due to their close proximity and the similar problems peers had. Research studies confirm the importance of having a female confidante not only for women but for older men as well (Nussbaum, et al., 1989).

The importance of supportive networks of families and friends offers even more reason for women to develop accommodation strategies and wide female networks to assist them throughout the lifespan. Having a female to confide in has been reported to make a positive impact upon women's adjustment to aging (Lowenthal & Haven, 1968). Learning to depend upon peer relationships also helps women adjust to interpersonal losses, especially as they age (Poulin, 1984).

The mutual exchange of comfort for older women was linked to both physical and emotional kinds of communication support such as taking in the mail and newspaper for close neighbors, calling regularly to inquire about needs or general health, offering transportation assistance for shop-ping and appointments, and sharing news received from media sources or conveyed by others. Other forms of meaningful communication included private nonverbal signals exchanged between interactants to alert others if someone was in need of assistance.

One interviewee expressed her feelings about what she expected to receive from a peer friendship by saying: "I don't have to tell them why I'm calling or explain why I don't want to come downstairs. We understand each other pretty well."

Health

Any discussion of aging and daily living inevitably turns to concerns about health, both mental and physical. Health concerns were expressed directly when the question was posed: "What concerns do you have for your future?"

The majority of participants (84%) mentioned the fear of becoming a burden to a family member. Their responses were tied to a negative anticipation of losing the degree of independence they were presently experiencing. Frequent references about observed memory impairments and the dread of some form of senile dementia surfaced during the interviews. Here are some typical responses:

"I couldn't stand to be waited on hand and foot by someone. My mother, when she got sick, insisted we go about our business and only tend to her at her house for certain hours of the day and night. I didn't understand her feelings then but I do now." Another participant reported: "I hope I don't have to deal with a long illness; I don't think I could take that." Call it self-empowerment or resilience but, about 83% of the participants in this study were convinced that they alone were responsible for the quality of their own aging future. One 60-year-old woman admitted:

> My son said to me last year that he didn't want me to think of moving in with him when I got as old as my mother. He said he'd get me an apartment or move me into senior housing. Well, I was very hurt at the time and thought about it for too many nights. Now I think I understand what he means. On my refrigerator I have this saying: 'The best things you can give your children are roots and wings.' I always loved that but it's been very hard to accept the wings part.

Health problems are reported to produce greater stress in older people than in younger adults (House & Robbins, 1983). Women seek more medical care than men, spend more time in health facilities, use more drugs for health care, and are the primary caregivers for others (Marieskind, 1980). Studies further suggest that "older women spend more than one third of their median income on medical expenses" (Mercer & Garner, 1989, p. 40). Many women are forced to deal with financial hardship in order to qualify for medicaid or to take care of a prolonged illness of a life partner (Sidel, 1986).

Widowhood

As the number of older women increases, so will the number of widows in our country. Older women's life expectancy, as compared with men, suggests they may have as long as 30 years to be without a partner (Thorson, 1995). Losing a life partner is one of the most crucial lifetime losses and adds considerably to the change and stress an older woman experiences. Without the availability of a trusted partner, many older women turn to others, who become substitute family members. In this sample of 80 older women, 41% were widows. The older the woman was, the more likely she was to be living in group housing or with a family member. One widow discussed her situation in these words:

> I've been a widow for 15 years. My husband was killed in the war. I never thought anything like this would happen to me, but I made it... Only thing that bothers me is that oldtimer's disease (Alzheimer's) you hear so much about. Every time I forget where something is, it about scares me to death.... What would I do? Honey, I guess somebody would have to take care of me. You just have to do the best you can....

Monk (1988) indicated that aging, loneliness, and communication are interrelated in such a way that loneliness increases with age, particularly among women. Among the causes are retirement, loss of income, the "empty nest syndrome", and widowhood. Only about 1% percent of women over age 65 experiences marriage, and may confront poverty, illiteracy, and chronic medical problems (Sidel, 1986). The percentage of widows between ages 65–74 is approximately 35.3% and rises to 65.7% for women aged 75+ (Thorson, 1995).

Variables that seem to create a smoother adjustment to widowhood include maintaining church attendance, or strong religious beliefs, and having a confidante (Lowenthal & Haven, 1968). These variables are also accommodation strategies that individuals use to ease their entry into a different cultural group (Gudykunst & Kim, 1992).

CONCLUSION

Older female models can be found in our culture although we do not always take the time to expose ourselves to them. The greater the exposure the more likely we are to understand and identify with them. To become interested and responsive to another cultural group communicates a message of willing involvement. Kim (1988) suggested that age is a variable that may impede cultural adaptation. Older individuals with a preference for the familiar and with long-term personality problems may find accommodation to new cultural and behavioral issues more difficult (Gudykunst & Kim, 1992).

In the next century, older women may throw off the cloak of invisibility that age stratification (Riley et al., 1972) and ageism have used to cover them. Older women's open communication style can be extended to people from different cultures and generations to celebrate similarities and female behavior synchronization. Increased life expectancy offers older women more time to develop Erikson's (1959) generativity stage in which older people become involved in establishing and guiding younger generations. Using this stage, older women can create a world family surrounding them as they move through their own aging.

Successful cultural adaptation is the culmination of intrapersonal and interpersonal communication negotiations people undertake to achieve self-confidence in a new role. When an older woman is able to effectively cross the tight rope of cultural acceptance, she can experience greater acceptance of her aging position. As Gudykunst and Kim (1992) suggested, "Psychological health is an important consequence of cumulative adaptive experiences over time" (p.228).

The health and behavior of older women in the future will probably reflect some of the same concerns of today.

1. More older women may be called back into the work force either by necessity or a desire to serve others.
2. Taking care of the elderly and acting as communication partners will continue to be a major need satisfied by older women in a paid or voluntary role.
3. Older women without close family members will continue to have financial difficulties having their needs met.
4. More educated and politically aware older women may serve as test participants in health and drug trials, in government and military roles, and in general positions of authority.
5. Teaching about the end of life and bereavement will increase so that death is viewed as a natural and inevitable consequence of life.
6. Integrating generations will expand through shared activities, housing, and local organizations.
7. With the possibility of more elderly female victims of dementia and other illnesses, men will have to be trained as caregivers to share a role usually relegated to women.

8. Women will prepare for widowhood in their middle years.
9. Constant and close relationships with women of all ages may create a strong sisterhood for women to depend on throughout their lifetime.
10. Education will become part of an older woman's lifestyle.

As life expectancy of the American woman continues to increase, problems remain: poverty, loss of intimate partners, and adjustment to a life alone. In 1985, the U.S. Population Survey found half of the women 75 or older lived alone. An important function for older women is to combat ageism, which creeps into society's communication and behavior. Older women can speak more forcefully and detail the interpersonal support they look for in others. With current national political rumblings about pushing back the retirement age until age 70, the aging years will take on added significance. Older women will find more reasons to exercise personal and cultural values of aging.

Women can become respected advisers and teachers of those younger, and their daughters will then become apprentices for their own aging. Women's choice of ego integrity (Erikson, 1978) at this stage, along with McCrae's (1982) coping strategies, may become the visible signs of aging self-worth in every culture.

REFERENCES

Atchley, R. (1994). *Social forces and aging* (7th ed.). Belmont, CA: Wadsworth.

Baker, N. (1985). Reminiscing is group therapy for self-worth. *Journal of Gerontology, 11*, 21–24.

Bateson, C. (1995, May). My mother, my daughter. *Washingtonian*, 57–60, 133–136.

Butler, R. (1979). *The other woman: Continuities and discontinuities.* Washington, DC: U.S. National Institute on Aging.

DuLude, L. (1987). Getting old: Men in couples and women alone. In G. H. Neimiroff (Ed.), *Women and men: Interdisciplinary readings on gender* (pp. 323–339). Toronto, Canada: Fitzhenry and Whiteside.

Erikson, E. (1959). Identity and the life cycle: Selected papers. *Psychological Issues, 1*, 18–164.

Erikson, E. (1978). *Adulthood.* New York: Norton.

Gudykunst, W., & Kim , Y. Y. (1984). *Methods for intercultural communication research.* Beverly Hills, CA: Sage.

Gudykunst, W., & Kim, Y. Y. (1992). *Communicating with strangers* (2nd ed.). New York: McGraw-Hill.

Hooyman, N. R., & Kiyak, H. A. (1987). *Social gerontology; A multidisciplinary perspective.* Newton, MA: Allyn & Bacon.

House, J. S., & Robbins, C. (1983). Age, psychosocial stress, and health. In M. W. Riley, B. B. Hess, & K. Bond (Eds.), *Aging in society: Selected reviews of recent research* (pp. 175–197). Hillsdale, NJ: Lawrence Erlbaum Associates.

Kim, Y. Y. (1988). *Communicating and cross-cultural adaptation: An integrative theory.* Clevedon, England: Multilingual Matters.

Levine, G. (1992). *Construction of the self.* New Brunswick: Rutgers University Press.

Lowenthal, M. F., & Haven, C. (1968). Interaction and adaptation: Intimacy as a critical variable. *American Sociological Review, 32*, 20–30.

Marieskind, H. I. (1980). *Women in the health care system; Patients, providers, and programs.* St. Louis: Mosby.

McCrae, R. R. (1982). Age differences in the use of coping mechanisms. *Journal of Gerontology, 37,* 454–460.

McCrae, R. R., & Costa, P. (1986). Personality, coping, and coping effectiveness in an adult sample. *Journal of Personality, 54,* 385–405.

Mercer, S., & Garner, J. (1989). An International overview of aged women. In J. Garner & S. Mercer (Eds.), *Women as they age* (pp. 13–45). Binghamton, NY: Haworth.

Monk, A.(1988, May–June). Aging, loneliness and communications. *American Behavioral Scientist, 31,* 532–563.

Nussbaum, J., Thompson, T., & Robinson, D. (1989). *Communication and aging.* New York: Harper & Row.

Portnoy, E. (1994, November). *Older women speak.* Paper presented at Speech Communication Association Conference, New Orleans, LA.

Portnoy, E. (1993, March). *Images of aging.* Paper presented at the Association of Gerontology in Higher Education Conference, Louisville, KY.

Poulin, J. (1984). Age segregation and the interpersonal involvement and morale of the aged. *The Gerontologist, 24,* 266–269.

Ries, P., & Stone, A. (Eds.). (1992). *The American woman* 1992–93. New York: Norton.

Riley, M. N., Johnson, M., & Foner, A. (1972). Elements in a model of age stratification. In M. W. Riley, M. Johnson, & A. Foner (Eds.), *Aging and society, 3, a sociology of age stratification* (pp. 3–26). New York: Russell Sage.

Sidel, R. (1986). Who will need me…Who will feed me when I'm 64? *New Directions for Women, 17*(1), 1–24.

Sontag, S. (1972, September). The double standard of aging. *Saturday Review of Literature 95,* 29–38.

Thorson, J. (1995). *Aging in a changing society.* Belmont, CA: Wadsworth.

U.S. Bureau of the Census (1992). *Current population reports,* Series p. 25, No. 1092. Washington, DC: U.S. Government Printing Office.

Wood, J. (1993). *Who cares? Women, care and culture.* Carbondale, IL: Southern Illinois University Press.

Wood, J. (1994). *Gendered lives.* Belmont, CA: Wadsworth.

APPENDIX

Interview Questions

Directions: Please circle the one response you think best answers each question. These questions are a guide for your interviewer to ensure that the important informational topics are introduced. The interviewer will explore some of your answers with you in order to gain more information.

1. How often do you think about the past?
   (a) constantly
   (b) very often
   (c) occasionally
   (d) very seldom
   (e) never

2. Generally, you would describe your memories as:
   (a) very pleasant
   (b) pleasant
   (c) neutral
   (d) unpleasant
   (e) very unpleasant

3. Your favorite time period for most memory recall is:
   (a) childhood
   (b) teenage years
   (c) young adulthood
   (d) middle age
   (e) other (explain)

4. How do your prefer to communicate your memories?
   (a) Always share
   (b) sometimes share
   (c) undecided
   (d) do not think of sharing
   (e) never share

5. How satisfied are you with your own aging?
   (a) very satisfied
   (b) satisfied

    (c) undecided
    (d) dissatisfied
    (e) very dissatisfied

6. Which group do you prefer sharing memories with?
    (a) family
    (b) friends about your age
    (c) younger people
    (d) others (explain)
    (e) I don't share

7. What is your primary use in recalling the past?
    (a) receive needed information
    (b) bring back pleasurable memories
    (c) share conversation with others
    (d) occupy your time
    (e) other (explain)

8. Do you enjoy listening to another person's reminiscence?
    (a) very much
    (b) most of the time
    (c) undecided
    (d) Not much
    (e) not at all

9. Do you think your story narratives about the past are worth preserving?
    (a) definitely
    (b) probably
    (c) undecided
    (d) probably not
    (e) absolutely not

10. As you look back on your life, are you:
    (a) very well satisfied
    (b) satisfied
    (c) undecided
    (d) dissatisfied
    (e) very dissatisfied

11. Looking at your aging years, are you:

(a) very well satisfied
(b) satisfied
(c) undecided
(d) dissatisfied
(e) very dissatisfied

12. What do you consider an older woman needs at this time in her life? Please give an example or examples...

13. Name at least 5 major concerns you have at this time in your life. Try to give an example of each.

14. In your opinion how does the media depict older women?
    (a) very satisfactorily
    (b) satisfactorily
    (c) no opinion
    (d) not satisfactorily
    (e) very unsatisfactorily

15. Do the people representing older women in print media (magazines) and on television appear to be:
    (a) very realistic models
    (b) realistic models
    (c) no opinion
    (d) unrealistic models
    (e) very unrealistic models

16. Which of the following adjectives describe your life at this time?
    (a) very active
    (b) active
    (c) no opinion
    (d) inactive
    (e) very inactive

17. List your favorite activities.

18. Who directs your activities at this time of life?
    (a) spouse
    (b) other family member
    (c) friends
    (d) members of organizations

(e) yourself

19. Can you name four roles which you have now?

20. Do you presently engage in volunteer activities of any kind? Please describe.

21. Which adjective best describes your feeling about this volunteer activity?
    (a) Very rewarding
    (b) rewarding
    (c) no opinion
    (d) unrewarding
    (e) very unrewarding

22. Who provides the most personal and emotional support for you now?
    (a) family
    (b) spouse
    (c) aging friends
    (d) professionals (lawyer, doctor, accountant, etc.)
    (e) other (explain)

23. Do you have any regrets about an activity which you have not participated in thus far, but would like to experience?

24. Regarding your physical appearance are you:
    (a) very satisfied with it
    (b) satisfied
    (c) no opinion
    (d) dissatisfied
    (e) very dissatisfied

25. Please share one of the compliments you have received about your appearance since you became a senior citizen.

26. What has given you the greatest pleasures in your life?

27. What has given you the greatest regrets?

28. If you had to list five concerns about your future, what might they be?

29. What terms best describe the number of close friends you have at this time?
    (a) a great many
    (b) many
    (c) no opinion
    (d) few
    (e) very few

30. What do you regard as the most significant things which have helped you to adjust to the aging process?

31. What is your overall impression of your participation in this semester-long interview process?
    (a) very satisfactory
    (b) satisfactory
    (c) no opinion
    (d) unsatisfactory
    (e) very unsatisfactory

32. Would you be willing to participate in another student interview process in the future?
    (a) definitely yes
    (b) yes
    (c) uncommitted
    (d) no
    (e) definitely not

(These specific questions were required within the interviews. In addition, all interviewers were encouraged to use them as initiators of conversation in order to probe for specific examples and situations.)

Aging and Infotainment Technologies: Cross-Cultural Perspectives

Norbert Mundorf
University of Rhode Island

Jennings Bryant
The University of Alabama

Winifred Brownell
University of Rhode Island

A father in his 70s called his son regularly after his wife's death. His calls consisted primarily of accounts of his health problems, and the tone of his conversations indicated some depression. His son, an expert with computers, recommended that his father buy one. Because his father had musical talent, the son recommended a peripheral device with an electronic keyboard. After the computer purchase, the father's conversations focused on his computer, his various accomplishments in new musical compositions, and questions about the computer and software. The father's spirits have significantly increased (Mundorf & Brownell, 1994).

A 70-year-old woman routinely complained to her daughter about her health and various frustrations in her life. She had faced a number of life-threatening problems, so these complaints were warranted. After some encouragement, she enrolled in an entry level computer course with a diverse population of adults. During the period she was enrolled in the course, she enthusiastically told her daughter about her latest computer skills and accomplishments. Afterwards, she bought her own computer system and began to use it with her children and grandchildren. Then she acquired a modem to explore Internet connections. Her spirits have significantly increased, despite continuing health problems (Mundorf & Brownell, 1994).

Individual characteristics, notably demographic factors such as gender, age, and culture influence the acceptance and adoption of communication technologies. In the "Information Age," the ability to manage information technologies is a critical condition for one's professional and private success (Salvaggio & Bryant, 1989). For an ever-increasing number of people, computers, telecommunications, and information networks are essential for effective job performance in the corporate environment . Outside the office and after retirement, electronic formats for banking, shopping, dating, reading magazines, communicating, and accessing health care are gaining acceptance (Ogozalek, 1991). Because of the importance of technological competence, gender, age, and cultural biases are considered issues of concern in the use of and attitudes toward computers and related communication technologies.

Adults over 55 years of age have had dramatically different exposure to new technologies than the 18- to 22-year-olds who attend college today (Baig, 1994). College students learn and work in an environment where access to new technologies is encouraged and expected. In the past, students had to learn about new communication technologies once they enrolled on campus; families did not own expensive video or communications equipment that was only found in television studios or major corporations. Once personal computer, video, and communication systems were developed, and the costs came down, access increased to new technologies. Today, college students arrive on campus with experience gained on video equipment that they used in high school, camps, social organizations, work, or in the home. Answering machines and CD players are now relatively common in student residences.

In contrast to the current college population, most older adults have had more limited and qualitatively different experiences with new communication technologies. While many devices were becoming affordable to the average American household, older adults were retiring and facing limited incomes. After functioning well for decades without the technology, many adults over 55 may not see a fax, VCR, personal computer, or compact disc player as an essential tool or appliance. Mundorf, Meyer, Schulze, and Zoche (1994) reported that older Germans were more reluctant than younger adults to purchase a new appliance or household technology.

Older adults are more likely than younger adults to be limited in their mobility and ability to perform vital social and business transactions; they are also more likely to be socially isolated. Nussbaum, Thompson, and Robinson (1989) projected that personal computers (and presumably electronic mail systems) may be used in the future by the elderly as a supplement to face-to-face encounters. They suggested that an electronic communication system may help the aged neutralize environmental and physical barriers while allowing them to fulfill interpersonal needs. Moreover, they suggested that "the elderly who take time to learn about computers are simultaneously developing practical skills and conversational skills with which the younger generation are familiar" (p. 78), enhancing possibilities for intergenerational relationships. The Alabama Information Age Task Force Report (Bryant,1991) offered some scenarios portraying a variety of positive uses of new communication technologies by older adults. Among their recommendations, the Task Force endorsed providing access to telecommunications and data bases for older adults to enhance the quality of their lives.

Seniors are now taking advantage of online access networks in greater numbers. Key sources that provide online discussions specifically geared to older adults, offer access to classes, and give opportunities to communicate with other seniors on common issues of interest are SeniorNet Online through America Online, the Retirement Living Forum through Compuserve, and Seniors Bulletin Board through Prodigy. A variety of anecdotal reports in the media describe examples of adults 70 and over who have formed friendships and even romantic encounters online. Such reports cite older adults who praise the access to fascinating company and the opportunity to keep their minds alive through good conversation. Over 16,000 seniors communicate on SeniorNet alone, and there are over 50 learning centers across the country providing instruction to older adults on computer usage (Nodell, 1994). Nursing homes in Peoria, Illinois, are installing computers with modems so that residents can access electronic "penpals" and gain information from online services.

This chapter explores the opportunities and problems associated with the use of infotainment technologies by older adults. It discusses empirical research that compares aging and younger population groups in the United States, Germany, and Croatia. The age differences found are both gender and culture-specific. The chapter elaborates on a theoretical model, which analyzes characteristics of technologies including interactivity, personalization, agency, selectivity, and iconicity and applies them to older users.

FEATURES OF NEW INFOTAINMENT SERVICES

Theoretical models of new information technology acceptance so far have added little to the understanding of how older adults adopt such technologies. One approach toward understanding interactive technologies that is suitable for this group of users was proposed by Bryant and Love (1996). Components of the model, such as interactivity, personalization, agency, selectivity, and iconicity can be applied to raise questions about the specific situation of older users.

Selectivity

A key feature of new services is their ability to provide a wide selection of choices to the user. With regard to computer use, a large number of software and online services are available from which the older adult can pick. The same will eventually be true for interactive television. No longer are users limited to the choice between three remarkably similar situation comedies on ABC, CBS, or NBC. In the future, they will be selecting from scores of different options within each of perhaps a dozen different genres, some of which may be new or, at least, hybrids. As older persons are used to consuming many hours of various media, it is unclear what the effect of this choice will be: Will they be overwhelmed, will they take advantage of the variety offered, or will they ignore it? What is the effect of no longer viewing a program simultaneously with many peers when it is possible to choose any program at any time in a video-on-demand setting? Psychologically, how will viewers respond when they can narrow their choices to media they really like, to genres they prefer, to characters they really care about, to settings and situations that are germane to their lives? Will this potential for selectivity broaden or deepen the entertainment experience? Will it alter media use by older adults in significant ways? Will it bring them closer to younger generations or isolate them even more?

Diet

Closely related to selectivity is the notion of *diet*. Diet refers to the composition of information that users select and can include variations in type of programming (e.g., entertainment, education, or information) between types of media (e.g., print vs. electronic), between reception formats (e.g., audio, video, AV), and the like. Will older users choose challenging and interesting content, which will keep them mentally active and socially involved, or will they stay with conventional shallow and passive entertainment (Landler, 1994)?

Interactivity

The concept of *interactivity* is the element of information technology most often discussed in the trade and popular presses, and logically, the capacity to respond to other messages, act on them, and the like should alter the infotainment experience qualitatively. For older users, interactivity may be a way to remain active and involved. It could present appropriate mental challenges after retirement and might even become part of the process of separation from work life, which is traumatic for many. However, who will choose the way of interaction? Will it be limited to those who are active and involved anyway, or will it help those who are otherwise isolated and have no feasible alternatives? The Internet, for instance, has provided access to a whole world of possible communication partners to those who may otherwise be shy or inhibited. It also offers a chance to ignore age, social status, and even gender.

Agency

Agency refers to the degrees of control one possesses in relation to a technology or system. Again, such control may empower older users, who have lost 'agency' in the workplace and family. Kautzmann (1990), for instance, found increased feelings of self-esteem and mastery as a result of exposure to computers in a therapy setting for older people. This might also affect consumption of entertainment media. Will users really want to select the denouement, or resolutions, of our dramas, select the personalities and physical characteristics of our soap opera heroes, or alter the lyrics to our popular music? If so, will this shift the boundaries of what we call "infotainment"?

Personalization

Older people in particular have experienced increasing *depersonalization* in their lifetime, from the vanishing of mom-and-pop stores and corner bars to the demise of close-knit neighborhoods and extended families. In general, electronic media have contributed to this depersonalization. Mass media messages typically have been addressed "to whom it may concern." To a certain extent, a combination of agency and interactivity are attributes of *personalization*. Direct marketing innovations have caused consumers to expect quasi-personalization (e.g., not "Dear Occupant" but "Dear Fred and Wilma Flintstone"). The next generation of media will permit true customization of messages along a number of lines. Will this trend be able to counteract some of the increasing anonymity, or will it simply contribute to greater "cocooning"? In entertainment, how much personalization is desired? How salient is too salient? How real is too real? Is personalization the enemy of the willing suspension of disbelief, long believed to be essential to certain types of entertainment?

Dimensionality

In the digital world, messages are not only infinitely malleable but they can also have many different dimensions. Looked at overly simply, will we always desire a *multi*media experience, or will we sometimes prefer to only read text or to only listen to music without the videos? How much multidimensionality is desirable for maximal enjoyment under what context and social situation? Will the new multimedia environment be designed by twenty-something programmers for the MTV and Nintendo Generation, or will there be options available that cater to the tastes and lifestyles of older users?

ELECTRONIC INFORMATION SERVICES
FOR OLDER ADULTS

Computers present challenges to many older adults, not the least of which is the fear of computers and "technophobia." Many in this age group grew up during the golden days of radio. Relatively few technical devices or appliances were commonly available in households of the 1940s and 1950s.

New technologies and organizations have the potential to make older adults avid computer users. Many online services provide special forums to seniors at special rates to get older citizens interested and "logged on." Slowly, networks of older computer users have been established. One example is the online user-services network called SeniorNet, which is the largest organized group of its kind. It is available commercially on America Online. Table 3.1 presents selected and other demographic information on SeniorNet subscribers.

The mission of SeniorNet is to build a community of computer-using adults age 55 and older. SeniorNet provides information and instruction about computer technologies so that older adults can use their new skills to benefit themselves and others. SeniorNet members have access to special computer training sessions and computer-related publications that cater to their special needs. In addition, SeniorNet offers members off-line benefits, including low-cost, friendly introductions to basic computer skills at SeniorNet Learning Centers.

SeniorNet also provides various discussion groups, in which members can talk about virtually any subject they wish. They include Collectibles, Cooking/Recipes, Crossword Puzzles and Games, Elderhostel, Employment, Environment, Flying, Gardening, Genealogy, Investments, Jokes and Clever Quips, the Media, Pets, Politics, Recreational Vehicles, Retirement Issues, Sex, Travel, and Writing.

TABLE 3.1
Demographic and Other Characteristics of SeniorNet Members

Characteristics	Percentage
Gender:	
Male	52
Female	48
Age:	
55–65	36
66–75	51
Over 76	13
Education Level:	
Grade School	1
High School	14
Some College	30
College Degree	19
Some Post College or Graduate Degree	36
Employment Status:	
Working Full-Time	12
Working Part-Time	19
Not Working or Retired	68
Computer Ownership:	
Yes	64
No	36
Type of Computer (of those owning computers):	
IBM-Compatible	78
Apple	17
Other	5
Computer Uses:	
Word Processing/Writing	57
Personal Finance	33
Telecommunications	25
Business Operations	22
Hobbies	21
Games	17

Source. SeniorNet WWW server, URL: http://www.SeniorNet.com

In addition to SeniorNet, there are other online services designed for older people. Prodigy offers a "Family of Choice," an online support group for grieving spouses (Rovner, 1995). Table 3.2 presents selected WorldWide Web sites of interest to many older citizens. All contain links to even more sites that the elderly might find interesting.

Options for the Physically Challenged Elders

In spite of their great potential, computers have presented considerable problems to physically challenged elders. Physical challenges tend to occur more frequently with age. Some technologies developed for the physically challenged are particularly suitable for older persons. Largely due to

TABLE 3.2
World Wide Web Sites of General Interest to Older and Physically Challenged Users

Sites
SeniorNet
http://www.SeniorNet.com.
http://www.SeniorNet.com/SeniorNet at Honolulu Community College
http://www.hcc.hawaii.edu/SeniorNet/SeniorNet.html
Senior Information—Blacksburg (VA) Electronic Village
http://www.bev.net/community/seniors/
Boulder Colorado Seniors Page
http://bcn.boulder.co.us/community/senior-citizens/center.html
The CyberSenior Review
http://bcn.boulder.co.us/community/senior-citizens/cybersenior-0395.html
Senior Group Newsletter
http://bcn.boulder.co.us/community/senior-citizens/seniorgroup/center.html
ANSWERS: The Magazine for Adult Children of Aging Parents
http://www.service.com/answers/cover.html
Adopt A Grandparent Program
http://hanksville.phast.umass.edu/misc/Grandparents.html
Seniors Computer Information Project
http://www.mbnet.mb.ca/crm/
Canadian Association of Retired Persons
http://www.mbnet.mb.ca/crm/lifestyl/advoc/carp.html
Health Related WWW Sites
Alzheimer Web
http://werple.mira.net.au/~dhs/ad.html
The Stroke And Aging Research Project
http://www.columbia.edu/~dwd2/
National Institutes of Health
http://www.nih.gov/
Index of Health-Related Sites on the Net
http://nearnet.gnn.com/wic/med.toc.html

(continued)

TABLE 3.2 (cont.)
Government Agencies

Social Security Administration Online
        http://www.ssa.gov/The Health Care Financing Administration
        http://www.ssa.gov/hcfa/hcfahp2.html
U.S. Department of Health and Human Services
        http://www.os.dhhs.gov/
GSA's Catalog of Federal Domestic Assistance Programs
        http://www.sura.net/gsa.html
WEB Server for the Visually Handicapped
        http://biomed.nus.sg/vh/vh.html
New Vista Ranch
        http://www.wizard.com/new.vista.html
National Library Service for the Blind and Physically Handicapped
        http://lcweb.loc.gov/nls/nls.html
Handicapped
        http://www.neosoft.com/internet/paml/groups.H/handicapped.html
Conference and Workshop Information
        http://www.cs.rpi.edu/conference/
HUMANICA OY
        http://www.otech.fi/otech/Humanica.html
Library for the Blind
        http://www.nypl.org/branch/central_units/lb/LB.html

arthritis and loss of flexibility, many older people do not have the dexterity or agility to use essential parts of current computers, such as the keyboard or mouse. Slowly, this is beginning to change; computer interfaces are becoming more user friendly. Features that aid the physically impaired are becoming available but usually at a considerable surcharge.

Several types of devices, including voice recognition software and hardware, aid the physically challenged in using computers. These technologies are still in the developmental stages and still have a lot of aspects that need to be worked out. Voice recognition technologies remain fairly expensive and as such, are not a practical application for the average user. Another technology, created by Berkeley Systems, transforms text on screen into digitized voice, which is particularly suitable for the visually challenged. Windows 95 also has some features, at additional cost, that help handicapped users. Among these features are keyboard remapping, developmental voice recognition, and speech synthesis.

Another technology that offers advantages to all users is Optical Character Recognition (OCR). OCR enables the computer to recognize letters, numbers, symbols, or pictures that come in from a foreign source (i.e., a scanner or a fax). This, in conjunction with digitized voice software, allows people with a variety of physical constraints to send and receive information. In particular, further development of this technology can circumvent use of the alphanumeric keyboard, a barrier to computer use for many, in particular, older users.

Microsoft has developed other handicapped-specific access. "Access-DOS" accommodates the physically challenged through software-based modifications. The software:

- Provides for single-fingered typing of SHIFT, CTRL, and ALT key combinations;
- Ignores accidental keystrokes;
- Adjusts the rate at which a character is repeated when one holds down a key or turns off character repeating completely;
- Prevents extra characters from being typed if one unintentionally presses a key more than once;
- Enables one to control the mouse pointer by using the keyboard;
- Enables one to control the computer's keyboard and mouse by using an alternate input device;
- Provides a visual cue when the computer makes sounds;
- Provides extensive online help.

"AccessDOS" also accommodates single-handed users by allowing keyboard layout designed especially for them. It also provides all of its written documentation on audio cassettes and floppy disks. There have also been some advances in recent years for people who do not have the use of their hands. These technologies remain very expensive due to limited demand. Currently, they are specially built at high cost. Some of these technologies include orally controlled point-and-click devices and the previously mentioned voice recognition software (Microsoft Corporation, 1993). The Trace Research and Development Center at the University of Wisconsin-Madison helps disabled people by describing special applications designed to meet their needs. The other option is the National Information System (NIS), which is an information and referral center for people with disabilities.

ACCEPTANCE OF INFORMATION TECHNOLOGY

Despite evolving options for older adults, one expects younger adults, who have had greater access and experience, to report a higher acceptance of new communication technologies than older adults. Many older adults have revealed a reluctance to accept change, and new communication technologies typically introduce dramatic changes in how we interact with other people. In reviewing research on work situations and relocation, Zeithaml and Gilly (1987) concluded that older employees tend to resist change in general and technology in particular. Kerschner and Chelsvig (1981) found that older respondents in a study on marketing technology were unlikely to have used calculators, computers, VCRs, automated teller machines, video games, and cable television.

Regardless of the widespread perception that older persons are reluctant to accept change, marketing groups, both from a public policy and a business point of view, are now gaining interest in older adults for the following reasons: The group over 55 is growing more rapidly than other age groups, older adults often have discretionary income and purchasing power, and they are a group with clearly identifiable and accessible needs (Zeithaml & Gilly, 1987). Researchers must establish what factors influence acceptance by older adults of new communication technologies.

Gelb (1978) concluded in a study of the "gray market" that older adults are not homogeneous; therefore, some subgroups may be more interested in information technologies than others. It is reasonable to expect that some forms of communication technologies are more acceptable than others to certain older adults. One such area concerns safety issues and security systems. The "smart house" uses technology to increase comfort, health, and safety in a living environment by incorporating communication and control systems to maximize the independence and function of older adults. Czaja (1988) noted that the smart house can reduce the risk of injuries from falls, burns, poison gases, crime, and fires while increasing security, communication, and entertainment. Given the needs and fears of older adults, forms of technology that enhance feelings of security are more likely to gain acceptance. Shostak (1994) pointed out that Artificial Intelligence (AI) could aid home or nursing care with the help of electronic agents serving the comfort and needs of older residents.

In a study of three retailing technologies, Zeithaml and Gilly (1987) found that older adults enthusiastically accepted electronic fund transfer, rejected automatic teller machines, and passively accepted grocery scanners. They found that older adults adopted technologies when advantages were offered and communicated. Other older adults who were most likely to adopt new communication technologies include those "higher in income, those living in multiunit dwellings, and those who are exposed to print media" (Zeithaml & Gilly, p. 66). This finding reinforced earlier research that established the acceptance of electronic fund transfer by older adults and their dependence on print media for word about innovations in technology.

Groves and Slack (1994) found that exposure to two 15-week training sessions significantly increased the enthusiasm of older infotainment technology users; they also noted a slow progression in functional skills. Ogozalek (1991) pointed out that computers can help enhance sensory and cognitive abilities, which decline in old age. Groves (1990) reported an increase in positive attitudes and life satisfaction in a small sample of elders using computers. In a therapeutical setting, Kautzmann (1990) demonstrated increased feelings of self-esteem and mastery in older patients using computers.

Nevertheless, there is a great need to tailor hardware, software, training, and networking to users, particularly older users, of information technology (Mundorf, Westin, & Dholakia, 1993). Morgan (1994) suggested that designers of computerized products target their work toward the special characteristics of older populations. Temple and Gavillet (1990) failed to reduce anxiety through a computer confidence course in a senior center, although computer literacy increased. The SeniorNet demographics reported in Table 3.1 also demonstrate that access to computer communication tends to be focused around the segment of educated older users.

Technology, Age, and Gender

Older consumers tend to be more reluctant to use emerging technologies than their younger counterparts. This tendency is somewhat confounded with gender effects, because men across age groups feel more comfortable with most technologies than do women (Meyer & Schulze, 1993, 1994). Some of these age differences are apparently the result of societal misconceptions. New communication and information technologies such as electronic shopping, banking and mail, video phones, telemedicine, and security systems may help older adults transcend environmental and social barriers (Nussbaum, Thompson, & Robinson, 1989). Unfortunately, older adults are also generally more reluctant to use such technologies (Kerschner & Chelsvig, 1981; Zeithaml & Gilly, 1987).

Some authors (Lockheed, 1985; Rogers, 1986) expressed concern that women might be at a disadvantage in the use of information technologies because their patterns of preference and usage differ from those of men. Gender differences materialize even in the use of more traditional technologies such as television. Besides age, gender is the strongest predictor of television content preferences (Beville, 1988). Ferguson (1991) and others found ample evidence for a male bias in remote control use. Zillmann, Weaver, Mundorf, and Aust (1986) suggested that entertainment provides a vicarious way of experiencing male-female differences that have dissipated in real life. Gender-specific behavior may have lessened in the work sphere, but it is still exhibited while viewing or reading entertainment messages.

Gender differences exist in later life that could influence the usage of new communication technologies. Men tend to taper off contact with social friends after retirement, but older women have and maintain more extensive ties in a diverse social community (Babchuk, 1978; Clark & Anderson, 1967; Rawlins, 1992; Roberto & Scott, 1986; Spakes, 1979). Unlike men, women make friends throughout their lifespan, including as older adults (Rawlins). One intriguing opportunity in technology for women involves online services with e-mail and their possibilities for seeking, nurturing, and maintaining friendships. Women maintain contact with friends across geographical distances and, therefore, might be more likely than men to explore and exploit the social possibilities of online conversations services and forums. Computer-mediated communication allows women an opportunity to maintain, enhance, and seek relationships and, perhaps, encourages men to maintain ties after retirement.

However, gender differences in computer use still stretch across private and public spheres (Arch & Cummins, 1989; Kiesler, Sproull, & Eccles, 1985; Venkatesh & Vitalari, 1986, 1987). Rogers (1986) claimed that new information technologies, especially computers, have caused gender inequalities and even reversed some of women's gains in the workplace. He argued that the male bias in math and science has extended to computers. Brownell and Mundorf (1990) noted that college males report higher usage levels of word processing, electronic mail, and statistical analysis than women. This survey confirmed findings from earlier research that men show greater use of computers, electronic mail, and similar activities.

Several authors have suggested that this bias is a function of cultural and social influences as well as software design and user interface factors. Notably, the presence of well-defined structures in the computing environment has been shown to mitigate gender differences. Kiesler et al. (1985) suggested that social circumstances and software content are instrumental in perpetuating the male bias. They contended that entertaining computer software is often designed in such a way that men find it more appealing based on content (war games, contact sports) and structure (spatial cues). Recently, information services have emerged that appear to have a relatively stronger following among women (Carey, 1991).

In several cases, an adequate teaching environment and ample computing resources have led to a disappearance of the male technology bias. It might be that such a softening of the gender bias results from new software content and structure that has considerable appeal to women. Miura (cited in Kubey & Larson, 1990) pointed out that girls become more involved with software applications that they find socially or intellectually meaningful, but boys prefer action-oriented applications. Meyer and Schulze (1993, 1994) report that males tend to be interested in technology for its own sake, whereas females look toward the benefits provided by the software.

In order to better understand how users relate to different technologies, it might be important to explore perceived groupings of various information and entertainment media and gender-based familiarity with these technologies. Users may perceive a screen-based information service as more similar to the telephone or television than to a computer system. The telephone and television are used more by women (Mundorf, Meyer, Schulze, & Zoche, 1994).

Technology and Cross-Cultural Comparison

A critical factor influencing the acceptance of and response to infotainment technologies internationally is culture. Differences between consumers of information technology products and services from different cultures could arise from a variety of sources, including political and social trends as well as educational, environmental, legal, and historical factors.

Differences in responses toward information and entertainment technologies among three different nations have been examined. Two of these nations were industrialized and new information technologies were commonly available (the United States and Germany); the third, Croatia, was on the periphery of the former East Bloc, and its economic development was further slowed by neighboring ethnic conflict.

The United States and Germany represent comparable income levels and penetration of common consumer technologies (Mundorf, Dholakia, Dholakia, & Westin, 1996; Westin & Mundorf, 1995) but different lifestyles. Some of the contextual patterns observed in contemporary Germany are attributable to the unification of East and West Germany and the resultant merger of two very different economic and infrastructure systems. Germany is economically advanced and has a well-trained workforce. However, in some respects, it is more traditional than the United States. Extended families tend to live closer together, female employment is somewhat lower, and work and private life are more clearly separated. Computer use in the workplace is high, but the use of technologies for communication and in the private sphere is somewhat less widespread than in the United States.

Widespread telephone penetration in private homes was not achieved until the late 1970s. Computer networking is also less common outside the research community. Finally, the ecological movement in Germany is strong; it tends to direct the focus of technology use toward its compatibility with the environment.

Croatia was part of the relatively open former Yugoslavia and, like most former East Bloc countries, has experienced an infusion of marketing of western technologies. Diffusion of technologies has been slow due to economic limitations. As a result, older Croatians have grown up in a world largely deprived of advanced technology and have only recently experienced its influx. Western products are now heavily marketed, particularly to the younger generation. Lifestyles of teenagers and young adults are becoming more similar to American youth. In addition, Croatian society is still characterized by extended families living closely together, which makes it less urgent to even use the telephone to keep in touch with other family members.

Results of a large scale international survey investigating the acceptance of new information technologies revealed that Americans are more familiar with technologies than are Germans (Mundorf & Brownell, 1994) and Croatians (Fortin, Mundorf, Westin, & Vranesevic, 1995). In the study, attitudes and orientations toward information and entertainment technologies of American, German, and Croatian consumers in different age groups were compared. American and German samples were chosen because they represent comparable income levels and penetration of common consumer technologies but different lifestyles. The study was extended to Croatia because, as an example of an emerging economy, it was anticipated to provide insights regarding attitudes toward technology in newly evolving markets. The "Familiarity and Lifestyle Survey," an instrument developed to investigate familiarity with, preferences for, and attitudes toward information technology, was administered to 212 college students and to 244 older adults in the United States. The questionnaire was then translated into German and Croatian and then administered to 84 college students and 50 older adults in Germany, and to 500 students and 500 older adults living in Croatia. All participants volunteered to participate in this study. Both the younger and older participants from each country were involved in their respective communities and completed the questionnaire without assistance. For details of the study, see Fortin, Mundorf, Westin, and Vranesevic (1995).

Surprisingly, the study demonstrated that German and Croatian levels of familiarity with technology move at a similar level. For emerging technologies, Americans showed greater familiarity compared to Germans and Croatians. For the more common types of technologies (TV and phone based), older Americans also showed greater familiarity than Germans and Croatians. In contrast to overall trends, older German males displayed a more positive attitude toward technology compared to their college-age counterparts. A related study revealed that in German households with younger women, the transfer of technology from the workplace to the home was found to be more likely to occur (Mundorf, Meyer, Schulze, & Zoche, 1994). German males were still the more prevalent technology users. They dominated the use of VCRs, CD Players, computers, and fax machines; were more interested in the inner workings of the technologies; used them for recreation such as games; and were more likely to repair them than were women. Whereas men were more interested in playing with the technologies, women regarded them as tools serving a particular purpose.

The intention to use conventional telephone technology (including cordless) was greater for Americans than for citizens of the two other countries. Croatians showed a clear linear pattern related to age, but for Americans and Germans, the middle-aged group showed the greatest intention to use, followed by the younger group and then the group over 50 years of age. An age effect materialized for the composite measure of computing. Apparently, those of college age are much more familiar with computers and related technologies than older groups—regardless of country or gender.

Overall, males tended to be more familiar with technologies than were females, younger participants displayed greater familiarity than older ones, and Americans were more familiar with technologies than were Germans. Across cultures, men were more technology oriented than women. This gender effect was not found for phone technologies. Probably, women feel a relatively greater level of comfort with these compared to other technologies, which results in familiarity levels similar to that of males. The data supported the view that American consumers were more familiar with most information technologies than were German consumers. This difference was especially pronounced for U.S. college students. Americans showed a greater propensity to use information technologies than did Germans or Croatians.

Americans showed significantly stronger agreement with three general statements pertaining to the role of technology in life. Germans revealed significantly greater concern than Americans did with specific technological advances, notably in the areas of the environment, medicine, human life, and society. Americans conceded that it improves our quality of life and gives us control over nature. Germans tended to be more skeptical of the role of technology in society than Americans, especially as far as specific societal areas are concerned (e.g., medicine and the environment). However, Americans were concerned with the danger of losing essential human qualities due to technological innovations. German college students were far more conservative regarding the acceptance of technologies than their American counterparts. They are roughly at the same level as older Germans. Finally, the study confirmed that across cultures, men are more technology oriented than women. As could be expected from greater telephone usage by women in both countries, this effect was not found for telephone-oriented technologies.

Americans displayed a greater degree of technology seeking compared to German respondents. Overall, students showed greater technology seeking than their older counterparts.

Current research reveals generally greater technology acceptance by men compared to women, by younger compared to older users, and by Americans compared to Germans and Croatians. In light of these patterns, it may be desirable to design and market technologies in such a way as to increase their acceptance by women and older users. Also, cultural differences in attitudes toward technologies might be addressed.

CONCLUSION

As diffusion of new technologies increases in private homes, older adults gain greater access to a variety of infotainment systems that have the potential to reduce their isolation, facilitate friendships across geographical distances, provide information on a variety of concerns, and generally improve their quality of life. Access to information and other users through online services and the WorldWide Web have helped attract thousands of older users to computer and communication technologies, even if they face the physical challenges often associated with aging.

The Bryant and Love (1996) model of infotainment technology use identifies how characteristics such as Selectivity, Diet, Interactivity, Agency, Personalization, and Dimensionality can benefit and attract older users. This model suggests directions for future research to explore acceptance and usage behavior of older users.

Although socioeconomic status is a critical predictor of technology use, this chapter has discussed research showing the importance of age, gender, and culture. Older adults are less likely than younger adults to acquire and use technologies. Across generations, a male bias in technology use still exists, although it seems to be lessened in some areas. By and large, women are more interested in the functionality and less impressed by the technical intricacies of a technology.

Technology use across cultures, in particular among older users, is little understood. This chapter presents some data comparing three cultures in terms of familiarity with and attitudes toward technology. Despite economic advances, German consumers tend to be less active users of, and less familiar with, some information technologies. Ironically, German patterns of diffusion are more similar to those of Croatia, where it is somewhat slower than in the United States. This difference is especially pronounced in the older group.

ACKNOWLEDGMENT

The authors wish to thank Jay Silver for his help with online research.

REFERENCES

Arch, E. C., & Cummins, D. E. (1989). Structured and unstructured exposure to computers: Sex differences in attitude and use among college students. *Sex Roles, 20,* 245–254.

Babchuk, N. (1978). Aging and primary relations. *International Journal of Aging and Human Development, 9,* 137–151.

Baig, E. (1994, July 25). Sending seniors into cyberspace. *Business Week,* 91.

Beville, H. M. (1988). *Audience ratings.* Hillsdale, NJ: Lawrence Erlbaum Associates.

Brownell, W. E., & Mundorf, N. (1990). *Student attitudes toward computers and the willingness to communicate online.* Unpublished manuscript.

Bryant, J. (1991). *Alabama Information Age Task Force report.*

Bryant, J., & Love, C. (1996). Entertainment as the driver of new information technologies. In R. R. Dholakia, N. Mundorf, & N. Dholakia (Eds.), *New infotainment technologies in the home* (pp. 91–114). Mahwah, NJ: Lawrence Erlbaum Associates.

Carey, J. (1991, October 23). *Consumer adoption of new communication technologies.* Lecture, University of Rhode Island.

Clark, M., & Anderson, B. G. (1967). *Culture and aging.* Springfield, IL: Thomas.

Czaja, D. J. (1988). Safety and security of the elderly: Implications for smart house design. *International Journal of Technology and Aging, 1,* 49–66.

Ferguson, D. A.(1991, November). *Gender differences in the use of remote control devices.* Paper presented at the annual convention of the Speech Communication Association, Atlanta, GA.

Fortin, D., Mundorf, N., Westin, S., & Vranesevic, T. (1995). The Impact of country, age, and gender on familiarity with and attitudes toward information technology. In R. R. Dholakia & D. Fortin (Eds.), *Proceedings of the first conference on telecommunications and information markets: Living and working in cyberspace.* (pp. 40–49). Kingston,RI: Research Institute for Telecommunications and Information Marketing.

Gelb, B. D. (1978). Exploring the gray market segment. *MSU Business Topics, 26,* 41–46.

Groves, D. (1990). Computer-assisted instruction with senior citizens. *Journal of Instructional Psychology, 17*(3), 172–177.

Groves, D., & Slack, T. (1994). Computers and their application to senior citizen therapy within a nursing home. *Journal of Instructional Therapy, 21*(3), 221–226.

Kautzmann, L. (1990). Introducing computers to the elderly. *Physical and Occupational Therapy in Geriatrics, 9*(1), 27–36.

Kerschner, P. A., & Chelsvig, K. A. (1981). *The aged user and technology.* Paper presented at the conference on Communications Technology and the Elderly: Issues and Forecasts, Cleveland, OH.

Kiesler, S., Sproull, L., & Eccles, J. S. (1985). Pool halls, chips, and war games: Women in the culture of computing. *Psychology of Women Quarterly, 9,* 451–462.

Kubey, R., & Larson, R. (1990). The use and experience of the new video media among children and young adolescents. *Communication Research, 17,* 107–130.

Landler, M. (1994, March 14). Are we having fun yet? Maybe too much. *Business Week,* 66.

Lockheed, M. E. (1985). Women, girls, and computers: A first look at the evidence. *Sex Roles, 13,* 115–122.

Meyer, S., & Schulze, E. (1993). *Projektergebnisse: technikfolgen fuer familien.* [Project results: Effects of technology for families]. Duesseldorf: VDI-Technologiezentrum.

Meyer, S., & Schulze, E. (1994). *Alles automatisch: Technikfolgen fuer familien.* [Everything's automatic: Effects of technology for families]. Berlin: Edition Sigma.

Microsoft Corporation (1993). *Microsoft Windows & MS-DOS users guide,* 381–385. Redmond, WA: Microsoft Press.

Morgan, J. M. (1994). User interface design for older adults. *Interacting with Computers, 6*(4), 373–393.

Mundorf, N., & Brownell, W. (1994, November). *Age, gender and culture and the acceptance of information technology.* Paper presented at the Speech Communication Association Convention, New Orleans, LA.

Mundorf, N., Dholakia, R. R., Dholakia, N., & Westin, S. (1996). Germand and American Consumer Orientations to Information Technologies: Implications for marketing and public policy. *Journal of International Consumer Marketin,* 125–144.

Mundorf, N., Meyer, S., Schulze, E., & Zoche, P. (1994). Families, information technologies, and the quality of life: German research findings. *Telematics and Informatics, 11*(2), 137–146.

Mundorf, N., Westin, S., & Dholakia, N. (1993). Effects of hedonic components and user's gender on the acceptance of screen-based information services. *Behavior & Information Technology, 12*(5), 293–303.

Nodell, B. (1994, June 3). Seniors go on-line to educate, find pals. (Hayward, CA) *Daily Review, 42,* p. D2.

Nussbaum, J. F., Thompson, T., & Robinson, J. D. (1989). *Communication and aging.* New York: Harper & Row.

Ogozalek, V. (1991). The social impacts of computing: Computer technology and the graying of America. *Social Science Computer Review, 9,* 655–666.

Rawlins, W. K. (1992). *Friendship matters: Communication, dialectics, and the life course.* New York: deGruyter.

Roberto, K. A., & Scott, J. P. (1986). Friendships of older men and women: Exchange patterns and satisfaction. *Psychology and Aging, 1,* 103–109.

Rogers, E. M. (1986). *Communication technology.* New York: The Free Press.

Rovner, S. (1995, July 23). Prodigy group offers support for grieving spouses. *Providence Sunday Journal,* p. E5.

Salvaggio, J. L., & Bryant, J., Eds. (1989). *Media use in the information age: Emerging patterns of adoption and consumer use.* Hillsdale, NJ: Lawrence Erlbaum Associates.

Shostak, A. B. (1994, July 11). Artificial intelligence and the fragile elderly: Doing the 'smart' thing...soon. *Brown University Long-Term Care Quality Letter,* 3–4.

Spakes, P. R. (1979). Family, friendship, and community interaction as related to life satisfaction of the elderly. *Journal of Gerontological Social Work, 1,* 279–293.

Temple, L., & Gavillet, M. (1990). The development of computer confidence in seniors: An assessment of changes in computer anxiety and computer literacy. *Activities, Adaptation and Aging, 14*(3), 63–76.

Venkatesh, A., & Vitalari, N. P. (1986). Computing technology for the home: Product strategies for the next generation. *Journal of Product Innovation and Management, 3,* 171–186.

Venkatesh, A., & Vitalari, N. P. (1987). A post-adoption analysis of computing in the home. *Journal of Economic Psychology*. 161–180.

Westin, S., & Mundorf, N. (1995). Adoption of information technology: The impact of age, gender, culture. *Proceedings of the 6th International Conference of the Information Resource Management Association*, 66–67.

Zeithaml, V. A., & Gilly, M. C. (1987). Characteristics affecting the acceptance of retailing technologies: A comparison of elderly and nonelderly consumers. *Journal of Retailing*, 49–68.

Zillmann, D., Weaver, J., Mundorf, N., & Aust, C. (1986). Effects of an opposite-gender companion's affect to horror on distress, delight, and attraction. *Journal of Personality and Social Psychology*, *51*, 586–594.

II

CROSS-GENERATIONAL COMMUNICATION AND AGING

INTRODUCTION

Part II focuses on the communication between generations within the framework of their cultures. Three American cocultures (Hawaiians, Arabs, and Mormons) were examined in regard to their familial relationships with their elders. Chapter 4 examines how the use of pidgin by Hawaiians reaffirms the mutual interdependence between generations in promoting and maintaining cross-generational continuity. Chapter 5 seeks to ascertain the attitudes of younger Arab Americans toward their elders while taking into account the cultural diversity among them. Chapter 6 looks at family mentoring across generations by considering elder parents and the mentoring relationships that may exist among these parents, their children and grandchildren among the Mormons.

These co-cultures greatly differ from each other in many regards, yet they are similar in their emphases on these familial relationships with their elders. The overriding theme of this section is to show that language, attitudes, and mentoring can serve as the links for maintaining cross-generational continuity in this multicultural society. Although the means may differ co-culturally throughout the society, the goal remains the same, which is maintaining cross-generational continuity for the betterment of all.

4

Pidgin To Da Max: A Bridge Toward Satisfying Cross-Generational Communication Among the Hawaiians

Diane M. Kimoto
American Red Cross

Mahalo! Mai-Tai! Luau! Don Ho singing "Tiny Bubbles" in Waikiki. For many haoles (i.e., Caucasians), these terms conjure pleasant memories and impressions of Hawai'i. However, these terms fail to capture the *kaona,* or "inner meaning," of Hawai'i that is best expressed in Hawaiian Creole English. According to local Hawaiians, this language expresses a spirit of aloha (Haas, 1992). Individuals who adopt this language, commonly referred to as pidgin, find that it involves them in the establishment of social criteria necessary for the construction of culture (Stoller, 1985).

Hawai'i is distinctive for yet other reasons. It is a state where the mother tongue of over 42% of the population is something other than Standard American English (Haas, 1992). As a consequence, Hawai'i is "the only place in the world" (Bickerton, 1984, p. 174) where it is still possible to interview surviving speakers of a localized pidgin alongside younger speakers of the same language. Clearly, then, it is imperative that we examine how "interaction with younger generations provides elders with the opportunity to exchange information about, and come to terms with, their lives" (McKay, 1993, p. 177). The overall goal of the chapter is to explore how local Hawaiians promote cross-generational continuity through their use of Hawaiian Creole English. The chapter also seeks to expand the canonical definition of pidgins and creoles by examining their role (i.e., the verbal exchange of experiences) in the multistaged, dynamic acquisition of culture. Consistent with this view, Hawaiian Creole English functions as a collective memory for the local island culture and cross-generational continuity takes shape through the notions and themes that are consistently repeated by a group of speakers. The chapter begins by reviewing current literature in the areas of pidginization, the social construction of cultural identity, cross-generational continuity, and modes of analysis. It proceeds by discussing the results and concludes with a summary of important findings.

AN OVERVIEW OF THE PIDGINIZATION OF HAWAI'I

Basic Definitions

A pidgin may be defined as the simple language that results when individuals do not share a first language (Bickerton, 1984; Meyerhoff & Niedzielski, 1994). As such, pidgins function primarily to "facilitate the conduct of commerce between different linguistic groups" (Meyerhoff & Niedzielski, p. 313). Creoles, on the other hand, refer to pidgins that have evolved into the first language of a group of individuals (Bickerton; Meyerhoff & Niedzielski). Often, creoles arise when individuals are forced to interact on a permanent basis and must converge on some common means of communication.

Hawai'i's History

The pidginization of Hawai'i may be traced back to when Captain James Cook landed in the Hawaiian Islands in 1778 (Day, 1987; Schutz, 1994). Upon this first sailing to Hawai'i, Captain Cook, who regularly recruited sailors from various ports of call, brought along a Tahitian sailor he had picked up while visiting Tahiti. Because he had never met a Hawaiian before, Captain Cook relied upon the Tahitian sailor to communicate with the local Hawaiians in a Polynesian-based language somewhat similar to Hawaiian. Through a modification of contextually based words and gestures, "Cook's encounter was perhaps the first documented use of what might be termed a pidgin" (Day, p. 164).

During the period from 1805 to 1876, both Hawaiian Maritime Pidgin and Plantation Pidgin prospered as a means for promoting the major industries of Hawai'i (Day, 1987). From 1805–1852, Hawaiian Maritime Pidgin was employed by individuals who were interested in trading for sandalwood with China and by those seeking their fortunes in the whaling industry. As such, it was "heavily Hawaiian, both in vocabulary and grammar" (Day, p. 165). Hawaiian Plantation Pidgin, which prospered from 1852 to 1876, promoted the interests of the sugar cane industry and the numerous

Chinese and Japanese laborers who came to work the cane fields. However, this latter pidgin is most "noteworthy in the history of Hawai'i" because it reflected a gradual shift from "a Hawaiian-based pidgin to an English-based pidgin" (Day, p. 171).

After the American annexation of Hawai'i in 1898, English was mandated as the official language of the Hawaiian Islands. Still, pidgin remained the language of choice for many Hawaiians (Bickerton & Wilson, 1987; Reinecke, 1969). Unsure as to which language to learn in any depth, the local islanders expanded this primitive pidgin into Hawaiian Creole English, which is spoken to this day (Bickerton & Odo, 1976).

Hawai'i's linguistic history has reflected how pidgin has affected and been affected by the social and interpersonal events of its speakers. For the pidgin and creole speakers of Hawai'i, "social reality is based on the historicity of this store of experiences" (Stoller, 1985, p. 5). It is this interplay of events that serves as a model for the acquisition of culture and the knowledge necessary for a people to orient themselves in the world (Berger & Luckmann, 1966; Stoller).

THE SOCIAL CONSTRUCTION AND CONTINUITY OF CULTURAL IDENTITY

The last few decades have seen a movement toward a deeper analysis of the changes that pidgins and creoles bring about "when they cease to function solely as an intergroup tool of communication and become an ingroup tool of speaker identity as well" (Meyerhoff & Niedzielski, 1994, p. 315). According to Stoller (1985),

> Ethnic identity reflects the social construction and acquisition of culture where a tacit agreement determines what is real and not real in any given society…and communication creates meaning as opposed to merely messages and in this way aids the individual in understanding personal and social experiences. (p. 5)

The tacit agreement as to what constitutes reality for a group of individuals is conveyed as much through the sharing of a mutual language as through the system of rules governing the recognition and ascription of meaning for terms, locations, ideas, and activities within the stream of conversation (Schegloff & Sacks, 1973). Consequently, the acquisition or construction of culture is both an intrapersonal and interpersonal process as it describes the manner in which the human mind interprets socially constituted knowledge.

Following the guidelines established by Meyerhoff and Niedzielski (1994), this chapter employs the term of *ethnolinguistic vitality* in explaining the relationship between a pidgin-speaking community and its cultural identity. Ethnolinguistic vitality refers to the perceived legitimacy of one's ethnic group as it relates to the status of one's language in the community, the relative numbers of speakers of the language, and the level of governmental support for the maintenance of this language (Giles, Bourhis, & Taylor, 1977). Pidgins and cultural identities associated with perceptions of high ethnolinguistic vitality will likely prosper. In contrast, those associated with perceptions of low ethnolinguistic vitality will most certainly fail to creolize (Meyerhoff & Niedzielski, 1994).

Intrinsically associated with the concept of stability is the notion of continuity. Continuity theory posits that as individuals grow older, they are predisposed toward maintaining consistency in personal habits, commitments, and preferences (Atchley, 1972). "Continuity is an adaptive response to both internal and external pressures" (Atchley, 1985, p. 238). Internal pressures toward continuity originate within an individual's need to build a stable foundation of viewpoints from which judgments and future predictions may be made. External pressures for continuity emanate from a need to fulfill the various social roles occupied by the individual. In striking a balance between these pressures, "continuity, then, is viewed as a healthy capacity to see inner change as connected to an individual's past and the sense of self-satisfaction achieved is relevant not only to that individual but others with whom he or she is associated" (Atchley, 1989, p. 184).

Continuity is also achieved through satisfying cross-generational communications where the elderly can feel a sense of contentment in knowing that their knowledge and experiences will continue to influence the lives of younger individuals (Atchley, 1989; McKay, 1993). For example, it is through personal interaction, such as with our elders, that we learn how to identify and assign meaning (Giles, Fox, Harwood, & Williams, 1994; Potter & Wetherell, 1987). "Consistent with a lifespan perspective, then, continuity becomes an integral aspect of individual development" (McKay, p. 177).

CONTINUITY OF HAWAI'I'S LOCAL CULTURE: A DYNAMIC INTERDEPENDENCE

Ingroup Identification

"Hawai'i has an evolving 'local' culture which represents the contributions of several ethnic traditions" (Rezentes, 1993, p. 390). In local terms, this language is called a *kapakahi* or chop suey mixture of many different people and customs (Simonson, Sakata, & Sasaki, 1986). In fact, when asked whether the roots of some pidgin words were more Japanese, Hawaiian, or English in nature, Rachel Kepepe, a local resident from Kaua'i, responded by saying:

> So we use the Hawaiian, Chinese, and English all together, in one sentence, see? And they ask me if that's a pidgin word, I say no, maybe that's a Japanese word. It is all mixed together in order to make a sentence for them to understand you. (Bickerton & Wilson, 1987, p. 70)

Thus, the local pidgin English, which borrows various cultural constructs from standard English, Hawaiian, and other languages, is a good example of how polyethnic groups have together formed a "new" ingroup language (Nagel, 1994; Rezentes, 1994).

Pidgin characterizes the local Hawaiian culture in that it reflects anything that is typical of the manner in which people do things in Hawai'i. It is also extremely rich in words from particular domains that are deemed important to the local culture. For example, the word *aloha* may only signify 'welcome' for a tourist, but for a local, it may "signify 'love,' 'affection,' 'good-will,' and may perhaps be twisted into 'thank you' or 'gratitude'" (Schutz, 1994, p. 208). The use of pidgin "provides an important means of preserving and passing on knowledge"; (Silva, 1989, p. 86) it also provides a means for exhibiting cultural pride.

Ethnolinguistic Vitality

According to Nist (1976), individuals speak the local Hawaiian pidgin (basilect) rather than the more formal acrolect of Standard American English because they are "socially disadvantaged Americans who have no more than a grade school education and are little better than innocent bystanders on the linguistic scene" (p. 205).

What has transpired since the 1970s has been a rebirth of Hawaiian pride, entitled *Hawaiiana* (Haas, 1992; Rezentes, 1994; Silva, 1989). The following statement is an illustration of that renaissance. It reaffirms the legitimacy of the local island culture and the language that represents its *kaona*. According to Pukui (1949),

> There were always two things to consider: the literal meaning and the *kaona*, or "inner meaning." The inner meaning was sometimes so veiled that only the people to whom the chant belonged understood it, and sometimes so

obvious that anyone who knew the figurative speech of old Hawai'i could
see it very plainly. (p. 247)

Cross-Generational Continuity

In cultures such as Hawai'i, which emphasize an oral tradition, cultural
continuity is promoted through the communication of mutual values and
ideas (Ong, 1980). Bickerton and Odo (1976), Tamir (1979), and Stoller
(1985) believed that the field of pidgin and creole studies contributed much
to this understanding by emphasizing the fact that satisfying cross-generational communication also promoted cultural stability and consistency.
Cultural practices and traditions are embedded within individuals' communication through what Burton and Stack (1993) called kinscripts, or prescribed patterns of family interaction.

> Kinscripts encompass three culturally defined domains: kin-work, which is
> the labor and the tasks that families need to accomplish to survive from
> generation to generation; kin-time, which is the temporal and sequential
> ordering of family transitions; and kinscription, which is the process of
> assigning kin-work to family members. (p. 103)

Hawai'i's elders are regarded as valuable resources in the education
of younger generations in that they are the keepers and conveyors of
kinscripts (Schutz, 1994; Sumida, 1985; Welford, 1983). For example,
through their everyday interactions, Hawaiian elders familiarize younger
generations with the local pidgin language and its associated rules
system, and children acquire a familiarity with home, community speech
events, knowledge of real-world events, and patterns of socialization
(Haas, 1992; Kawakami & Au, 1986; Schutz; Speidel, Tharp, & Kobayashi, 1985).

METHOD

As mentioned earlier, the chapter hoped to gather information rather than
provide empirical validation. In light of this goal, a sample of 19 individuals
(9 females and 10 males) was deemed appropriate. The participants were
recruited from a midsize shopping mall in the Honolulu area on a weekday
afternoon by two students from a local community college during the
summer of 1995. Prospective participants were informed that the survey,
which would take about 10 minutes to complete, was part of a project
dealing with cross-generational communication and the use of pidgin. The

food court section of the shopping mall was considered a primary location for recruitment because of its central location and attraction for individuals from various walks of life. All participant responses were presented to a graduate student, who was trained in the coding of qualitative responses, in order to spot-check the researcher's coding of continuity themes, thus ensuring a more valid set of findings (Kaid & Wadsworth, 1989; Stempel & Wesley, 1981).

A review of the literature (Mokau, 1994; Rezentes, 1993) suggested that the topic areas of language (pidgin), family caretaking, and impressions of Hawai'i were appropriate in identifying the local Hawaiian culture. The following questions, as shown in the Appendix, were posed before each participant: (a) What does it mean for you to take care of your grandparents? (b) Why do you speak pidgin? (c) With whom do you speak pidgin? and (d) Explain three things that make Hawai'i special for you. Finally, general demographic information pertaining to each participant was gathered: (a) educational background, (b) age, (c) length of residency in Hawai'i, and (d) socioeconomic status.

ANALYSIS OF CULTURAL CONTINUITY

In advancing the position that individuals' cultural identities are influenced through a cross-generational use of pidgin, it is essential to examine the degree to which Hawaiian Creole English is spoken by local Hawaiians, the use and function of this language, and the manner in which notions of continuity are embedded within responses regarding family caretaking and personal impressions of Hawai'i. Through this approach, notions of continuity will take shape as individuals provide "descriptions of their roles, relationships, and accounts of information exchanged with others" (McKay, 1993, p. 178).

Pidgin: It's the Way Local People Communicate

According to the demographics in Table 4.1, 16 of the 19 participants who indicated that they spoke pidgin were considered as local Hawaiians for the purposes of this study. The participants explained that their acceptance and usage of pidgin were promoted through early exposure in the home, which was reinforced through continued familial and relational interaction. In the next two examples, the individual responses of participants were separated by arrows (i.e.,→) and presented sequentially from eldest to youngest. These

TABLE 4.1
Background of Respondents

Value Label	N	Percentage
Lived in Hawai'i (years)		
less than 20	4	21
20–29	12	63
30–39	1	5
60+	2	11
Gender		
Male	10	53
Female	9	47
Age (years)		
less than 20	1	5
20–29	8	42
30–39	4	21
40–49	2	11
60+	4	21
Educational Background		
High school	1	5
High school graduate	3	16
College	8	42
College graduate	4	21
Graduate school	2	11
Other	1	5
Social Economic Status		
Medium	19	100

N = 19

examples, which illustrated how local Hawaiians from various generations used the same pidgin words and expressions in their everyday communications, suggested that continuity between generations can be enhanced through similar language use. For instance, in the first example, notice how certain terms, such as *da kine* (i.e., an all-inclusive term for anywhere, anytime, anyhow, and anykind) and *bruddah* (i.e., friend), were employed to extend the cultural understanding between generations.

With whom do you speak pidgin?

All people (po'e) born in Hawai'i, da kine → friends, classmates, Filipino adult workers → family members who reside in Hawai'i, da kine → only those local bruddahs who understand it → non fluent English speakers, like locals → family/friends → everybody in ya da kine.

Pidgin may also serve as an important link between generations by promoting the sharing of common rules governing the patterning of conversations (Schegloff & Sacks, 1973). Participants as young as 12 and as old as 73 commented how they easily conversed with one another.

Why do you speak pidgin?

Brought up with pidgin → Because I want to get to know people (po'e) and communicate → To communicate. Be understood and understand what is being said → Because that is the way I was brought up and the language spoken in the 'ohana (family) → As a simplified means of communication, with emphasis placed more on content than diction → It is a simple way to communicate wit'ou complex sentence structure and words. Eliminates jargon → Because that is what I grew up with, habit → Just raised with it and exposed to it while growing up.

Pidgin may also facilitate cross-generational continuity in that it provides a public demonstration of cultural pride. In fact, the most detailed explanations about pidgin utilization came from individuals who have attended college and are aware of the acrolect status associated with Standard American English.

Kiana is a 24-year-old female who has lived her entire life in Hawai'i, as does the majority of her family. She considers Hawai'i both her birthplace and home. Kiana comes from a middle-income background and has attended college. She feels most comfortable speaking pidgin with family and close friends and chronicles the history of local Hawai'i when she details *why she speaks pidgin*:

It was a language that was formed back during the time of bartering. There were so many different races stopping over plus many immigrants who were brought here to work. It was a means of communication between different cultures. The only way they could communicate was to speak in broken English, thus yielding Pidgin English. But now, I think it is used to distinguish yourself as being local. It's a way the local people (po'e) communicate. What's important to know is when to use it and when to turn it off.

The usage of pidgin as a cross-generational tool extends beyond shared notions of language use and function. It continues into the formation of a collective memory pertaining to personal roles and relationships in the family.

Family Caretaking: Notions of 'Ohana

Embedded within the pidgin language are kinscripts regarding family caretaking. As a culture built upon the transmission of common values and "tasks that families need to accomplish to survive" (Burton & Stack, 1993, p. 103), the following responses provided by local Hawaiians, presented in sequential order from eldest to youngest, illustrate a continuity in cultural norms regarding the unquestioned giving back to one's own, a sign of respect for *'ohana.*

What does taking care of grandma and grandpa mean to you?

Taking care of them, I guess → Obligation → Feeling of owing to them without owing, though → Making sure that they are well-fed, neat and clean and that they have transportation to wherever they need to go, they are happy and able to travel anytime and anywhere without financial burdens → It's a must. No questions asked. You make time to do what needs to be done → It is like a family obligation but not a duty to perform, that means a lot to me, learning our family history, heritage, and customs; from my tutu kane (grandfather) gave me a sense of identity → Watching out and caring for them because they have raised my parents; so as the younger generation we are indebted to show loving care and tenderness toward our grandparents. The patriarchs of 'ohana (family), kupuna-elders. Founders of the 'ohana deserve the respect of all generations → no questions asked, simply a giving to my tita (grandmother) and tutu kane (grandfather) → My grandparents are extremely important—I would take great interest in making sure that my grandparents are happy, content, and healthy → Taking care of them the way they took care of me when I was a baby.

Once again, it is interesting to note how many different pidgin terms the participants associate with the notion of family caretaking, thus establishing it as an essential component of the local Hawaiian culture. Together, these results emphasize the strength attributed to cultural tales advanced through familial communications (Stoller, 1985) and the stability of cultural rule systems (Woolford & Washabaugh, 1983).

Impressions of Hawai'i: E'Hawai'i Au

The findings from this study reveal that local Hawaiians focused on four general themes in describing their impressions of Hawai'i: the island's beauty and the island culture as home, people, and food. The following examples were selected, and sequentially placed from eldest to youngest because they characterized the typical manner in which similar pidgin words and expressions have been used by successive generations of local Hawaiian men and women. In turn, these examples suggested that even casual communications served to maintain cultural continuity (Atchley, 1972, 1985, 1989; McKay, 1993).

> Salu, a 73-years-old man, explained that he liked Hawai'i because of its friendly people (po'e) and good food. He grew up in Hawai'i, therefore it would always have a feeling of nostalgia and proximity.

> Aunty JoJo, a 67-year-old woman, associated Hawai'i's specialness with its climate and people (po'e) more free—you don't have to really dress up; You feel more like you talk to people (po'e)—you don't feel, like what you say uptight.

> Keoki, a 44-year-old man, commented that Hawai'i was special to him because of Buggahs! Brahs! (Friendly people (po'e)—especially on the outer islands); weather and outdoor activities that Hawai'i presents; Because E'Hawai'i Au (I am Hawaiian) and this is my home.

> Kalena, a 24-year-old woman, revealed that Hawai'i was special since it was the place of her birth, the history, culture, and music that makes it unique, the beauty of the islands—weather, beaches, mountains. My home!

> Keka, a 12-year-old boy, said he liked Hawai'i's atmosphere. Everyone here helps each other. Aloha spirit; all of my family and friends are here; food and beauty of the islands.

Each of these examples contains at least two of the four general themes regarding impressions of Hawai'i. For some individuals, these impressions may be experienced individually, as in one's appreciation of the island's beauty, its weather, beaches, or outdoor activities. On the other hand, the appreciation of people, family, a local style, or racial harmony may be more of an interpersonal activity. Thus, it appears that some tacit agreement exists that allows individuals to understand what constitutes reality (Stoller, 1985).

CONCLUSION

The purpose of this chapter is to explore how cross-generational continuity is promoted through the use of Hawaiian Creole English. In addition, the chapter seeks support for the notion that pidgin and creole languages influence the shaping of one's cultural identity through a verbal exchange of experiences. The implications from these findings suggest several answers.

Local Hawaiians are brought up speaking pidgin. Through daily interactions with family and close friends, individuals acquire their cultural identity and social rules of behavior. Possibly, it is the simplistic nature of pidgin with its greater emphasis upon content rather than structure that allows individuals from different generations and backgrounds to communicate so readily. Perhaps, pidgin serves as an important link between generations because it promotes common rules that govern the patterning of conversations. Maybe, pidgin's significance rests upon its usage as a tangible expression of cultural pride. No matter which reason is discussed, the fact remains that the use of pidgin promotes intergenerational and cultural continuity.

Through the use of pidgin, a collective memory surrounding family caretaking and personal impressions of Hawai'i has developed. In addition, this collective memory also carries with it a system of rules governing the interpretation and recognition of "inner meanings," such as the understanding of kinscripts and *E' Hawai'i Au.* This more tacit connotation promotes reality and extends the cultural continuum across generations. It appears that notions of cross-generational continuity and cultural identity are embedded within everyday conversations of everyday experiences.

Although the findings associated with this chapter indicate satisfying intergenerational communications, that is not the norm. Cross-generational communication is often hindered by patronizing or overaccommodating talk (Giles, Fox, Harwood, & Williams, 1994). These communication events occur bidirectionally in that young people often patronize (i.e., talking loudly as if all elders have poor hearing) and overaccommodate (i.e., speaking slowly and down to elders) the elderly. According to Giles, Fox, Harwood, and Williams,

> Many of the problems associated with cross-generational communication reside within socially constructed images and stereotypes of individuals, and that these originate in the activities of categorizing and assigning meaning to categories. (p. 148)

Consequently, it is essential that we investigate those communities that have successfully negotiated a bypass through this dilemma. It is also imperative that we "examine how older people actually talk and are talked to by younger people" (Giles, Fox, Harwood, & Williams, 1994, p. 137). Findings from such studies could advance efforts to promote the development of social skills for the elderly (Mokau, 1994; Welford, 1983) and the transition of nonstandard English-speaking students to Standard American

English speakers (Feldman, Stone, & Renderer, 1990; Kawakami & Au, 1986; Sumida, 1985).

What is presented in this chapter lays a foundation from which to examine how the use of pidgin reaffirms the mutual interdependence between generations in promoting and maintaining cultural and cross-generational continuity. In order to grasp the full meaning of this phenomenon, more detailed empirical and ethnographic examinations need to be pursued in order to understand aging as a communication-based production of collective experiences. It is hoped that the information provided here has sparked that interest.

REFERENCES

Atchley, R. C. (1972). *The social forces in later life: An introduction to social gerontology.* Belmont, CA: Wadsworth.

Atchley, R. C. (1985). *Social forces and aging.* Belmont, CA: Wadsworth.

Atchley, R. C. (1989). A continuity theory of normal aging. *The Gerontologist, 2,* 183–190.

Berger, P., & Luckmann, T. (1966). *The social construction of reality.* Garden City, NJ: Doubleday.

Bickerton, D. (1984). The language bioprogram hypothesis. *Behavioral and Brain Sciences, 7,* 173–221.

Bickerton, D., & Odo, C. (1976). *Change and variation in Hawaiian English.* Honolulu, HI: University of Hawai'i.

Bickerton, D., & Wilson, W. H. (1987). Pidgin Hawaiian. In G. G. Gilbert (Ed.), *Pidgin and creole languages* (pp. 61-76). Honolulu, HI: University of Hawai'i.

Burton, L. M., & Stack, C. B. (1993). Conscripting kin: Reflections on family, generation, and culture. In P. A. Cowan, D. Field, D. A. Hansen, A. Skolnick, & G. E. Swanson (Eds.), *Family, self, and society: Toward a new agenda for family research* (pp. 103–114). Hillsdale, NJ: Lawrence Erlbaum Associates.

Day, R. R. (1987). Early Pidginization in Hawai'i. In G. G. Gilbert (Ed.), *Pidgin and creole languages* (pp.163-176). Honolulu, HI: University of Hawai'i.

Feldman, C. F., Stone, A., & Renderer, B. (1990). Stage, transfer, and academic achievement in dialect-speaking Hawaiian adolescents. Special issue: Minority children. *Child Development, 61,* 472–484.

Giles, H., Bourhis, R., & Taylor, D. (1977). Toward a theory of language in ethnic group relations. In H. Giles (Ed.), *Language, ethnicity, and intergroup relations* (pp. 307–348). London: Academic.

Giles, H., Fox, S., Harwood, J., & Williams, A. (1994). Talking age and aging talk: Communicating through the life span. In M. L. Hummert, J. M. Wiemann, & J. F. Nussbaum (Eds.), *Interpersonal communication in older adulthood* (pp. 130–161). Thousand Oaks, CA: Sage.

Haas, M. (1992). *Institutional racism.* Westport, CT: Praeger.

Kaid, L. L., & Wadsworth, A. J. (1989). Content analysis. In P. Emmert & L. L. Barker (Eds.), *Measurement of communication behavior* (pp. 197–217). New York: Longman.

Kawakami, A. J., & Au, K. H. (1986). Encouraging reading and language development in cultural minority children. *Topics in Language Disorders, 6,* 71–80.

McKay, V. C. (1993). Making connections: Narrative as the expression of continuity between generations of grandparents and children. In N. Coupland & J. F. Nussbaum (Eds.), *Discourse and lifespan identity* (pp. 173–186). Newbury Park, CA: Sage.

Meyerhoff, M., & Niedzielski, N. (1994). Resistance to creolization: An interpersonal and intergroup account. *Language and Communication, 14,* 313–330.

Mokau, N. (1994). Life themes of native Hawaiian female elders: Resources for cultural preservation. *Social Work, 39,* 43–49.

Nagel, J. (1994). Constructing ethnicity: Creating and recreating ethnic identity and culture. *Social Problems, 41,* 152–176.

Nist, J. (1976). The language of the socially disadvantaged. In L. A. Samovar & R. E. Porter (Eds.), *Intercultural communication: A reader* (pp. 204–217). Belmont, CA: Wadsworth.

Ong, W. J. (1980). Literacy and orality in our times. *Journal of Communication, 30,* 197–204.

Potter, J., & Wetherell, M. (1987). *Discourse and social psychology: Beyond attitudes and behavior.* London: Sage.

Pukui, M. K. (1949). Songs (Meles) of old Ka'u Hawai'i. *Journal of American Folklore, 62,* 247–258.

Reinecke, J. (1969). *Language and dialect in Hawaii.* Honolulu, HI: University of Hawai'i.

Rezentes, W. C. III. (1993). N Mea Hawai'i: A Hawaiian acculturation scale. *Psychological Reports, 73,* 383–393.

Schegloff, E. A., & Sacks, H. (1973). Opening up closings. *Semiotica, 8,* 289–327.

Schutz, A. J. (1994). *The voices of Eden.* Honolulu, HI: University of Hawai'i.

Silva, K. (1989). Ka'akai o te Henua 'Enana: History of the land of men. *The Journal of Polynesian Society, 98,* 85–90.

Simonson, D., Sakata, K., & Sasaki, P. (1986). *Pidgin to da max.* Honolulu, HI: Bess Press.

Speidel, G. E., Tharp, R. G., & Kobayashi, L. (1985). Is there a comprehension problem for children who speak nonstandard English? A study of children with Hawaiian-English backgrounds. *Applied Psycholinguistics, 6,* 83–96.

Stempel, G. H., III., & Wesley, B. H. (Eds.). (1981). *Research methods in mass communication.* Englewood Cliffs, NJ: Prentice-Hall.

Stoller, P. (1985). Toward a phenomenological perspective in pidgin and creole studies. In I. F. Hancock (Ed.), *Diversity and development in English-related creoles* (pp. 1–12). Ann Arbor, MI: Karoma.

Sumida, J. I. (1985). Language development in the Hawai'i "Follow-Through-Project." *Journal of Reading, Writing, and Learning Disabilities, 1,* 71–79.

Tamir, L. M. (1979). *Communication and the aging process.* New York: Pergamon.

Welford, A. T. (1983). Social skills and aging: Principles and problems. *International Journal of Aging and Human Development, 17,* 1–5.

Woolford, E., & Washabaugh, W. (1983). *The social context of creolization.* Ann Arbor, MI: Karoma.

APPENDIX

Cross-Generational Communication Amongst Hawaiians

How is it that young and old can talk to one another without conflict or patronization? The reason for the lack of cross-generational conflict can be traced to the use of Hawaiian Creole English, or pidgin. Through the use of pidgin, cross-generational communication becomes a verbal exchange of experiences. Please take a few minutes to answer the following questions. Circle answers where appropriate. If you need more room, please use the back of the sheet. Thank you!

1. How long have you lived in Hawaii?_____

2. Why do you speak pidgin?_____

3. With whom do you talk pidgin?_____

4. What does it mean to you to take care of grandma and grandpa?_____
_____

5. Explain 3 things that make Hawai'i special to you._____
_____
_____

6. Gender: Male____   Female____

7. Age:____

8. Educational background:_____

9. Social economic status: Low____   Middle____   High____

5

Trends in Cross-Generational Communication Among Arab Americans

Hana S. Noor Al-Deen
University of North Carolina at Wilmington

The older population, aged 65+, has increased rapidly worldwide during this century. In 1990, the United States ranked second after China regarding elders, with 31.6 million people and 63.4 million people respectively (U.S. Department, 1991). By the year 2030, the prediction is that one of every five people in the United States will be aged 65+ (U.S. Department, 1991). This fast-growing segment of the U.S. population has inspired a great deal of attention from various organizations, interest groups, and the government. As a case in point, the U.S. federal government has increased funds for the National Institute on Aging (NIA) from $248,938,000 in fiscal year 1991 to $445,823,000 in fiscal year 1996 (Budget, 1990–95). Such an increase represents an overall jump of approximately 79% in funding.

Given the fact that American society is made up of various cocultures, one must observe such groups within the context of their cultural framework in order to understand the communicative patterns of the groups. The purpose of this chapter is to assess the quality of communication, herein explained by positive and negative attitudes, that younger Arab Americans hold toward their elders and to ascertain the magnitude to which cultural diversity among younger Arab Americans has an impact on the quality of communication that they extend toward their elders.

PERSPECTIVES ON AGING

During the last 4 decades, social gerontological theories were developed to examine the social and behavioral aspects of aging while focusing on adaptation of elders to the aging process (Markides & Mindel, 1987).

Despite their contribution, these theories "are still in the formative stage" (Cockerham, 1991, p.69). Theories from other areas of the social sciences are borrowed for the study of aging. One of the most useful is the exchange theory. It "is based on the assumption that human beings act or behave in ways that maximize rewards and minimize costs" (Markides & Mindel, p. 30). The "exchange theory components such as cost, reward, reciprocation, profit, reinforcement, power, and distributive justice" (Sussman, 1985, p. 443), notably "have roots in hedonistic doctrine, utilitarian economics, and the psychological theory of reinforcement provides (Sussman, 1985, p. 417), logical explanations of family–elderly…linkage" (Sussman, 1985, p. 443). "When rewards are not proportional to investments over the long term…individuals tend to feel angry with social relations, instability is created, and the propensities for conflict increase" (Lipman, 1982, p. 196). Lipman explained that "rewards may assume a wide gamut of forms: social approval;…self-reinforcement of values through conformity; and attainment of those items that are highly valued in their culture" (p. 196). Doyle (1987) illustrated two kinds of reinforcement: extrinsic and intrinsic. The "extrinsic reinforcement occurs when an outside reward follows an act", whereas "intrinsic reinforcement means the activity itself is rewarding" (Doyle, p. 336). The "experience of totally absorbing activity has been called task-centered (in contrast to ego-centered) activity" (Doyle, p. 337). So, the extrinsic reward can become "as a means to an end", and the intrinsic reward can become "as an end in itself" (Doyle, p. 337).

Whether the reward is materialistic, such as an inheritance, or nonmaterialistic, such as social praise for meeting cultural obligations, it has an impact on the quality of communication that younger people extend to their elders. The quality of communication is considered "the major issue in intergenerational exchange" (Cibulski & Bergman, 1981, p. 250). Tamir (1979) advocated that "the quality not quantity of communication is the key to personal well-being" (p. 149). Bengtson, Cutler, Mangen, and Marshall (1985) pointed out that "while the primary concern…is on the frequency of contact, another relevant factor to consider is the type of interaction" (p. 319). "Formal and ritualistic contact (such as family reunions and ceremonies) versus informal interaction (brief visits or discussions) may have qualitatively different effects upon lineage members" (Bengtson, et al., p. 319). Hummert, Nussbaum, and Wiemann (1992) "found a positive relationship between the quality and frequency of elders' relational interaction and their life satisfaction" (p. 416).

The quality of communication, for this study, is explained by positive and negative attitudes. An attitude is a "predisposition to act in a positive or negative way toward the attitude object" (Littlejohn, 1989, p. 84). Doyle (1987) noted that, according to modern social psychologists, "attitudes, mental structures concerning an object or issue, have cognitive, affective and action components. They may be central or peripheral, more or less salient, and more or less crystallized" (p. 328). "Social situations...may influence attitudes through the relations between the people involved" (Doyle, p. 303). Samovar, Porter, and Jain (1981) mentioned that "attitudes are learned within a cultural context. Whatever cultural environment surrounds us helps to shape and form our attitudes, our readiness to respond, and ultimately our behavior" (p. 45). "Attitudes, positive or negative, are an unavoidable aspect of human life" (Nussbaum, Thompson, & Robinson, 1989, p. 16). They do affect the quality of communication.

RATIONALE AND RESEARCH QUESTIONS

The cultural diversity of Arab Americans makes them an excellent group to study. Regardless of its origin or the degree of its variation, cultural diversity is substantially based on the acculturation of Arab Americans (Noor Al-Deen, 1994). "Acculturation refers to the reciprocal modifications that occur when individuals from two or more different sociocultural systems come into contact" (Spindler, 1977, p. 31). It represents "those changes that individuals make in their affective and cognitive identity and in their interactive behavior as they deal with life in a new cultural environment" (Ellingsworth, 1988, p. 259).

The acculturation of Arab Americans has been derived from the influence of both traditional Arab cultural values and American cultural values. For example, the communicative pattern of the traditional Arab family is vertical, that is, downward communication and upward communication from older to younger members, and vice versa (Barakat, 1985). "Downward communication often takes the form of orders, instructions, warnings, threats, reprehension, shaming" by the elders toward the young (Barakat, p. 37). "Upward communication, on the other hand, often takes the form of silence, pleas, appeals, apologies, explanations, inquires, etc." (1985, p. 37). Elders among traditional Arabs, as in many traditional groups, "act as models for behavior and sources of authority on values, history,...skills within the culture," customs, traditions, and so forth (Zandi, Mirle, & Jarvis, 1990, p. 163).

Nevertheless, "societal modernization as a whole...is negatively related to overall attitudes toward the aged" (Tamir, 1979, p. 100). Indeed, the "aged become increasingly useless with the advances of modern technology, and it is likely that with further modernization, subsequent generations will feel less favorably towards their elderly members" (Tamir, p. 100). Cockerham (1991) further elaborated by stating that "modernity appears to have adversely affected the status of the aged" (p. 62). He added that such a process "change[s] the roles of the elderly and reduce[s] the status and esteem they are accorded" (Cockerham, p. 62). Still, critics of modernization say that "Japan is one of the most modern and industrialized nations in the world, yet the status of the aged has remained quite high" (Cockerham, p. 62). Despite such criticism, the modernization effects appear to be more acute on western cultures than on eastern cultures.

Arab Americans basically can be grouped into those American citizens who were born in the United States and have been living in this country for generations and those naturalized citizens and permanent residents who were born in the Middle East and have been living part of their lives in the United States. The following research questions (RQs) are raised herein in order to examine the quality of communication that younger Arab Americans extend toward their elders.

RQ1:   Do Arab Americans have a positive or a negative attitude toward their elders?

RQ2:   Would any of the variables gender, age, education, marital status, country of origin, and duration in the United States (GAEMCD) have an impact on the attitudes of younger Arab Americans toward their elders?

METHOD

Sampling

The sample was randomly drawn from the database for the southeastern United States (i.e., North and South Carolina) of the American-Arab Anti-Discrimination Committee (ADC). The ADC was founded in 1980 by U.S. Senator James G. Abourezk. Because the population of North Carolina is virtually twice that of South Carolina, two thirds of the sample were drawn from the former state. Four hundred surveys were mailed out to Arab Americans on August 16, 1993, requesting anonymous responses. A week after the mailing, responses started to arrive and continued until September 27, 1993, when they effectively stopped. This was considered the official closing date for the waiting period. No follow-up was conducted due to certain limitations.

Although a mailed survey has some advantages in comparison to other research methods, a low response rate is one of its typical disadvantages. An acceptable response rate can be evaluated differently. For instance, Babbie (1986) indicated that a response rate of 50% is adequate, 60% is good, and 70% is very good. Wimmer and Dominick (1994) pointed out that "a typical survey (depending on area and type of survey) will achieve a response rate of 20%–40%" (p. 124). Hsia (1988) denoted that "generally returns fall within a range between 10% and 25%, if no elaborate enhancement or incentive is given" (p. 126). For this study, the response rate was 37%. Such a response rate is not high, although it is reasonable for a mailed survey, considering the following restriction that was put on the age of the participants.

Operationalization

In this study, "older people" were defined as individuals aged 65 and above. Younger people who participated in this study, however, were adults of ages 54 and below. Those surveyed were cordially asked not to participate if they were aged 55+. Such a request was deemed necessary because age 55 is considered a benchmark for designating the older population according to U.S. Department (1991). Nonetheless, suffice it to say that a definitive gauge for "old age" remains a somewhat elusive concept throughout much of the literature.

The survey was developed with the intention of gauging the quality of communication that younger Arab Americans extend toward their elders. Included in the 29 items of the survey is the NAD aging scale which consists of 20 items (Noor Al-Deen, 1993). The NAD aging scale was designed for assessing positive and negative attitudes of younger Arab Americans toward their elders using a 5-point Likert scale, where scores could range from a high of (5) 'strongly agree' to a low of (1) 'strongly disagree' The positive attitude items were composed of respect, help, responsible, communicate, time, pleasant, advice, live, trust, and closer. Essentially, participants were asked about their predispositions toward their elders, such as respecting them, helping them, acting responsibly toward them, communicating with them, spending time with them, perceiving them as pleasant, seeking their advice, liking to live with them, trusting them, and feeling close to them.

Meanwhile, the negative attitude items consisted of no self-respect, no feeling, resentful, interfere, unhappy, gossip, care, argue, no change, and problem. Here, younger people were asked if they perceived their elders as having no self-respect, having no feeling toward others, being resentful, interfering in others' lives, being unhappy, being gossips, requiring constant care, being argumentive, refusing to change, and having health problems.

The nine remaining items of the survey can be illustrated as follows: One of them was intended to rate overall communication on a 10-point semantic differential scale with (1) 'extremely poor ' and (10) 'excellent.' The next two items were related to whether the respondent is currently living with an older person plus if the older person is financially independent. The purpose of these two items was to ascertain whether the presence of older people and the financial dependency of such individuals had an impact on the younger members' attitudes toward them. In addition to demographics (gender, age, education, and marital status), two final items were incorporated (country of birth and duration in the United States for foreign-born American citizens and permanent residents). These two items may serve to explain the magnitude to which cultural diversity, which is due to acculturation, among younger Arab Americans has an impact on the quality of communication that they extend toward their elders.

Statistical Analysis

The quality of communication that younger people extend towards their elders was examined through correlation coefficients and multiple regression. The reliability of this research was measured by alpha for the positive and negative attitudes. The reliability coefficient shows that the internal consistency for the positive attitude was .78, and it was .72 for the negative attitude. Such results demonstrate that the intercorrelation among the variables within the group of positive or negative attitude is satisfactory.

RESULTS

Focusing on the highest percentage for each category of the attributes of Arab Americans who completed the surveys, the basic study data can be summarized as follows: seventy percent were males, 33% were between ages 45 and 54, 57% have earned a graduate school degree, 81% were married, and 60% of the participants were born in the Middle East (see Fig. 5.1). Those who were born in the Middle East are either naturalized U.S. citizens or U.S. permanent residents, and two thirds of them have been in the United States for less than 25 years.

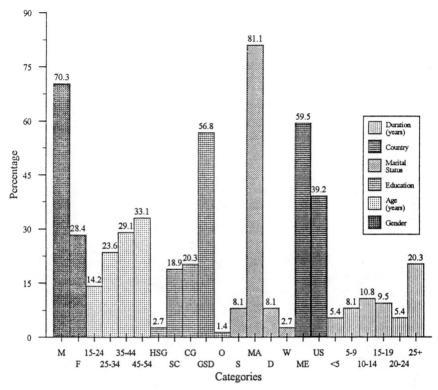

FIG. 5.1. Demographic Characteristics.
M = male, F = female; HSG = high school graduate, SC = some college, CG = college graduate, GSD = graduate school degree, O = other; S = single, MA = married, D = divorced, W =
widow(er); ME = Middle East, US = United States.

RQ1 is basically intended to examine the overall attitudes of younger
Arab Americans toward their elders. Essentially, younger Arab Americans
maintained that they offer a good quality of communication toward their
elders, and their attitudes are relatively positive. Specifically, the majority
of the respondents rated their overall communication with their elders 7 and
above on a scale from (1) being the lowest to (10) being the highest.
Excluding two respondents who rated their overall communication as
extremely poor, none of the respondents rated their communication with
their elders below the midpoint 5.

Regarding their positive attitude toward their elders, most of the surveyed Arab Americans strongly agreed with respecting their elders, as
shown in Table 5.1. In fact, respect ($M = 4.76$, $SD = .43$) was ranked the
highest on a scale that ranged from (1) being the lowest 'strongly disagree'

TABLE 5.1
Means and Standard Deviations of Attitudes

	Mean	SD
Positive		
Respect	4.76	.43
Help	4.57	.57
Responsible	4.57	.66
Communicate	4.49	.73
Time	4.46	.76
Pleasant	4.14	.76
Advice	3.88	.98
Live	3.49	1.16
Trust	3.29	1.04
Closer	2.99	1.01
Negative		
No self-respect	1.53	.88
No feeling	1.56	1.04
Resentful	2.03	1.02
Interfere	2.21	1.07
Unhappy	2.39	1.17
Gossip	2.65	1.09
Care	2.69	1.17
Argue	2.96	1.12
No change	3.60	1.01
Problem	3.63	1.15

Note. N = 148.

' to (5) being the highest 'strongly agree '. However, the respondents did not feel very close ($M = 2.99$, $SD = 1.01$) to their elders. Only 22% of the surveyed Arab Americans have their elders living with them, and roughly 23% of the participants indicated that their elders were financially dependent on them. For the negative attitude, meanwhile, younger Arab Americans agreed on the fact that their elders have health problems ($M = 3.63$, $SD = 1.15$). However, they strongly disagreed over the point that their elders have no self-respect. Indeed, no self-respect ($M = 1.53$, $SD = .88$) was ranked the lowest on a scale that ranged from (1) being the lowest *strongly disagree* to (5) being the highest *strongly agree.*

Pearson correlations were calculated for both positive and negative attitudes. For the positive attitude, the results indicate that there is no significant correlation between trusting their elders and any of the remaining variables displayed in Table 5.2. However, it was found that a very high significant relationship ($r = .83$, $p < .01$) exists between communicating with their elders and spending time with them. This may be supported by the fact that about 43% of the respondents scaled such communication between 7 and 8 out of 10 on a scale from (1) being the lowest to (10) being the highest. Such results may indicate that a sound relationship exists between younger Arab Americans and their elders.

Meanwhile, Pearson correlations for the negative attitude showed a substantial relationship ($r = .48$, $p < .01$) between their elders requiring constant care and refusing to change (see Table 5.3). Equally important, a substantial relationship ($r = .48$, $p < .01$) was obtained between viewing their elders being unhappy and being resentful. It is noteworthy that the variable that exhibited the fewest significant relationships with the rest of the negative attitude was that of having no self-respect. Such results may manifest that although younger Arab Americans realize that their elders have difficulties, they hold their seniors in high regard.

RQ2 sought to predict the effects of the variable(s) GAEMCD on both the positive and the negative attitudes of younger Arab Americans. Based on the analysis of multiple regression (see Table 5.4), the results show that GAEMCD has no significant effect on the positive attitude ($F = 1.94$, $p < .087$). R^2 reveals that only 14% of the variation in the positive attitude is accounted for by GAEMCD. Still, the multiple regression analysis demon-

TABLE 5.2
Pearson Correlation Matrix for Positive Attitude

Variable	Re	He	Rs	Co	Ti	Pl	Ad	Li	Tr	Cl
Respect		.45**	.25**	.17*	.26**	.19*	.06	.18*	-.13	-.01
Help			.37**	.32**	.24**	.28**	.15	.23**	-.07	-.18*
Responsible				.19*	.16	.34**	.11	.13	-.08	-.17*
Communication					.83**	.46**	.43**	.55**	-.01	.23**
Time						.45**	.50**	.55**	-.08	.24**
Pleasant							.46**	.57**	.13	.17*
Advice								.47**	.10	.22**
Live									-.03	.31**
Trust										.38**
Close										

Note. $N = 148$; *sig. $p < .05$; **sig. p 01; 2-tailed test.
Re = Respect, He = Help, Rs = Responsible, Co = Communication, Ti = Time, Pl = Pleasant, Ad = Advice, Li = Live, Tr = Trust, Cl = Close.

TABLE 5.3
Pearson Correlation Matrix for Negative Attitude

Variable	Ns	Nf	Re	In	Un	Go	Ca	Ar	Nc	Pr
No self-respect	.27**	.31**	-.16	.25**	.09	.02	-.01	.01	.02
No-feeling		.45**	.10	.34**	.06	.33**	-.08	.29**	.04
Resentful			.31**	.48**	.17*	.45**	.24**	.44**	.18*
Interfere				.06	-.02	.24**	.29**	.29**	.18*
Unhappy					.33**	.19*	.09	.34**	.24**
Gossip						.30**	.28**	.16	.12
Care							.24**	.48**	.14
Argue								.11	.33**
No change									-.06
Problem									

Note. N = 148; *sig. p <. 05; **sig. p < .01; 2-tailed test.
Ns = No self-respect, Nf = No feeling, Re = Resentful, In = Interfere, Un = Unhappy, Go = Gossip, Ca = Care, Ar = Argue, Nc = No change, Pr = Problem.

strats that GAEMCD has a significant effect on the negative attitude ($F = 2.20$, $p < .053$), as displayed in Table 5.5. In particular, country of birth evinced a significant independent effect on the negative attitude with ($t = -2.92$, $p < .005$). Its coefficient of (-11.3) indicates that individuals who were born in the Middle East displayed less negative attitude toward their elders than those who were born in the United States. In other words, the negative attitude declined because the majority of the participants came from the Middle East. As mentioned previously, about two thirds of younger Arab Americans were born in the Middle East, and nearly two thirds of these

TABLE 5.4
Regression Analysis of Positive Attitude with Demographics

Variable	B	SE B	Beta	T–test	Sig. T
Gender	−2.75	1.43	−.22	−1.926	.0583
Age	−.59	.60	−.13	−.979	.3311
Education	−.38	.63	−.07	−.600	.5508
Marital status	2.47	1.58	.18	1.566	.1218
Country	1.24	3.65	.04	.341	.7344
Duration	−.53	.39	−.18	−1.359	.1786
(Constant)	43.99	5.76			

Note. N = 148; $R^2 = .14$, F = 1.94, Sig. .087, p < .05.

TABLE 5.5
Regression Analysis of Negative Attitude with Demographics

Variable	B	SE B	Beta	T-test	Sig. T
Gender	1.55	1.51	.12	1.028	.3074
Age	– .58	.63	–.12	– .923	.3594
Education	.41	.67	.07	.608	.5451
Marital status	.48	1.67	.03	.287	.7748
Country	–11.30	3.86	–.34	–2.924	.0047
Duration	– .04	.42	–.01	– .086	.9319
(Constant)	35.24	6.10			

Note. $N = 148$; $R^2 = .16$, $F = 2.20$, Sig. .053, $p < .05$.

have been in the United States for less than 25 years. R^2 shows that 16% of the variation in the negative attitude is accounted for by GAEMCD.

CONCLUSION

Basically, younger Arab Americans maintain that they extend a good quality of communication toward their elders, and their attitudes are relatively positive although some of them perceive their elders negatively to some degree. The positive predisposition may stem from the fact that younger Arab Americans, whether born in the Middle East or in the United States, are taught to extend a positive attitude toward their elders. These younger Arab Americans are not particularly different from those of the Indian culture wherein "children though born and raised in America were encouraged to follow the traditional values of their families' culture" (Zandi, Mirle, & Jarvis, 1990, p. 161). Adhering to such behavior, younger people are often bestowed with an extrinsic reward of social praise for meeting cultural obligations, so extending a positive attitude toward their elders may have such an extrinsic reward for younger Arab Americans while it simultaneously offers them an intrinsic gratification through feeling good about themselves.

The positive attitude of younger Arab Americans may also be influenced by the composition of the participants in this study. The majority of them fall into the categories of middle aged, highly educated, and born in the Middle East. In all likelihood, middle age people are inclined to envision themselves as soon being in a situation similar to the current one of their elders. This might help to improve their predisposition toward their elders. Education might also be considered a significant factor in improving the attitudes of the younger generation toward their elders. For example, "education is recognized by Lebanese-American informants as a primary cause of the changing attitudes of the younger generations toward care of their aging relatives" (Shenk, 1990, p. 156).

Despite the fact that younger Arab Americans maintain that they hold a positive attitude toward their elders and select respect as the leading variable for such an attitude, they do not feel very close to them. Moreover, their responses indicate that they perceive their elders as having health problems and as being reluctant to change when the negative attitude was examined. This attitude might be better explained through the cultural diversity that exists among Arab Americans. According to traditional Arab cultural values, a negative attitude toward one's elders should not be held or revealed, despite the ailments and/or problems of the elders. It is the duty of younger people to offer a positive attitude toward their elders and to meet the expectations of their elders in the best possible way (Noor Al-Deen, 1994). Elders most often live with their offspring regardless of physical or financial independency. Yet, this study reveals that more than three fourths of these younger Arab Americans indicate that their elders are independent. Although one might take into consideration that the majority of the participants are immigrants and their elders are still overseas, it is important to recognize that independence is an American cultural value. This was explained by Tamir (1979), who noted that "our society holds independence and personal utility in high esteem" (p. 99). This is clearly a departure from traditions that can be illustrated by Shenk (1990):

> While the values of respect for elders and caring for one's aging parents has been maintained into the second and third generations, the meaning of these values is different for members of each generation, with varying behavioral expectations attached to those values. The Lebanese-American immigrants expected to provide physical care for their aging parents. ... Members of the second generation often anticipate providing actual physical care for their aging parents, although less often bringing their parents into their homes. By the third generation, the filial expectation is more often provision of emotional support and financial assistant, rather than physical care—and sometimes at a distance. (p. 156)

This study shows that the attitudes of younger Arab Americans appear to be influenced, to a large degree, by traditional Arab cultural values more than by American cultural values. This may be due to the fact that the majority of these individuals are immigrants and the traditional cultural values are still potent. Nevertheless, should the makeup of the respondents differ or should a similar study be conducted on older Arab Americans asking them about their perceptions of the attitude of their juniors toward them, the results might be different. Despite limitations, this type of research may prove to be of value, particularly because we are living in a multicultural society wherein the older population is growing rapidly.

ACKNOWLEDGMENTS

Sincere gratitude is extended to Professor Richard David Dixon of the University of North Carolina at Wilmington and Professor Gary Copeland of The University of Alabama for their insightful comments and helpful suggestions regarding this chapter. Special appreciation is expressed to Charles Richard Ward, Assistant Vice-Chancellor for Academic Affairs of the University of North Carolina at Wilmington, for providing computer software and help in producing the graph for this chapter. Genuine thanks go to Lamia Doumani, Office Manager of the American-Arab Anti-Discrimination Committee for securing a mailing list concerning this project. A final word of thanks is conveyed to the numerous Arab Americans in North Carolina and South Carolina who graciously participated in this survey.

REFERENCES

Babbie, E. R. (1986). *The practice of social research.* Belmont, CA: Wadsworth.
Barakat, H. (1985). The Arab family and the challenge of social transformation. In E. W. Fernea (Ed.), *Women and the family in the Middle East: New voices of change* (pp. 27–48). Austin, TX: University of Texas.
Bengtson, V. L., Cutler, N. E., Mangen, D. J., & Marshall, V. W. (1985). Generations, cohorts, and relations between age groups. In R. H. Binstock & E. Shanas (Eds.), *Handbook of aging and the social sciences* (2nd ed., pp. 415–449). New York: Van Nostrand Reinhold.
Budget of the United States Government: Fiscal Year 1991-96. (1990–95). Washington, DC: U.S. Government Printing Office.
Cibulski, O., & Bergman, S. (1981). Mutuality of learning between the old and the young: A case study in Israel. *Aging and Society, 1,* 247–262.
Cockerham, W. C. (1991). *This aging society.* Englewood Cliffs, NJ: Prentice-Hall.
Doyle, C. L. (1987). *Explorations in psychology.* Monterey, CA: Brooks/Cole.
Ellingsworth, H. W. (1988). A theory of adaptation in intercultural dyads. In Y. Y. Kim & W. B. Gudykunst (Eds.), *Theories in intercultural communication* (pp. 25–279). Thousand Oaks, CA: Sage.
Hsia, H. J. (1988). *Mass communications research methods: A step-by-step approach.* Hillsdale, NJ: Lawrence Erlbaum Associates.
Hummert, M. L., Nussbaum, J. F., & Wiemann, J. M. (1992). Communication and the elderly: Cognition, language, and relationships. *Communication Research, 19*(4), 413–422.
Littlejohn, S. W. (1989). *Theories of human communication.* Belmont, CA: Wadsworth.

Lipman, A. (1982). Minority aging from the exchange and structuralist-functionalist perspectives. In R. C. Manuel (Ed.), *Minority aging: Sociological and social psychological issues* (pp. 195–201). Westport, CT: Greenwood.

Markides, K. S., & Mindel, C. H. (1987). *Aging & ethnicity.* Beverly Hills, CA: Sage.

Noor Al-Deen, H. S. (1993). *The NAD aging scale.* Unpublished scale.

Noor Al-Deen, H. S. (1994). Understanding Arab Americans: A matter of diversities. In A. Gonzalez, M. Houston, & V. Chen (Eds.), *Our voices: Essays in culture, ethnicity, and communication* (pp. 18–23). Los Angeles: Roxbury.

Noor Al-Deen, H. S. (1994, November). *Cross-generational communication: A comparative analysis.* Paper presented at the annual meeting of the Speech Communication Association, New Orleans, LA.

Nussbaum, J. F., Thompson, T., & Robinson, J. D. (1989). *Communication and aging.* New York: Harper & Row.

Samovar, L. A., Porter, R. E., & Jain, N. C. (1981). *Understanding intercultural communication.* Belmont, CA: Wadsworth.

Shenk, D. (1990). Aging in a changing ethnic context: The Lebanese-American family. *Ethnic Groups, 8*(3), 147–161.

Spindler, L. S. (1977). *Culture change and modernization.* Prospect Heights, IL: Waveland Press.

Sussman, M. B. (1985). The family life of old people. In R. H. Binstock & E. Shanas (Eds.), *Handbook of aging and the social sciences* (2nd ed., pp. 415–449). New York: Van Nostrand Reinhold.

Tamir, L. M. (1979). *Communication and the aging process: Interaction throughout the life cycle.* New York: Pergamon.

U.S. Department of Health and Human Services. (1991). *Aging America: Trends and projections* (DHHS Publication No. 91-28001). Washington, D C: Author.

Wimmer R. D., & Dominick, J. R. (1994). *Mass media research.* Belmont, CA: Wadsworth.

Zandi, T., Mirle, J., & Jarvis, P. (1990). Children's attitudes toward elderly individuals: A comparison of two ethnic groups. *International Journal of Aging and Human Development, 30*(3), 161–174.

6

Mentoring Across Generations: Culture, Family, and Mentoring Relationships

Pamela J. Kalbfleisch
Arlyn Anderson
University of Wyoming

A woman "said that her mother lived with her in her old age, weak and unable even to comb her hair. 'She'd say "My darling daughter, your blessing will be that your daughter will do the same for you as you do for me." And she was right.' " (Silverman, 1994, p. 274)

Leadership is about demonstrating by doing—and that include[s] sweeping the floor. (Silverman, 1994, p. 274)

In the last 30 years, the study of mentoring relationships has become a popular area of research in communication, education, business, and in many other academic disciplines. Virtually every academic discipline and every applied profession has published research on mentors and mentoring as well as advice for conducting these relationships (Kalbfleisch, in press). Popular press articles proclaim "Get ahead! Find a mentor!" (Keyton & Kalbfleisch, 1993), whereas scholarly research documents the monetary gains associated with having someone take you under their wing and shepherd you through the organization or profession (Fagenson, 1989; Whitely, Dougherty, & Dreher, 1991, 1992).

The concept of mentoring, however, did not begin with business, industry, or the advance of the professions. The first mentor who appears in written mythology was Mentor, the adviser to Odysseus. Mentor was trusted with the instruction of Odysseus's son Telemachus when Odysseus went off to war (Homer, 1960). In other words, Mentor was a surrogate parent for Telemachus. The term *mentor* refers to the original Mentor. The process of mentoring is the process of instructing, or assisting one who needs guidance.

Mentors are described as people who provide others with advice, support, information, and professional sponsorship; people who share their values and help others gain access to influential networks (Olian, Carroll, Giannantonio, & Feren, 1988). Protégés are the beneficiaries of the mentors' advice and sponsorship. According to Kalbfleisch and Davies (1993), "proteges receive guidance from their mentors and may in turn support them as their knowledge grows and the mentoring relationship develops" (p. 399).

Great individuals throughout history have had mentors who have helped them along the way (Kalbfleisch & Keyton, 1995). For example, both U.S. presidents James Madison and James Monroe had former U.S. President Thomas Jefferson as a mentor (Bushardt, Fretwell, & Holdnak, 1991). There are also examples of famous mentors and protégés throughout sports, politics, and the arts (Kalbfleisch & Keyton).

One of the common problems noted by Brown (1985), Kalbfleisch (1991), Kalbfleisch and Davies (1991), and Kalbfleisch and Keyton (1995) is that women often have trouble finding mentors in business and academe. However, Kalbfleisch (in press) noted that many professional women have indicated that their fathers were their mentors. In other words, Kalbfleisch (in press) identified women who did not have mentors in their workplace as citing their fathers as helping them get ahead by giving their advice and their support. This suggests that another avenue of mentoring and social support, which has been overlooked by both the scholarly literature and the popular press, is available, that is, the mentoring that occurs within family relationships.

The typical view of family relationships is one in which the parents are doing all the giving and the children are the recipients of all the parents' nurturance (Fine, 1992; Fish & Osborn, 1992; Tiesel & Olson, 1992). Children are portrayed in much of the scholarly research as a drain on the parents, both financially and emotionally (Rodman & Sidden, 1992; Schvaneveldt & Young, 1992). However, Vogl-Bauer and Kalbfleisch (1995) indicated that children did contribute to the overall quality of family life.

The Vogl-Bauer and Kalbfleisch (1995) study is unique in that it looks at parents and children as coparticipants in social support and family maintenance. Taken in light of the Kalbfleisch (in press) discovery that professionals cite parents as assisting them in their careers, it appears that mentorship in families deserves a closer examination.

The study presented in this chapter begins this scrutiny by presenting a look at mentoring within family relationships. Specifically, this chapter looks at family mentoring across generations by considering elder parents and the mentoring relationships that may exist among these parents, their children, and grandchildren. Kalbfleisch (in press) noted that professionally, mentors may have several layers of protégés, grand protégés, and great-grand protégés. People who have mentors will often mentor others; therefore, mentors who begin the chain of social support might expect several generations of protégés to follow. This chapter considers whether generational mentoring is part of a family relationship.

Further, in order to effectively study the development of these family relationships, we chose the Mormons because they place strong emphasis on the family, both in religion and culture. This cultural group exists in isolated pockets in the western United States as well as in more cosmopolitan and international locations worldwide. The following research questions were developed for the study presented in this chapter.

R_1: Do elder parents in Mormon families identify mentoring relationships with their children? If so, what are the characteristics of these relationships?

R_2: Do elder grandparents in Mormon families identify mentoring relationships with their grandchildren? If so, what are the characteristics of these relationships?

R_3: Do elder parents in Mormon families perceive their children as reciprocating social support or other helping behaviors?

R_4: Do elder grandparents in Mormon families perceive their grandchildren as reciprocating social support or other helping behaviors?

R_5: What effect does the church have on mentoring relationships within Mormon families?

Elders and Their Families

Even though Lewis (1990) argued that there is a lack of theoretical foundation and methodological study of elders, research and published findings can provide a distinct image of elders and their relationships with their families. Concerning their offspring, generational composition and the family networks of elders can be complex. For example, as Brubaker (1990) noted, a 70-year-old widow may have a retired 50-year-old son with children leaving home, and she may also have a 30-year-old daughter who has just married and is beginning a family.

Peterson (1989a) claimed that elders enjoy high levels of contact with their families through letters, phone calls, and visits; that weekly visits are common. Personal visits are dominant when traveling distances are short (less than 4 hours), but when distances are greater, phone calls become the primary method of contact even though the actual number of calls does not increase (Connidis, 1989).

One frequently addressed aspect concerning the relationships between elders and their descendants is the support between generations. Brubaker (1990) and Lewis (1990) identified the notion of reciprocity with the support between elders and their successive generations. Lewis noted that when elders provide some form of help to their adult children, it is given with the expectation that the child will aid the elder during any future emergency. Also, most of the support that offspring provide for aging parents is of an emotional or psychological nature (Peterson, 1989a). When particularly special assistance is needed by elders, a middle-aged daughter will usually provide the help if it is not already provided for by a spouse or a professional (Connidis, 1989). This is especially the case when the elder is the mother (Walker, Shin, & Bird, 1990).

With a shift in focus from elders to grandparents, it appears that the two are not always the same. Becoming a grandparent occurs primarily in midlife instead of during the older years (Connidis, 1989; Peterson, 1989b). Peterson observed modal ages for grandparents to be 50 for women and 52 for men. If elders are categorized as age 65 and older (as in this study), then it can be reasoned that although elders may be grandparents, not all grandparents are elders. Therefore, grandparenting in the older years usually involves relationships with grandchildren between the ages of older teenagers and young adults (Connidis, 1989), a point supported to some degree by Brubaker (1990).

Another theme rather common to the grandparenting research is the notion of roles filled by grandparents or descriptions of the relationships they have with their grandchildren (Connidis, 1989; Roberto, 1990). Peterson (1989b) noted that much of this research focuses on topologies to describe grandparent roles. The fun-seeker, parent surrogate, role model, historian, and mentor were some of the roles he identified in the research.

It was the research by Kornhaber and Woodward (1981) that identified grandparents as mentors and role models that was of particular interest for the study presented in this chapter. Mentoring grandparents were those who had close, warm relationships with their grandchildren. These grandparents were seen by the grandchildren as someone to be like, and as someone to go to for advice. Kornhaber and Woodward also suggested that these mentoring "grandparents teach [grand]children ways of working with the basic materials of life: food, clothing, shelter, and transportation, plus how to deal with the world outside the home" (p. 171).

The mentor and role model grandparents made up only 5% of the grandparents sampled in the Kornhaber and Woodward (1981) study. Nevertheless, the value of grandparents or elders in the lives of younger generations can have a distinct impact on the younger generation's future lives. People adapt to the aging process through their interaction with others, and a person's internal conceptualization of the aging precess is socialized into his or her mental makeup early in life (Giles, Coupland, Coupland, Williams, & Nussbaum, 1992). A child's future role as a grandparent is shaped by his or her own parents' and grandparents' example in that role (Roberto, 1990). Kornhaber and Woodward claimed that grandparents can provide a real example (as opposed to one seen on television or heard of in stories) of what being a grandparent is like. They also argued that positive relationships with grandparents provide positive attitudes toward aging in the minds of grandchildren, and negative stigmas associated with aging diminish.

To conclude this section on elders and grandparenting, a few points are worth reviewing. Elders enjoy continued contact and interaction, often in some form of support, with their families. And as grandparents, elders can have a significant influence on their grandchildren, especially in terms of the grandchildren's views and anticipations of becoming grandparents themselves.

Mormonism

The existence of the Mormons as a unique cultural entity can be established and even traced back to the 1830s and the church's[1] early origins when the Mormons were seen as peculiar and unexplainably different from others surrounding them in Missouri and Illinois (Ericksen, 1922). Lamar (1972) supported this claim and asserted that in early Mormondom in Utah (where the church members moved after being harassed in the Midwest), "the local subculture was not necessarily western and certainly not 'cowboy' western" (p. 140). Hill and Allen (1972) attributed the Mormons' theocratic governing system, plural marriages, and general communal living as reasons for why many non-Mormons viewed the Mormons as not belonging to the

---

[1]The Church of Jesus Christ of Latter-Day Saints is the formal name of the church. The term *Mormon* is the moniker for a member of this church.

typical American culture. Today, the Mormons still occupy a general position in society that separates them from the world around them. Along with their conservative nature and practices, their tight-knit and close system, and their family doctrines and practices, the Mormons provide a unique cultural system in which to investigate the concepts of mentoring with regards to the elderly.

Beginning with their conservative nature, Mormons characterize a number of values or behaviors that reflect earlier generations. Hill and Allen (1972) described Mormonism today as "what America was, not what it is becoming" (p. 145) and that Mormons have worked to maintain ideals and values that are more characteristic of 19th century America. Teachings on sexual behavior and the sexual practices of the church and its members strongly suggest a conservative nature. Plural marriages have long been forbidden, and sexual abstinence before marriage, and strict fidelity after marriage are heavily promoted in the church (Bennion, 1991). Research findings concerning the pre-marital sexual behavior of Mormons suggest that Mormons generally do practice these more conservative approaches to sexual behavior (Heaton, 1992; Thomas, 1983). In addition to the afore-mentioned notions on sexual teachings and behavior, Mormons are also taught to abstain from coffee, tea, alcohol, and tobacco (Church of Jesus Christ of Latter-Day Saints, 1981). Mormons are also encouraged to pattern their families after traditional family characteristics, from encouraging more traditional roles to having larger families (Arrington & Bitton, 1979; Bennion, 1991; Conley, 1990; Cracroft, 1991; Thomas, 1983).

A second uniqueness of Mormonism is the tight-knit closeness of their system. Mormons sought "a close-knit community free from...outside influences" (Hill & Allen, 1972, p. 3) early in their history. Their early persecutions in Missouri and Illinois and their isolationist tendencies after migrating to Utah helped build a strong sense of solidarity and group cohesion (Arrington, 1972; Ericksen, 1922). Also, today, as in the past, the church represents a set of doctrines that permeate all facets of a person's life (Arrington, 1972; Bennion, 1991; Cracroft, 1991; Ericksen, 1922; Hill & Allen, 1972). The members of the church also make a substantial offering of their time to the church because the bulk of the work done within the church is performed by its lay members. Especially at the local level, nearly all officers, teachers, youth leaders, and various other service positions are filled by members who receive no salary for their efforts (Arrington, 1972; Arrington & Bitton, 1979; Bennion, 1991).

Finally, the last characteristic of Mormonism worth noting that sets it apart from other cultures is its notion of the family. According to Cracroft

(1991), the church "is held together by the roots of the family" (p. 107). Marriage and family life receive a high degree of attention within Mormonism (Bennion, 1991; Cornwall & Thomas, 1990). Arrington (1972) observed that "the eternality of the family relationship and the overwhelming importance of the family in the church and society has become the single most important theme of Mormon sermons in this century" (p. 172). According to church teachings, marriages solemnized in Mormon temples are binding for eternity and that the family structure permeates all the realms of existence (premortal, mortal, and postmortal) as outlined in Mormon theology (Church of Jesus Christ of Latter-Day Saints, 1981; Thomas, 1983).

To conclude the discussion on Mormons, suffice it to say that this religious group clearly provides a unique and distinct culture that is separate from others. Forced to draw on each other from their earliest beginnings, the presence of a clear group identity has been a part of their entire history. Their conservative nature goes even further to set the Mormons apart. As both Cornwall (1989) and Thomas (1983) noted the strong intergenerational ties and support systems within Mormon families, particularly the larger ones, it appears that the culture of Mormonism offers excellent conditions in which to apply and expand the notions of mentoring, especially with regards to the elderly.

METHOD

Participants

Participants for the study were selected from one stake within a small community (village population approximately 25,000) in the western United States. A *stake* in Mormon congregational structures is one size above the smallest congregational structure, the *ward*. Several wards will form a stake. The stake from which this sample was taken was composed of six wards, three of which were made up entirely of university students. Because the targeted sample required the respondents to be 65 or older, these respondents were drawn from the three remaining nonuniversity wards. Forty-seven names of older church members age 65 and older were provided by the stake president (the presiding officer of the stake). A researcher then telephoned the individuals on the list and asked them to participate in a study examining the relationships among older members of the church and their children and grandchildren. Twenty-five individuals agreed to participate in the study.

Interview

Once selected, respondents agreed to meet for approximately one hour to be interviewed. All interviews, with one exception, were conducted in the homes of the participants. The one exception was conducted in an office on the campus of the local university. The respondents were initially asked some general demographic questions regarding themselves and their families (see Appendix). This allowed the participants to relax somewhat as they discussed nonthreatening information about themselves and their progeny with the interviewer.

Once this preliminary information had been gathered, the interviewer then read the Olian et al. (1988) and Kalbfleisch and Davies (1993) definitions of mentors and protégés. After the definitions were read, the participants were asked if they felt the descriptions applied to their relationships with their children. Specifically, the respondents were asked if they felt they had a mentoring relationship with their children. Because all respondents felt that the definitions did apply or that they had experienced a mentoring relationship with their children, all participants were asked to describe some of the characteristics of their mentoring relationships (see Appendix). This same line of questioning was also pursued in regards to the respondents' relationships with their grandchildren (see Appendix). To conclude the interview, all respondents were asked to describe how their membership in the Mormon church affected their mentoring relationships with both the children and the grandchildren.

Analysis

The information from the interviews was recorded in notes taken by the interviewer during the sessions and on audiotape. The responses to the interviewer's questions were categorized using Bulmer's (1979) analytic induction method. The descriptive phrase was the unit of analysis categorized using Bulmer's procedure. In the cases where several descriptive phrases from one respondent held together as one thought, these phrases were unitized as one phrase for analysis. The responses were examined to determine the number of descriptive phrases that fell into the domain of the five research questions in this study (i.e., areas and methods of mentoring children and grandchildren, support from the children and grandchildren, and the church's influence on mentoring relationships). The base number of phrases for each research question was established with a count of the phrases in the domain of each question.

Using analytic induction, the descriptive phrases were placed into general themes within the domain of each research question by two coders. The areas in which elders mentor(ed) their children produced 100 descriptive phrases that were grouped into three broad categories—Psychosocial, Work/Survival Skills, and Education/Careers. Intercoder reliability for this category using Cohen's (1960) Kappa was .81. The 76 descriptive phrases concerning methods of mentoring were categorized into two groups labeled as Verbalizing and Demonstrating, with an intercoder reliability of .77. The questions about support from the children yielded 74 responses that were divided between Physical Support and Emotional Support, with an intercoder reliability of .94.

The same categories for these three areas were used to categorize the responses concerning the elders' grandchildren. The questions concerning the areas of mentoring within the elder grandparent–grandchild relationship provided 46 descriptive phrases. The methods to mentor within this relationship produced 35 descriptive phrases, and concerning support from the grandchildren, the participants gave 30 responses. The intercoder reliability scores for the response dealing with these relationships are as follows: areas of mentoring .80, methods of mentoring .90, and support from the grandchildren 1.0.

RESULTS

Beginning with the demographic information obtained from the interviews, there are some characteristics worth noting. The majority of the participants were women ($n = 16$). All 9 of the men who participated in the study were married, but only 8 of the women were currently married. The remaining 8 women were either divorced or widowed. These particular findings support Brubaker's (1990) observations of marital conditions of the elderly. The average age of the respondents was 73.5 years. It should be noted that two respondents did not provide their ages. Of those who reported their ages, the oldest was 86, and the youngest was 67. Concerning their Mormon heritage, the average participant was between a third and fourth (3.46) generation member of the church. The high was five generations, of which there were 10 respondents. There were 6 first-generation Mormons. The total number of children identified by the 25 participants was 69. The average number of children per person or couple was 3.45, with a high of eight, and a low of one. The average age of these children was just under 45 at 44.9. The oldest was 64, and the youngest was 27. The gender split was nearly even, with 37 of the children being male and the remaining 32 being female.

In terms of grandchildren, all participants identified a total of 163 grandchildren. The average number of grandchildren per person or couple was just over eight at 8.1. The high was 16, and the low was 2. Concerning the ages of the grandchildren, five participants were unable to accurately recall the ages of their grandchildren, and two grandchildren had passed away. Excluding these two exceptions, the average age for the grandchildren was established at 18.1. The oldest grandchild was 37; three were found to share that age. The youngest was less than one. Seventy-nine of the grandchildren were identified as males and 84 as females.

Mentoring Children and Grandchildren

Whereas all the respondents identified their relationships with their children as being mentoring relationships, additional comments and descriptors were also introduced by the respondents. The largest group of these comments (25%) described the relationships with the children as strong, positive, or close. Eighteen percent of the responses qualified mentoring as an automatic extension of, or comparable to, the notion of parenting. Other responses (18%) described the amount or degree of mentoring as something that varies with each child. Along similar lines, 11% of the responses described mentoring as something that can vary with age (11%) or even with subject matter (3%). Finally, some of the responses (11%) even described the elder's parents as mentors.

When asked if the mentoring relationship as they witnessed it with their children was applicable to their grandchildren, most of the respondents described a mentoring relationship with the grandchildren that was less than the mentoring relationship enjoyed with the children. Almost half (48%) described the definition of mentoring as somewhat applicable to these relationships but to a lesser degree. Sixteen percent felt that they had a mentoring relationship with their grandchildren but only *through* their children, and 12% simply said that they did not have what they felt was a mentoring relationship with their grandchildren. However, there were some of the participants who felt that the mentoring description did apply to their relationships with their grandchildren. Twelve percent felt that their mentoring relationship with their grandchildren was equal with that of their children, whereas 12% felt that they enjoyed a stronger mentoring relationship with the grandchildren than with the children.

Some of the respondents offered explanations or reasons for why they felt there were differences in the degree of mentoring they provide for their grandchildren as it compares to that of their children. Geographical distance was cited by 44% of the participants as a reason for the difference. Four percent, who cited geographical distance as a reason also mentioned a large generational difference between them and their grandchildren as an additional reason. Also, 12% of these grandparents preferred to describe their relationships with their grandchildren as playful, or just enjoying the grandchildren.

For those who felt they had some degree of a mentoring relationship with their grandchildren, regardless of whether it was more or less of a mentoring relationship than they had with the children, in general, the responses simply mirrored those concerning the children. This is primarily due to the fact that most respondents simply referred back to the areas discussed with their children. As a result, the same categories were identified, and the divisions among the responses were very similar, with fewer responses.

Areas of Mentoring

Psychosocial. This area seems to be the primary focus of the mentoring efforts of elder parents with their children. When the respondents were asked to name the areas in which they tried to mentor their children, nearly half (48%) of the 100 descriptive phrases were judged to be Psychosocial

TABLE 6.1
Percentages of Total Responses by Groupings

Responses	Children	Grandchildren
Areas of Mentoring		
Psychosocial	.48	.46
Work/Survival Skills	.28	.24
Education/Careers	.24	.30
Methods of Mentoring		
Demonstrating	.58	.48
Verbalizing	.42	.52
Support From Children		
Emotional	.67	.77
Physical	.33	.20
None		.03

in nature (see Table 6.1). The primary focus of the efforts of elders in this area was to develop in their children a healthy sense of self and a healthy relationship with the world around them. The most referenced area in the Psychosocial realm was the religious development of the children, specifically as it pertained to the Mormon church. The following comment by one elder father captures the general attitude of respondents who believed it was important to mentor children in religious development:

> We felt that the [church] permeates all areas of our lives. It's difficult to mentor in any one area without mentoring in the religion. So by focusing our efforts in mentoring the children in their religion, we could mentor the children in most areas of their lives.

Other respondents talked about how important it was for them to teach their children to be active in the church, and others touched on how important it was to guide their children toward a temple marriage.

Another frequently referenced area in the psychosocial category was that of developing strong morals, and although this may appear similar to religious mentoring, these descriptive phrases were distinct. Responses regarding religious mentoring focused on those things that were more unique to the Mormon culture, such as temple marriages, serving proselytizing missions, and living the church's health code. Morals, as categorized here, had a much broader application as it addressed topics such as honesty, integrity, and sincerity. Although such notions are promoted by Mormons because their appeal and value are appreciated by many cultures, religious and nonreligious, they were kept separate from the religious mentoring in this analysis.

For elders' relationships with their grandchildren, the psychosocial category also dominated the areas of mentoring by occupying almost half of the responses (46%). Most of these are divided among mentoring in religion, morals, personal relationships, and self-esteem. The remaining responses dealt with mentoring the grandchildren in artistic areas and sports.

Work/Survival Skills. Responses in this category were geared more toward those things that provided the children a broad foundation considered necessary to survive in the world. The general theme of this category deals primarily with basics such as being able to work hard, solve problems, eat well, and live a healthy life. The following comment captures some of the intentions of the respondents as they addressed preparing their children to meet the world someday:

Once when working at the landfill, a fellow got a flat tire and asked me to call a tow truck. Instead of calling the tow truck, I taught him right there how to change his own tire. I showed him where the right tools were, how to loosen the bolts before you jack up the car, and then how to change the tire. He had his kids with him in the car, so I asked him, "What would you have done if this happened on the Interstate miles from anywhere with your kids in the back and no phone to call anyone?" Well, I always made sure the kids could take care of themselves, so that nothing like this could happen to them.

With 24% of the responses, work and survival skills were the least emphasized by the respondents in their comments about mentoring relationships with the grandchildren. Work and survival skills that were described by the grandparents were providing financial support, instructing in domestic skills, housing a grandchild, instilling a good work ethic, and promoting self-sufficiency.

Education/Careers. The responses within this category seemed to emphasize mental or intellectual stimulation as well as the discovery of the right career so that the children might enjoy a sense of satisfaction in their chosen profession. Although the area of careers might appear more at place in the Work/Survival Skills category, it was placed in this section because the advice and instruction given to the children regarding careers was focused more on applying a child's background to something specific, much like earning a degree or working in a certain field. This section addressed those responses that expand the mind and help one find a niche in the world. Some of the respondents talked of moving near the university in an attempt to make higher education more available to their children; others spoke of how they encouraged their children to make learning a lifelong pursuit. The following comments also prove insightful as to the nature of the perceived importance of these areas within these mentoring relationships:

I didn't think that the children's career choices should be directed by my career choice. I wanted them to choose their own enjoyable or rewarding careers, so I encouraged them to take an aptitude test or vocational inventory to see where their strengths and interests were.

After my son had looked at different career choices, I worked with him by encouraging him to look into a pharmacy program. At first he wasn't real excited about it. I even helped him fill out some of the forms to help him get into the program.

For grandparents mentoring their grandchildren, education and career mentoring comprised 30% of the respondents' descriptions. Education itself was the most commented on area within this category, followed by reading and job choices.

Methods of Mentoring

As Table 6.1 indicates, the methods used by the participants to mentor their children and grandchildren were grouped into two distinct categories—Demonstrating and Verbalizing. The responses that were grouped into the Demonstrating category dealt with those techniques used to specifically show the children and grandchildren the value of a particular idea or concept. Those methods falling into the Verbalizing category are those that described some way of vocalizing something of value to the children and grandchildren.

Demonstrating.   Just over half (58%) of the responses concerning how the participants actually mentored their children fell within this category. It includes such notions as being an example of desired values, attending church, providing hands-on learning, and supporting and attending the children's activities. Also mentioned were providing family activities that reinforced desired ideals. One respondent even mentioned the simple act of giving money to the children; another talked of setting up the oldest child as an example to the younger children—perhaps a form of meta mentoring. Following are some of the comments from the respondents as they spoke of how they demonstrated their values and supported their children:

> While we lived on a ranch, we made sure the children had plenty of hands-on instruction about what work on the farm was like. We taught them to milk and how to garden. They were usually given an animal to raise and care for and then slaughter. Not only did they learn about the work, but they also learned how to take care of themselves if they had to someday.

Verbalizing.   The Verbalizing category is composed of ways used to pass along values, advise, and inform, primarily through spoken communication. These took place on either interpersonal or group levels of communication and consisted mainly of lectures, conversations, and discussions. However, other methods named include holding Family Home Evening (a weekly event in Mormon households when the family gathers for a family-centered activity) and setting up rules, discipline, and punishments. A few respondents also mentioned frequently reading scriptures and praying with the children. The following help to illustrate:

Since we lived out on a ranch that was pretty far away, sometimes we couldn't make it to church. Usually the weather would keep us from making it in. But I still tried to teach my children church on Sundays. If we couldn't make it to church then we had church at home. Because of this, I always thought that I had been having Family Home Evening before the church asked us to.

For grandparents with their grandchildren, 52% of the responses in this area were categorized as verbal. These also included holding discussions or even lectures. Family Home Evenings and the establishement of rules, discipline, and punishments were also mentioned. One area noted that was not commented on when discussing the children was the teaching of and passing on of the values of the family heritage to the grandchildren.

Support From Children and Grandchildren

The responses concerning the support provided for the elderly respondents by their children and grandchildren were easily grouped into two categories—Emotional Support and Physical Support. Just as in the previous categories, many of the responses generated for this area were along the same lines as what was said about the children. One distinct exception was the comment that no support had been provided by the grandchildren. Beyond this, much was the same as with the children in that the responses were categorized into areas of emotional and physical support. The percentages were similar as well.

Emotional. The emotional support provided to the elderly participants by their children is clearly the bulk of the support that is provided. Just over two thirds (67%) of the responses fell within this group. The primary focus of these efforts emphasized efforts that ensured strong emotional support for the older parents by the children. Comments about visits, phone calls, letters, and general expressions of love made up the bulk of these responses. These were followed with comments about feeling secure that the children would provide any needed help, should occasion warrant, to deal with the grief and death of loved ones, and even to provide advice. A few mentioned how their children support their activities, maintain positive relationships among themselves, and even provide elders with grandchildren. Here are some of the comments in greater detail:

When my husband passed away, within three hours my daughter had arrived from New Jersey. My son arrived one hour after her. My daughter provided special emotional support by listening to me and just being a friend. My son took care of all the legal issues and logistics of my husband's passing. I don't know how I could have dealt with it all if they had not been there.

For support from the grandchildren, emotional support accounted for the vast majority of the responses (77%). In addition, these responses contained some of the more interesting comments describing the support behavior of the grandchildren in some of the relationships:

> When my wife developed Alzheimer's, my grandchildren began to research the subject so that they would be more informed about it and so they could help more effectively. They attended some workshops about the disease to be more informed. And they visited some care centers too. They also sent me a video about the disease.

> When my husband passed away it created such a void in my life. But then shortly afterwards, one of my granddaughters was born, and she helped fill that void so well. And while she didn't know what she was doing for me, I felt as if she was sent to help me. I have always felt that way.

When this last respondent was asked if she felt that this support should be attributed to her child, the grandchild's parent, for providing the grand-daughter, the respondent explained that she felt it really applied to the actual grandchild.

Physical.   The comments describing the physical support that the children provide for elder parents totaled 33% of all the support comments. These centered around actions that actually take care of the physical well-being of elder respondents. The largest portion of these responses were divided among health assistance, home care and maintenance, and the task of simply taking the parent on errands. Beyond these comments, a few talked of how their children have provided them with housing, assistance with finances, and help with the family business.

> After I became paralyzed, I moved in with my daughter for three months where she set up therapy for me. When I moved back to my own house, she helped to set up things here so that I can get around alright.

> Since my wife has come down with Alzheimer's, one of my daughters comes over when she can and helps with the food, cleaning, and other chores.

For perceived support received from grandchildren, physical support seemed to focus only on home care and generated 20% of the responses. Apparently, any of the participants needing health care or other forms of physical assistance were either getting this from their children or from other sources. One comment describing some home care assistance captures the value of supportive younger generations:

> When I decided to move back here, all I could get was this trailer. And it was in pretty bad condition. But all of my children and grandchildren came to fix it up. And with all of their expertise, I never had to pay anyone to do any of this work for me. They did all the electrical work, and the carpentry, and the plumbing, and anything that needed done. Even the mechanical. They did it all.

Whereas this comment crosses both generations of this respondent, it does show the active and enterprising role that the grandchildren played in helping with a housing need.

The Church's Influence on Mentoring

The vast majority of the participants felt that the church had either a distinctly positive (72%) or mildly positive (20%) effect on their mentoring relationships. One respondent felt that the church's influence was inconsequential, saying that the mentoring relationship was the same with or without the church. Only one respondent claimed a negative effect. Although quite committed to the church, this respondent was one of the first-generation Mormons and the only known person in her family to have converted to the church. Because of this and her children's negative regard for Mormonism, her membership in the church had placed somewhat of a wedge between her and her children. If the church is ever talked about by this respondent's children, it is referred to as "that church."

When asked to identify a specific doctrine or teaching of the church that played a distinct role in their mentoring relationships, the largest number of responses (44%) centered around Mormonism's emphasis on strong family ties or the eternal nature of family relationships. Some participants even cited the quotations mentioned earlier about the greater importance of the work performed within the home.

Those who did not specifically refer to the church's teaching on families, did cite a number of biblical teachings. The following list includes the passages that were mentioned:

> Proverbs 22:6. "Train up a child in the way…and he will not depart from it."

Matthew 6:33. "...seek ye first the kingdom of God...and all these things shall be added unto you."

1 Corinthians 10:13. "God...will not suffer you...above that [which] ye are able..."

Matthew 25:40. "...as ye have done it unto the least of these...ye have done it unto me."

Also mentioned were "The Golden Rule" and "The Ten Commandments." Two of the participants had no specific teaching, doctrine, or quote that they wanted to refer to, and one simply cited the teaching of the power of prayer.

CONCLUSION

It appears from the participants in this study that mentoring does exist in the family environment. Although the degree and nature of mentoring varied, all of the respondents felt that they had mentoring relationships with their children. Several respondents even noted that they felt their parents had been their mentors.

Participants also reported mentoring relationships with their grandchildren. However, for most of the respondents, these relationships did not appear to be as strong as they were with their own children. Children moving away and taking their children with them was the most frequently cited reason for not developing these relationships. Even so, one fourth of the respondents felt that they had distinct mentoring relationships with their grandchildren, with some of these respondents reporting that these relationships were as strong as the mentoring relationships that they had with their own children. Additionally, several respondents felt that they were mentoring their grandchildren through their own children.

The church affected the mentoring relationship in terms of the values that the elder respondents felt were important to teach their children, especially in terms of the church's doctrines and teachings. However, many of the values passed on to their children were similar to those that members of other cultures find desirable, such as being a caring, trustworthy, and responsible member of society.

The networking aspect of mentoring was not mentioned by these respondents, perhaps because specific interview questions were not formulated about introducing children and grandchildren to members of important networks. On the other hand, perhaps networks were not mentioned by the respondents because, in this case, the family and the church served as the network in which the respondents and their children were, for the most part, already members.

The support provided by the children and grandchildren for the respondents also closely matched the findings in other research. Peterson (1989a) noted that most of the support that offspring provide for their aging parents is of an emotional/psychological nature. Such was the case with the participants in this study.

The percentage of this sample that reported mentoring relationships between grandparents and grandchildren was larger than the study by Kornhaber and Woodward (1981). It is possible that the Mormon culture may have affected either the relationships themselves, or the reporting of these relationships. Nearly half of the participants in this study stated that the church's teachings on families strongly influenced their efforts to mentor both their children and grandchildren. On the other hand, the respondents may have reported these mentoring relationships or the church's influence on the development of these relationships because they felt such responses were more socially desirable for Mormons than not reporting these relationships or the church's influence on their formation. Also, the unique strength of intergenerational relationships within Mormon families may have affected the findings concerning the intergenerational mentoring relationships. Similar research done outside of Mormon circles should be conducted to provide more generalizable research on these mentoring relationships.

Even though the study provides a more accurate picture of how mentoring relationships are effected across generations within the Mormon culture, a few areas, particularly within research concerning aging and Mormonism, could have been addressed in more detail. For example, concerning aging and grandparenting, gender appears to play a role in the types and qualities of intergenerational relationships (Connidis, 1989; Kornhaber & Woodward, 1981; Peterson, 1989b; Roberto, 1990; Walker, Shin, & Bird, 1990). Although some of the responses from the participants showed patterns similar to those described in the literature, the pursuit of such responses was not an integral part of the study. As a result, the interviewer did not focus on gender differences in the interviews with the respondents.

Another limitation of this study was created because a researcher who was a member of the Mormon church conducted the interviews with the respondents. Although this greatly assisted the research team in gaining access to the participants, this same membership may have affected the respondents' answers. Although this researcher was from a different ward than the participants in this study, the possibility does exist that the respondents and the interviewer might have some future contact. As a result, the participants may have provided responses focused more closely to the church than they would have rendered to a non-Mormon researcher.

Further, the participants in this study were drawn from a pool provided by the stake president. The participants may have been more positively skewed toward active church membership than elderly church members who may not have been included in this pool of participants.

Finally, the research presented in this chapter was conducted from the perspective of the mentor, not the protégé. In other words, the children and grandchildren (protégés) may or may not have shared their parents' and grandparents' perspectives on their family relationship. Future research should focus on the perceptions of both sides of the mentoring relationship; in this case, the perspective of other family members would have increased the breadth of perspective on this culture, mentoring, and the relationships between elderly family members and their progeny.

In sum, the study reported in this chapter suggests that elder Mormons do have mentoring relationships with their children and, to a lesser extent, with their grandchildren. For both children and grandchildren, these relationships are characteristically comprised of psychosocial mentoring, work and survival mentoring, and education and career mentoring by elder family members. The methods used to advise, inform, assist, and pass values to children and to grandchildren included using demonstration and example, and using verbal communication that included lectures, conversations, and discussions. Elders reported receiving both emotional and physical support from their children and, to a lesser extent, from their grandchildren. Respondents reported that the Mormon church affected their mentoring relationships, particularly in the values that they conveyed to their children and grandchildren.

ACKNOWLEDGMENTS

The authors thank Jan Gierman, Len Fishman, and Gene Pratt for their assistance with this project. Correspondence concerning this chapter should be addressed to Dr. Pamela J. Kalbfleisch, Department of Communication and Mass Media, P.O. Box 3904, University of Wyoming, Laramie, WY 82071-3904. Electronic mail may be sent via Internet to PAMELAK@uwyo.edu.

REFERENCES

Arrington, L. J. (1972). Crisis in identity: Mormon responses to the nineteenth and twentieth centuries. In M. S. Hill & J. B. Allen (Eds.), *Mormonism and American culture* (pp. 168–184). New York: Harper & Row.

Arrington, L. J., & Bitton, D. (1979). *The Mormon experience: A history of the Latter-Day Saints.* New York: Knopf.

Bennion, L. (1991). A Mormon view of life. *Dialogue: A Journal of Mormon Thought, 24,* 59–68.

Brown, D. A. (1985). The role of mentoring in the professional lives of university faculty women. *Dissertations Abstracts International, 47*(1), 160A.

Brubaker, T. H. (1990). An overview of family relationships in later life. In T.H. Brubaker (Ed.), *Family relationships in later life* (pp. 13–26). Newbury Park, CA: Sage.

Bulmer, M. (1979). Concepts in the analysis of qualitative data. *Sociological Review, 27,* 651–671.

Bushardt, S. C., Fretwell, C., & Holdnak, B. J. (1991). The mentor/protégé relationship: A biological perspective. *Human Relations, 44*(6), 619–639.

Church of Jesus Christ of Latter-Day Saints (1981). *The doctrine and covenants of The Church of Jesus Christ of Latter-Day Saints.* Salt Lake City, UT: The Church of Jesus Christ of Latter-Day Saints.

Cohen, J. (1960). A coefficient of agreement for nominal scales. *Education and Psychological Measurement, 20,* 37–46.

Conley, L. J. (1990). Childbearing and childrearing practices in Mormonism. *Neonatal Network, 9,* 41–48.

Connidis, I. A. (1989). *Family ties and aging.* Toronto, Canada: Butterworth.

Cornwall, M. (1989). The determinants of religious behavior: A theoretical model and empirical test. *Social Forces, 68,* 572–592.

Cornwall, M., & Thomas, D. L. (1990). Family, religion, and personal communities: Examples from Mormonism. *Marriage and Family Review, 15,* 229–252.

Cracroft, R. H. (1991). "A profound sense of community": Mormon values in Wallace Stegner's Recapitulation. *Dialogue: A Journal of Mormon Thought, 24,* 101–113.

Ericksen, E. E. (1922). *The psychological and ethical aspects of Mormon group life.* Chicago: University of Chicago Press.

Fagenson, E. A. (1989). The mentor advantage: Perceived career/job experiences of protégés versus non-proteges. *Journal of Organizational Behavior, 10,* 309–320.

Fine, M. A. (1992) Families in the United States: Their current status and future prospects. *Family Relations, 41,* 430–435.

Fish, L. S., & Osborn, J. L. (1992). Therapists' views of family life: A delphi study. *Family Relations, 41,* 409–416.

Giles, H., Coupland, N., Coupland, J., Williams, A., & Nussbaum, J. (1992). Intergenerational talk and communication with older people. *International Journal of Aging and Human Development, 34,* 271–295.

Heaton, T. B. (1992). Demographics of the contemporary Mormon family. *Dialogue: A Journal of Mormon Thought, 25,* 19–34.

Hill, M. S., & Allen, J. B. (Eds.). (1972). Introduction. In M. S. Hill & J. B. Allen (Eds.), *Mormonism and American culture* (pp. 1–9). New York: Harper & Row.

Homer (1960). *The odyssey of Homer,* (E. Rees, Trans.). New York: Random House.

Kalbfleisch, P. J. (1991, November). *Gender Issues and Academic Mentoring.* Paper presented at the Seminar Series on Mentoring at the Annual Conference of the Speech Communication Association, Atlanta.

Kalbfleisch, P. J. (in press). *Mentoring as a personal relationship.* New York: Guilford.

Kalbfleisch, P. J., & Davies, A. B. (1991, April). *Mentors and protégés: Choices in partnership.* Paper presented at the annual meeting of the Southern States Communication Association (Top Three Paper), Tampa, FL.

Kalbfleisch, P. J., & Davies, A. B. (1993). An interpersonal model for participation in mentoring relationships. *Western Journal of Communication, 57*(4), 399–415.

Kalbfleisch, P. J., & Keyton, J. (1995). Power and equality in mentoring relationships. In P. J. Kalbfleisch & M. J. Cody (Eds.), *Gender, power, and communication in human relationships* (189–212). Hillsdale, NJ: Lawrence Erlbaum Associates.

Keyton, J., & Kalbfleisch, P. J. (1993). Mentoring: From a female perspective. *Mentor, 5,* 1–10.

Kornhaber, A., & Woodward, K. L. (1981). *Grandparents/ grandchildren: The vital connection.* Garden City, NY: Anchor Press.

Lamar, H. R. (1972). Statehood for Utah: A different path. In M. S. Hill & J. B. Allen (Eds.), *Mormonism and American Culture* (pp. 127–141). New York: Harper & Row.

Lewis, R. A. (1990). The adult child and older parents. In T. H. Brubaker (Ed.), *Family relationships in later life* (pp. 68–85). Newbury Park, CA: Sage.

Olian, J. D., Carroll, S. J., Giannantonio, C. M., & Feren, D. B. (1988). What do proteges look for in a mentor? Results of three experimental studies. *Journal of Vocational Behavior, 33,* 15–37.

Peterson, E. T. (1989a). Elderly parents and their offspring. In S. J. Bahr & E. T. Peterson (Eds.), Aging and the family, (pp. 175–191). Lexington, MA: Lexington.

Peterson, E. T. (1989b). Grandparenting. In S. J. Bahr & E. T. Peterson (Eds.), *Aging and the family* (pp. 159–174). Lexington, MA: Lexington.

Roberto, K. A. (1990). Grandparent and grandchild relationships. In T. H. Brubaker (Ed.), *Family relationships in later life* (pp. 100–112). Newbury Park, CA: Sage.

Rodman, H., & Sidden, J. (1992). A critique of pessimistic views about U.S. families. *Family Relations, 41,* 436–439.

Schvaneveldt, J. D., & Young, M. H. (1992). Strengthening families: New horizons in family life education. *Family Relations, 41,* 385–389.

Silverman, E. L. (1994). Women in women's organizations: Power or *Pouvoir?* A case study of leadership in the National Council of Jewish Women in Canada. In H. L. Radtke & H. J. Stam (Eds.), *Power/Gender: Social relations in theory and practice* (pp. 270–286). London: Sage.

Tiesel, J. W., & Olson, D. H. (1992). Preventing family problems: Troubling trends and promising opportunities. *Family Relations, 41,* 398–403.

Thomas, D. L. (1983). Family in the Mormon experience. In W. V. D'Antonio & J. Aldous (Eds.), *Families and religion: Conflict and change in modern society* (pp. 267–288). Beverly Hills, CA: Sage.

Vogl-Bauer, S. M., & Kalbfleisch, P. J. (1995, November). *The Impact of Perceived Equity on Parent/Adolescent Communication Strategy Usage and Relational Outcomes.* Paper presented at the annual convention of the Speech Communication Association (Top Four Paper), San Antonio, TX.

Walker, A. J., Shin, H., & Bird, D. N. (1990). Perceptions of relationship change and caregiver satisfaction. *Family Relations, 39,* 147–152.

Whitely, W., Dougherty, T. W, & Dreher, G. F. (1991). Relationship of career mentoring and socioeconomic origin to managers' and professionals' early career progress. *Academy of Management Journal, 34*(2), 331–351.

Whitely, W., Dougherty, T. W., & Dreher, G. F. (1992). Correlates of career-oriented mentoring for early career managers and professionals. *Journal of Organizational Behavior, 13,* 141–154.

APPENDIX
Elder Mentoring Questionnaire

Demographic Questions

1. What is your age?
2. How many generations back has your family been members of the church?
3. How many children do you have?
4. How old are these children?
5. How many of the children are (were) male(s), and how many are (were) female(s)?
6. How many grandchildren do you have?
7. How old are the grandchildren?
8. How many of the grandchildren are (were) male(s), and how many are (were) female(s)?
9. Do you have any great-grandchildren?
10. If so, how many?
11. How old are the great-grandchildren?
12. How many of the great-grandchildren are (were) male(s), and how many are (were) female(s)?

Mentoring Questions

Mentors: "people who provide advice, support, information, and professional sponsorship to their protégés; share their values; and help their protégés gain access to powerful networks" (Olian, Carroll, Giannantonio, & Ferren, 1988).

Protégés: "receive guidance from their mentors and may in turn support them as their knowledge grows and the mentoring relationship develops" (Kalbfleisch & Davies, 1993, p. 399).

After the interviewer read the aforementioned definitions, the following questions were asked of the respondents:
(Concerning the children)

1. With these definitions in mind, how well do you feel your relationships with your children compare to the definition of mentoring?
2. Could you elaborate on the areas you provide advice, support, and information to your children?

3. Is there an area in your children's lives that receives a greater mentoring focus? How about a second greatest, and so on?
4. What are some of the ways you provide advice, support, and information?
5. What are some of the ways you used to share your values with your children?
6. Are there ways in which your children provide some area of support for you?

(Concerning the grandchildren)
7. Does the definition of mentoring apply to your relationships with your grandchildren?
8. In what areas do you provide advice, support, and information to your grandchildren?
9. Is there an area that receives a greater mentoring influence than another?
10. Do the methods you use vary from those used with your children?
11. How do you try to share your values with your grandchildren?
12. Are there ways in which your grandchildren provide support for you?

(Concerning the church)
13. How do you feel your church membership has influenced or affected this relationship with your children?
14. How about with your grandchildren?
15. Are there any specific church doctrines, scriptural references, written passages, lessons, and so on, that have played a distinct role in this relationship with your children or grandchildren?

CROSS-CULTURAL COMMUNICATION AND AGING WITHIN ORGANIZATIONAL SETTINGS

INTRODUCTION

Part III gives a glimpse of cross-cultural communication and aging within various organizational settings. Selective communicative contexts within business organizations are discussed regarding the treatment of our elders in this society. Chapter 7 argues that elders in American organizations must cope with conditions that reflect societal and organizational value systems that are represented symbolically in simplified and generalized beliefs or stereotypes of elders. Chapter 8 advocates that the application of a cross-cultural communication perspective can be powerfully useful in categorizing the daily problems of elders in their care centers and in guiding the development of very practical solutions. Chapter 9 shows that changing sociocultural perspectives and the public health care system of the Indian Health Service have negatively impacted the sociocultural perspectives of aging Native American women's roles.

These organizations deal with elders as either employees (internal customers) or residents and patients (external customers). Thematically, this section reveals that many American organizations frequently contribute to the hardships that both internal and external elder customers must endure. This will hopefully entice organizations to reevaluate their posture toward elders in this epochal period of a changing customer base.

7

Cultural Views and Stereotypes of Aging in American Organizations

Larry W. Long
Daniel A. DeJoy
Manoocher N. Javidi
North Carolina State University

Akbar N. Javidi
University of Nebraska at Kearney

Although all industrialized cultures must deal with change due to techno-logical obsolescence and increased global competitiveness, does it neces-sarily follow that aging workers are "obsolescent," cannot change, and will cease to contribute to society and organizations after a certain chronological age? Or, can American elder employees' "shelf life" be extended by discov-ering the proper balance between work demands and personal needs? Have cultural beliefs about the relative influence of "nature" or "nurture" on the aging process influenced our view of elders?

We begin our response to these questions with the contention that American organizational and societal cultures have developed stereotypes of elders and the aging process primarily from an ontogenetic, or physi-ological, perspective, which implies that an employee's productivity and human resource value is a function of "nature." The alternative (which we clearly support) is that productivity and human resource value is or can be a function of social and organizational "nurture." We support this position with two propositions. First, cultures differ in terms of work and person emphasis, which has been somewhat reflected in cross-cultural differences in elder employment levels. Second, cultures contain beliefs about elders' contributions to societal and organizational goals, and these beliefs are symbolized in stereotypes. Often, stereotypes of elder American employees are inaccurate and undervalue elders as an organizational resource. We conclude the chapter with a set of recommendations for enhancing organizational outcomes by improving elders' working environments.

DIFFERENCES IN CULTURE:
WORK VERSUS PERSON EMPHASIS

A useful perspective for understanding value divergence and inherent consequences for members of organizations and social systems is derived by comparing the extent of emphasis on work versus personal needs. This distinction has been successfully employed in cross-cultural, psychological, sociological, organizational, and communication research.

Late 19th and early 20th century organizational designs were guidelines for behavior used to enhance total productive efficiency. Mid-twentieth century designs accounted for aspects of employee needs and incorporated them in contemporary organizational models to maximize employee satisfaction levels. Although probably unintended by their creators, earlier designs contained prescriptive guidelines with implicit assumptions about the suitability of elder employees for particularly demanding tasks. Later designs infrequently addressed the potential for tension when organizational and employee needs were simultaneously emphasized. A notable exception was the development of sociotechnical systems design; however, successful application of that approach, to date, has been infrequent.

A work emphasis over personal needs has been dominant in American organizations (Trompenaars, 1993). This orientation assumes output is a ratio of individual physical and intellectual attributes required and applied in order to transform input to output. Thus, high value is placed on an employee's *current* physical and intellectual strengths with respect to the task being performed. Because valued attributes emanate from current job role expectations rather than long-term career development needs of the individual, physical and intellectual barriers to work processes are assumed to be eliminated primarily through employee training or replacement.

Specific Organizational Cultures

Organizational creation and development tends to be a relatively deliberate activity, reflecting traditional organizational designs and the current state of technology required for managing and transforming physical, financial, human, and symbolic resources. As a result, organizations tend to be objective constructs that are moderated by societal values and beliefs. Organizational cultures can be differentiated by several components:

1. The general relationship between the employees and organization.
2. The vertical or hierarchical system of authority defining supervisory and subordinate relationships.
3. Employee perceptions of organizational destiny, purpose, and goals.
4. Societal values.

Long (1979) originally conceptualized organizational components along a continuum that ranged from role specialization to role exchange. Combined with the work versus person differences, these four components permit a differentiation of specific organizational cultures along two different dimensions: role specialization versus role exchange and work versus person emphasis. Figure 7.1 visually displays differences in the four types of organizational cultures that vary in terms of learning, change, operations, reward systems, conflict management, and motivational strategies (Javidi & Javidi, 1991; Trompenaars, 1993). Discernible differences in corporate culture existed when organizations in different countries were compared.

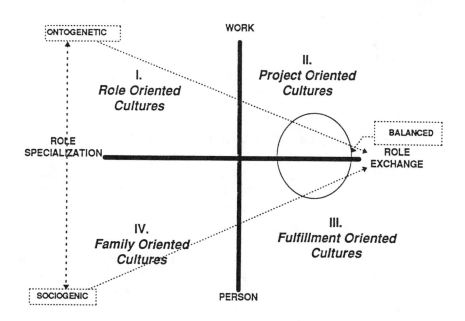

FIG. 7.1. Integrative framework: Sociogenic/ontogenetic perspectives of aging.

Trompenaars described these different cultures as role, project, fulfillment, and family oriented.

Role Oriented Cultures.   Role-oriented cultures were usually found in American organizations. Status was ascribed to superior roles that were distant yet powerful. Learning was achieved through logical, analytical processes. Promotion was a function of assuming a hierarchically higher position with much broader role definition, particularly in terms of power. Role specialization and work emphasis were dominant values.

The role-oriented organizational culture has emphasized and valued specialized work roles and employees who best fill those roles. The interesting paradox is that this emphasis on productivity is, by definition, a short-term goal (Cummings, Long, & Lewis, 1987). In contrast, emphasis on intermediate goals, or a focus on human resources development and adaptation are critical to long-term organizational efficiency. Interestingly, American organizations have often precluded identification of elder employees as a necessary human resource.

Project Oriented Cultures.   Project-oriented cultures were common in German and Danish corporations. Interactive employee relationships were the consequence of work processes rather than a function of social relationships. In other words, collaborative human relationships were work oriented. Status was achieved by project group members who contributed to total goal accomplishment. Heterogeneous groups often provided the means for task accomplishment. In this type of culture, work emphasis and role exchange and work collaboration were dominant values.

Fulfillment Oriented Cultures.   Fulfillment-oriented cultures were common in Swedish organizations where the corporation was often secondary to personal need-fulfillment. Here, the strategy was to insure that all employees spontaneously related to others. Status was achieved through creativity. Process orientations and cocreativity were promoted; management was characterized by enthusiastically providing constructive criticism. These organizations valued role exchange and personal emphasis.

Family Oriented Cultures.   Family-oriented cultures were common in India, France, and Japan. Relationships were defined holistically. In essence, individual membership was deemphasized, and harmonious group, or "family," outcomes were valued most. Consistent with patriarchal values, managers enacted a "fatherhood" role (Javidi & Javidi, 1991; Trompenaars, 1993). Thus, a dominant personal need for a supervisor in the hierarchy was to care for and make decisions for the subordinate. Consequently, this type of culture valued role specialization with a paternal emphasis on a subordinate's personal needs.

This typology of organizational cultures is consistent with earlier work conducted by Cummings, Long, and Lewis, (1987), who developed the Organizational Communication Design Matrix (OCDM) to compare organizational designs, assumptions, values, and related communication behaviors.

Older People and Organizational Cultures

Specific factors have significantly influenced conditions for elders in America's workforce. These include the weakness of kinship ties, rapidity in industrial and technological change that leads to obsolescence, a significant growth in the number of older people in America, and an emphasis on productivity and sacredness of work in the American culture (Clark & Anderson, 1967).

These factors have placed many aging Americans in a very difficult predicament. Elders have found themselves in organizational and societal cultures that exhibit little tolerance for employees who cannot keep up with innovation and maintain efficiency. At the same time, American organizational designs have considered elders as a resource with limited "shelf life." As a result, many elders eventually feel that they and their organizational life must come to an end because they are no longer able to measure up to those expectations so prized by their organization and society (Clark & Anderson, 1967).

Application of the "shelf life" cliché to older American employees provides a useful and, at the same time, ironic analogy for examining the circumstances of elder workers. For example, many food items, particularly fresh fruits and vegetables in a grocery store, are considered to have a short-term shelf life due to their perishable nature. However, certain processing procedures, such as canning or freezing, extend the shelf life of these items significantly. Many other processing and preservation techniques exist for prolonging freshness and usability of produce and other perishable items. The commonality across preservation techniques for perishables is that items are handled carefully in a controlled environment that insures maintenance of quality and a high level of consistency. In the United States, perishables with an appearance outside strict, limited tolerance levels will be rejected by consumers, whether the cause is due to mishandling, poor packaging, or natural forces of decay. Although American organizations have been successful in increasing the shelf life of nonhuman perishables, such outcomes for the elder employee have yet to occur due to myths surrounding the hiring, training, and retention of older workers (Clark, 1994).

In contrast to American organizations, other cultures have more effectively provided opportunities for elder employees. Clark (1994) compared employment experiences of elders in the United States and Japan, suggesting that American corporations might learn from the family-oriented culture in Japanese organizations. He noted that approximately 16% of the males over 65 remained in the American workforce, compared to over 37% of Japanese males. There appear to be at least three significant contributions to the variance (Clark). First, Japan's corporate economic and personnel policies reflect their desire to maintain a global competitive edge and recognition that elders desire to continue employment after retirement from their "career" job. Clark indicated that some companies reduced labor costs by selectively rehiring workers after mandatory retirement at wages that are 20% to 25% less than previous salary levels, a practice often illegal in the United States under the Age Discrimination in Employment Act. Despite this practice, however, the modal mandatory retirement age in Japan has increased from 55 to 60 during the past 20 years. Second, the homogeneous Japanese culture (Javidi & Javidi, 1991) reinforces an economy of interlocking firms that form trading groups that provide placement opportunities for retired workers (Clark). Third, there are a large number of self-employed workers in family businesses, and, because many Japanese firms offer lump-sum retirement options, some retirees will use these funds to purchase a business (Clark).

CULTURAL BELIEFS AND ELDER STEREOTYPES

Stereotypes can be efficient communication vehicles, but their misuse can create and perpetuate misunderstandings, leading to erroneous conclusions. Hooyman and Kiyak (1996) described stereotypes as "generalized and simplified beliefs about a group of people as objects" (p. 29). When individuals are stereotyped, they are assumed to possess or lack certain qualities, abilities, or behaviors because they are associated with some group.

At times, stereotyping is a useful strategy for efficiently processing, storing, and retrieving significant amounts of information. However, stereotyping is often misleading and unproductive. When labels or characteristics are attributed to a person or group based on limited information, individual attributes not commonly associated with the stereotyped category are overlooked. Also, stereotyped individuals may begin to believe these inaccurate assumptions about themselves and live up or down to the label.

Societal and organizational values are often reflected in the stereotypes used to describe elders. Hooyman and Kiyak (1996) noted that all societies define old age and determine its status according to certain criteria. These criteria naturally reflect the values of the culture. If growing older is perceived to have a detrimental affect on one's ability to engage in behavior highly valued by the society, then it is likely that stereotypes develop, and status is lowered within that context. Often, the valence of stereotypes covaries with organizational emphasis on work-centered versus person-centered values or differences in cultural beliefs. When stereotypes are negative, elders will feel they no longer have anything of value to exchange (Dowd, 1975). The intensity of this feeling is increased when negative stereotypes act as filters that influence evaluations of elder employees' actual and potential contributions to the company.

Cultural Interface and Stereotyping

Culture encompasses the collective mind of a society that guides its members' behavior and has a significant impact on stereotyping (Cummings, Long, & Lewis, 1987). As Moody (1993) noted, "what is honored in a country is cultivated there" (p. 27). Positive stereotypes are associated with groups that advance a culture's priorities; negative stereotypes arise when a group does not meet societal expectations. However, evaluations of people are not solely influenced by their country's macroculture. They are also influenced by membership in numerous "cultures" that are based on elements such as ethnic or national origin, religion, gender, geographic region, and age (Gollnick & Chin, 1990). Elder employees are simultaneously cast into multiple, overlapping "cultural" environments. Consequently, assimilated cultural stereotypes and their valence, positive or negative, might be used as a frame of reference for interpreting an elder employee's actual and potential human resource value to the society and organization.

To some extent, an organization's culture will reflect values that characterize the society in which it functions. In a country fostering capitalistic values, such as the United States, where strong emphasis is placed on productive efficiency and financial strength, many have argued that corporate values have determined the nature of social values. Nevertheless, societal and organizational differences may exist. For example, international businesses may adopt some characteristics of a "host" country while retaining characteristics of their "home" country. Furthermore, smaller, family-oriented businesses and larger, corporate entities in the United States have been shown to exhibit remarkably different value systems, particularly in emphasizing work-centered versus person-centered environments and organizational designs (Cummings, Long, & Lewis, 1987). Thus, organizational and societal culture may be separate (see Fig. 7.2), but there is a societal-organizational interface that may stimulate modifications in values and stereotypes or be mutually reinforcing. Thus, employees are members of societies and organizations that overlap and coexist in a global environment, and they may simultaneously belong to multiple, overlapping cultures. Cultural memberships are a function of many characteristics such as employment status, age, profession, educational status, and wealth, and they contribute to a stereotype's valence.

Organizations incorporate most societal values in their corporate cultures, yet values and stereotypes derived from the corporate culture may differ from societal culture. For example, a Japanese person working for an American company in Tokyo belongs to Japanese society and operates among its belief and value systems. That person is also a corporate employee and must function in ways consistent with the corporation and its cultural values to maintain employment. Although the American corporation may alter operating policies to facilitate functioning in Japan, it will

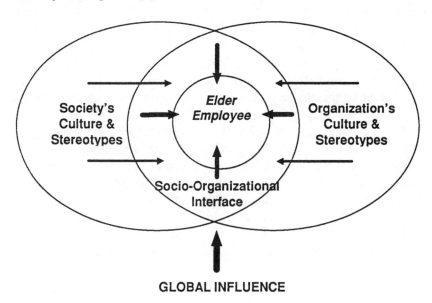

FIG. 7.2. Employee–society–organization interface.

retain most American policies to insure consistency with the home office in the United States. The outcome of this societal and organizational interface determines whether that employee operates in a role- or fulfill-ment-oriented organizational culture.

Stereotypes of Aging in the United States

What are some of the more common stereotypes of elders? McTavish (1971) reviewed a number of studies from the 1950s and 1960s on attitudes and stereotypes. He found that people often characterized elders as ill, tired, disinterested in sex, forgetful, poor at learning new material, grouchy, unproductive, and less willing to become involved in activities. In addition, other research found that elders are perceived as frail, slow, irritable, dependent, withdrawn, vague, and stagnant (Braithwaite, 1986). These negative stereotypes lead to *ageism* or the development of prejudice by one age group toward other age groups.

Stereotypes About Elder Employees

What are some of the more common stereotypes of older employees? Shea (1991) listed eight stereotypical notions or myths that we have:

1. Older people should retire to make way for younger employees.
2. Most older people are pretty much alike.
3. The basic job needs of older people in general are different from those of younger people.
4. As people age, they tend to focus on the past.
5. Most older employees cannot or will not alter behaviors to meet the changing needs of the organization. They prefer to coast and shy away from promotions or challenge.
6. Age is a disease—a slow but continuous process that cannot be reversed.
7. Old age is (or should be) a period of relative calm and stability—and that's what old people want.
8. As people age, they become more critical, complaining, and suspicious. (p. 30)

As we shall see, these myths have contributed to negative clichés and self-fulfilling prophecies.

A number of these views seem to reflect the assumption that many aging employees experience a growing dissatisfaction with work over the course of a career. The older employee becomes more critical and complaining, is oriented to the past "when life was better," tires of having to adapt to new situations and responsibilities, and longs for the peace and quiet of retirement. For example, some of the common clichés used to refer to older workers are: "You can't teach an old dog new tricks," "marking time," "ready for the gold watch," and "on the shelf."

Whereas the findings of earlier investigations pointed toward mostly negative perceptions of elders, recent studies suggest that attitudes may be shifting in a positive direction. Austin (1985), for example, reported that individuals ranked old age among the least disabling of various conditions on a scale of social distance. Also, some persons recognized that age had some advantages that could lead to positive stereotypes: Advancing years may bring a decline in physical abilities and attractiveness, but the years of experience often are associated with increased wisdom, kindness, and insight.

Those who interact with elders may contribute to the perpetuation or evolution of stereotypes. Coupland, Coupland, Giles, Henwood, and Wieman (1988) found that young interactants made statements to and asked questions of elder partners that actually elicited stereotypical behavior. In other words, intergenerational discourse led to a self-fulfilling prophesy or caused stereotypic behaviors. In addition, attitudes and assumptions about elders appeared to be influenced by such factors as the type of information available about a particular elder, whether the individual was judged solely on merit or in comparison to a younger person, and the context (for example, work related versus not work related). Generally, negative stereotypes dominated when little specific information about an elder was available, the context was not work related, and the elder was rated in comparison to a younger person (Braithwaite, 1986; Kite & Johnson, 1988). The last factor was particularly significant. For example, Kite and Johnson found that raters ignored stereotypic assumptions and focused on personal information when they considered a single elder target, but they ignored individuating information and relied on stereotypes when they compared an elder to a younger person.

STEREOTYPING ELDERS:
ONTOGENETIC VERSUS SOCIOGENIC VIEWS

Stereotyping does not necessarily end with labeling. Assumptions about causation often follow. In other words, a stereotype may encompass not only how a person will act or think but also why the individual behaves this way. Ross (1977) indicated that these faulty assumptions or fundamental attribution errors occurred when the perceptual focus was on behavior to the exclusion of the context or environment in which the behavior occurred. In the macroculture of the United States, the "biomedicalization" of aging (Estes & Binney, 1989) appears to have played a significant role in focusing attention on elder behavior. In this case, however, the emphasis has been on clinical phenomena such as organic pathologies and physiological etiologies to the exclusion of context or culture in which the person ages.

Ontogenetic View of Elders

The stereotype that aging is an irreversible, disease-like process reflects an ontogenetic view of development in which the various behaviors and developmental changes associated with aging are considered inherent properties of the aging organism. Thus, the stereotype of age as a disease suggests that older people behave as they do because that is what happens when people get older. Dannefer (1984) stated that "the implicit assumptions of the ontogenetic paradigm entail a view of change in adulthood as a natural property of the individual which tends to be uniform across individuals and relatively unaffected by context" (p. 109). In other words, older people are stereotyped as creatures who complain, are inflexible, long for the good old days, and so on, because that is the way they are.

Sociogenic View of Elders

In contrast, a sociogenic view of aging focuses on those *environmental and cultural* factors that may contribute to commonly observed behavioral changes characteristic of different developmental periods. For example, Dannefer (1984) suggested that patterns of behavior commonly associated with particular stages of development, such as the midlife crisis, are culturally defined and normed. With respect to aging employees in a corporation, he indicated that the organizational context in which the employees' careers unfold is a more important factor in determining productivity and job satisfaction than the biological influences of aging. In other words, many of the changes in employees' behavior and values are characteristic of different career stages and are artifacts of social structure. Often, changes might merely reflect self-fulfilling prophecies. Dannefer stated that:

> Sociological analysis of age effects needs to attend to the institutional forces that organize aging, and to questions of how normative expectations and

assumptions about aging influence and are influenced by these, and the extent to which age-related change in individual characteristics is produced by such processes. (p.112)

REALITIES VERSUS STEREOTYPES OF ELDER EMPLOYEE PERFORMANCE

Many investigations of elders' performance in organizations exist. Sterns and McDaniel (1994) provided a comprehensive meta-analysis of existing literature. They reviewed and analyzed data from studies representing thousands of participants. For example, evaluations of studies investigating relationships between age and job performance represented over 60,000 participants. Their evaluation of the research yielded several conclusions about elders' performance at work:

1. An extensive body of research indicates that age and job performance are by no means highly correlated. If performance does anything with age, it improves slightly, but the relationship is very weak.
2. Older adults learn less in training than younger workers, make more errors in training, and take longer to master the training material. However, the relevance of these findings [to the aging process] is not clear.
3. The research literature is fairly consistent in finding a weak negative relationship between age and turnover—that is, older workers are slightly less likely to change jobs than younger workers.
4. In reviewing the literature on accidents and aging in the workplace, occupational injuries were found to occur at a lower rate to older workers than to younger ones. Accident frequency declined steadily up to age 64 and then dropped even more sharply for workers over 65.
5. The job/worker match or mismatch and productivity relationship has been reviewed as well. Based on currently available data, there seems to be no major reason why middle-aged and elder workers cannot continue to be productive in most job situations. (p. 45)

Comparisons of aging to work processes and outcomes supported the contention that ontogenetically-derived stereotypes of elders are inaccurate. It was clear that current information supported the contentions that aging and productivity are not related, elder workers are more reliable, and elder workers are less likely to have work-related accidents when compared to younger employees. Finally, training differences were not equivocal and were based primarily on comparisons of 25-year-old workers to those 60 years of age and older.

Thus, our understanding of organizational principles and experiences with elders have led to the formulation of three major conclusions. First, many stereotypes about elders are ontogenetically-derived and inaccurate when generalized to the group as a whole. Second, stereotypes about aging and performance at work are generally inaccurate and potentially self-ful-filling prophecies, exacerbated in a negative direction. Third, negative stereotypes have been reinforced by societal and organizational belief systems.

CULTURAL FRAMEWORK AND PERSPECTIVES OF ELDER EMPLOYEES

How can productive efficiency for organizations and employee satisfaction for elders be enhanced? We propose a cultural framework (depicted in Fig. 7.1) that fosters consideration of a balance between ontogenetic and socio-genic perspectives.

Figure 7.1 visually displays the relationship between ontogenetic and sociogenic variables. As indicated earlier, role (Quadrant I) and project (Quadrant II) cultures place high emphasis on work outcomes; these organizations value work processes, so physical and mental attributes of employees are emphasized, and assessment is based on an ontogenetic perspective. In the extreme, this emphasis is at the expense of person-centered needs.

Fulfillment (Quadrant III)- and family (Quadrant IV)-oriented organizational cultures value person-centered issues and are found in societal cultures that make a concerted effort to adapt to life-phase needs and attributes of all members. Thus, the culture is compatible with sociogenic perspectives of aging. In extreme cases, this emphasis may displace appropriate levels of concern for work demands and requirements.

Obviously, extreme preoccupation with either perspective predisposes one to neglect the needs and realities of work processes or individuals. Thus, realistic integration of ontogenetic and sociogenic concerns requires a balance (see Fig. 7.1). Because Quadrants I and IV contain organizational structures that emphasize hierarchies of authority and role specialization, communication tends to be one way and downward. In order to achieve balance, while maintaining both efficiency and satisfaction levels, mutual, two-way interaction or role exchange is required. Thus, organizations must actively solicit input from elder employees at all organizational levels in order to separate fact from fantasy. In role-oriented organizations such as found in the United States, this reality occurs very infrequently.

Project- and fulfillment-oriented cultures, which in reality overlap in Quadrants II and III, emphasize an environment supportive of relational development based on work, personal needs, or a work/personal need balance through communication role exchange. These tenets are assumed by participative management and sociotechnical systems approaches.

Large-scale collaborative designs, such as those found in participative management and sociotechnical systems approaches, have not been implemented effectively on a large scale—they require a cultural belief and value shift, a feat not accomplished overnight or in the next fiscal quarter. For example, when role exchange is valued, individual employee development and growth is encouraged. This strategy may mean that production efficiency is sacrificed in the short run in the belief that significant long-term advantages will be realized by providing an environment that is more supportive or elder employee centered.

Although role specialization in American companies has contributed significantly to industrial productivity and to the solution of problems inherent in employee information and work overload, it has also created conditions of obsolescence and replaceability for many elder employees. In addition, the focus on efficiency of the corporation to the exclusion of individual employees' careers has perpetuated stereotyping myths, particularly as they have been reinforced by an inherent ontogenetic bias in American culture. As Shea (1991) noted, "while the behavior of every age group is stereotyped by others to some degree, no group is as negatively affected by such generalizations as the elderly; at least other age groups are expected to outgrow their idiosyncrasies" (p. 28).

Therefore, achieving an appropriate balance between biological needs and human resource assets of elder employees will not be an easy task. The cultural framework described here, however, provides a specific direction: Human resources management should become less job role focused and more employee centered. To illustrate, we draw on our personal experience with physical resources management:

Traditionally, the day after Thanksgiving has been a time for us to visit a friend's Christmas tree farm to select and cut down a tree. Since the owner was a professor of horticulture and did not live on the farm, the assumption was that he spent a minimum amount of time on the lot except for the period between Thanksgiving and Christmas. He found our naiveté amusing. "I'm here every weekend throughout the year, and so are most of my family members," he said. "How do you think these trees get to be so symmetrical in shape? They take years to grow, and they must be constantly pruned, supported, sprayed, and fertilized." (personal interview, April 12, 1996)

RECOMMENDATIONS

Recommendation One: Develop a Portfolio-Centered Rather Than a Job-Centered Philosophy for Human Resource Management. M o s t people cannot demonstrate the same levels of productivity and energy at 65 or 70 that they did when they were 30, but when people function in an environment (culture) that encourages flexibility, capitalizes on strengths that may vary with points in the life span, and promotes "portfolio careers," then the shelf life of many employees in American corporations might be extended dramatically. In other words, if corporate culture approaches aging from a sociogenic perspective (i.e., how we handle our employees will greatly influence how they age with us) rather than an ontogenetic view (i.e., age decays employee performance and attitude no matter what we do), then America's elder citizens may find renewed fulfillment in work, and its organizations may rediscover the wisdom and long-term perspective that comes with age.

Recommendation Two: Evaluate the Accuracy of Current Stereotype and Eliminate Inaccuracies. American organizations can take several steps in moving toward a more sociogenic view of aging. First, the cultural members need to reevaluate a number of stereotypical attitudes about older adults. Shea (1991) suggested that context should be considered with respect to many stereotypes: ". . . context is almost everything when one is attempting to understand and describe an individual's life status" (p.39). For example, if older people appear to look forward to the calm and stability associated with life after work, it may, in fact, be due to the desire to escape the monotony of their jobs. They are longing for something different, for excitement rather than calm.

Recommendation Three: Use Elder Employees as Consultants and Facilitators of Organizational Change. Elders' resistance to change is often a consequence of past experiences with poorly managed periods of organizational transition. As stated previously, individuals do not become old overnight. Elders have experienced a lifetime of change. If their organization has a track record of managing change inefficiently, not recognizing the efforts of employees in the change process, or seeming to change for change's sake, then it is understandable that older employees may be resistant to development efforts. In contrast, openly discussed, well-planned development efforts induce less stress, less ambiguity, and more support. Organizations should use advice and counsel from older employees who have experienced change. Elder employees are more likely to know when an organization is "reinventing the wheel" or "making the same mistakes that were made 15 years ago." Failure to consult with more seasoned employees results in increased resentment, isolation, and resistance to development efforts.

Recommendation Four: Nurture Job Role Flexibility and a Balanced Frame for Evaluating Performance. American organizations can learn and profit from other cultures where aging and work are viewed quite differently. For example, Leviathan (1983) described the role that work plays in the lives of elder residents in the kibbutz. In this cultural setting, where life expectancies are longer, individuals enthusiastically choose to work well into the later years of life. Leviathan noted an important difference between the kibbutz and the macroculture. In the kibbutz, changing work roles are encouraged into the late 1940s and early 1950s. As people age, there is continual "refitting" between jobs, skills, and needs. In contrast, job changing in American organizations tends to result in seniority loss, reduced benefits, and dramatically reduced income levels.

Recommendation Five: Develop "People Potential Centers."
According to Van der Erve (1993), the issue of career goals versus organizational goals is increasingly important as corporations struggle to deal with change and competitiveness. Because organizational change often leads to job role changes, he suggested that human resource departments become "people potential" centers that help employees to discover what they want to be (1993).

If organizations focused on helping people determine what they want to do in a career, resistance to change would decline. Over time, resources invested in elders (before they became elders) would have a greater payback simply because the employees would have a greater commitment to organizational goals. The result, then, would be greater productive efficiency and increased employee satisfaction.

CONCLUSION

Assumptions about what happens as employees age have often been analogous to the "naive" belief that seedlings, planted on a farm and left to their own genetic tendencies, need little or no intervention by the farmer to magically become beautiful, symmetrical trees that people want to take home and decorate for Christmas. Then, after Christmas, when the tree has become used up, dry, and brittle, it should be discarded. Organizations often treat employees in a similar way—they assume that new, younger employees will inevitably develop on the job and be productive through the first half of their careers. However, because biological aging is inevitable and cannot be altered by organizational intervention, elder workers' feelings and attitudes about their careers, organizations, and value to a company will become negative, reflecting deteriorating physiological processes. Hence, they should be "retired" or "discarded."

Organizations that do not continually cultivate employees often assume that after middle age there is an inverse relationship between aging and a satisfied, productive employee. This cultural belief reflects an ontogenetic perspective of aging employees and a belief that the primary determinants of attitude and performance are "...fixed by organismic requirements and constraints..." (Dannefer, 1984, p. 109). Essentially, these organizations treat elder employees as dysfunctional because aging is viewed as a sine qua non of biological processes that stimulate deteriorating attitudes about work, reduce personal motivation, and lower productivity.

Much like the horticulture professor who devoted much time caring and nurturing seedlings in order to develop Christmas trees, a few organizations have rejected the notion that biological aging beyond the middle years inevitably produces negative outcomes for an employee. These organizations have assimilated a sociogenic view of aging processes into their organizational culture, assuming that behavior and attitude are "... an artifact of social structure ... of the organization of work settings and of norms about ideal careers" (Dannefer, 1984, p. 110). These organizations "fertilize and prune," that is, they provide social structures that produce functional employees throughout their careers. How, then, can American organizations enhance *all* employees' careers so they will be a long-term asset rather than a liability?

REFERENCES

Austin, D. (1985). Attitudes toward old age: A hierarchical study. *The Gerontologist, 25,* 431–434.

Braithwaite, V. (1986). Old age stereotypes: Reconciling contradictions. *Journal of Gerontology, 41,* 353–360.

Clark, R. (1994). Employment costs and the older worker. In S. Rix (Ed.), *Older workers: How do they measure up*. Washington, DC: American Association of Retired Persons.

Clark, M., & Anderson, B. (1967). *Culture and aging*. Springfield, IL: Thomas.

Coupland, N., Coupland, J., Giles, H., Henwood, K., & Wieman, J. (1988). Elderly self-disclosure: Interactional and intergroup issues. *Language and Communication, 8,* 109–133.

Cummings, W., Long, L., & Lewis, M. (1987). *Managing communication in organizations: An introduction.* Scottsdale, AZ: Gorsuch Scarisbrick.

Dannefer, D. (1984). Adult development and social theory: A paradigmatic reappraisal. *American Sociological Review, 49,* 100–116.

Dowd, J. (1975). Aging as exchange: A preface to a theory. *Journal of Gerontology, 30,* 584–594.

Estes, C., & Binney, E. (1989). The biomedicalization of aging: Dangers and dilemmas. *The Gerontologist, 29,* 587–596.

Gollnick, D., & Chin, P. (1990). *Multicultural education in a pluralistic society.* Columbus, OH: Merrill.

Hooyman, N., & Kiyak, H. A. (1996). *Social gerontology: A multidisciplinary perspective* (4th ed.). Boston: Allyn & Bacon.

Javidi, A., & Javidi, M. (1991). Cross-cultural analysis of interpersonal bonding: A look at East and West. *Howard Journal of Communications, 3,* 129–138.

Kite, M., & Johnson, B. (1988). Attitudes toward older and younger adults: A meta-analysis. *Psychology and Aging, 3,* 233–244.

Leviathan, U. (1983). Work and aging in the kibbutz: Some relevancies for the larger society. *Aging and Work, 6,* 215–222.

Long, L. (1979). *An exploratory study of communication roles as predictors of job satisfaction and managerial preference.* Unpublished doctoral dissertation, University of Oklahoma, Norman.

McTavish, D. (1971). Perceptions of old people: A review of research methodologies and findings. *The Gerontologist, 11,* 90–101.

Moody, H. (1993). Age, productivity, and transcendence. In S. Bass, F. Caro, & Y. Chen (Eds.), *Achieving a productive aging society* (pp. 27–40). Westport, CT: Auburn.

Ross, L. (1977). The intuitive psychologist and his shortcomings: Distortions in the attribution process. In L. Berkowitz (Ed.), *Advances in experimental social psychology.* New York: Academic Press.

Shea, G. (1991). *Managing older employees.* Oxford: Jossey-Bass.

Sterns, H.L., & McDaniel, M.A. (1994). Job performance and the older worker. In S. Rix (Ed.), *Older workers: How do they measure up.* Washington, DC: American Association of Retired Persons.

Trompenaars, F. (1993). *Riding the waves of culture: Understanding cultural diversity in business.* Avon, Great Britain: Bath Press.

Van der Erve, M. (1993). *The power of tomorrow's management.* Oxford: Butterworth-Heinemann.

8

The Nursing Home and Retirement Community: A Cross-Cultural Communication Perspective

Christi L. Grooters
Winslow Court Retirement Community, Colorado Springs, CO

L. Brooks Hill
Trinity University

Penelope N. Long
North Carolina State University

The institutional elder-care system of American society fits generally on a continuum with three identifiable points. Anchoring one end of this continuum is the "nursing home," where clients are largely dependent on the staff who provide 24-hour skilled care. At the opposite end is the "retirement community," where the clients are largely independent, but care is readily available. Ranging in the middle of the continuum is the "assisted-living" environment, which involves variable dependence on the staff and includes partial care. Despite the common concern for aging and elders, extrapolation of research from place-to-place on this continuum requires careful adaptation.

The history of this field study provides some useful information about the emergence of the cross-cultural communication perspective it employs. Within this perspective, the first two authors began in 1990 to gather inductively examples of symbolic behaviors reflective of problems for patients in the nursing home environment. Those observations generated a set of preliminary categories that were reported in a paper at the annual convention of the Speech Communication Association (Cupach, Grooters, Hill, Long, & Long, 1992). Subsequently, these categories were used as an a priori framework for the examination of behaviors in the retirement community situation. Not only did the categories correspond to problems in this new context but they also provided directions for possible solutions to these problems.

This chapter reports the application of a cross-cultural communication perspective in the contexts of the nursing home and retirement community. Obviously, the suggested advice will require adaptation to fit the various situations of elder care, but it should be useful even in the family care environment. The structure of this chapter directly reflects its historical evolution. The first major section presents the derived categories of problems we observed in the nursing home and briefly anticipates how they were used in formulating practical approaches to resolution of the social problems they manifested. The second major section examines in more detail the training programs that evolved as partial solutions. A final section summarizes the chapter and projects conceptual and methodological refinements for the future application of this cross-cultural communication perspective.

CATEGORIES OF PROBLEM ANALYSIS

Our study of the nursing home environment identified five major problem areas, treated in the following sections as confounding symbolism, confronting stereotypes, interactional anxiety and uncertainty, negotiating social reality, and maintaining progress. Central to this cross-cultural communication perspective and the study of these five problem areas is the pervasive symbolic behavior of all parties involved. More specifically are the labeling, "metaphorizing," and mythmaking activities so interwoven in the processes of stereotyping (Kennan & Hill, 1979).

Confounding Symbolism

Labeling is the process of assigning a symbol to a thing, idea, or activity. Through labeling, we facilitate the psychological ordering of our universe and the social communication about that world. Because we have a finite set of labels and an infinite universe, we are forced to use metaphors as one means of expanding our referential system. By extending labels for the known, we can hypothetically capture the unknown. If the metaphor fits, the label will in time simply assume the additional meaning, and the creative aspect of the metaphor lapses. Until the metaphor is incorporated into everyday discourse, we continue to use the metaphor as a vehicle for creative management of the unknown. At an even broader level, we explain the unknown through the use of story lines replete with metaphors; this mythmaking activity permits us to capture even larger chunks of the unknown and to settle the anxiety about our limitations (Kennan & Hill, 1979).

The labels and other symbols used in the nursing home often function negatively and serve to inhibit adult–adult, rational interactions. Verbally, the residents are frequently addressed in demeaning ways that serve to dehumanize both the patient and the treatment. Similarly, the nonverbal behavior of the caregivers is often impersonal and condescending. The combined effect of this symbol abuse is to reduce the elders to children who are, in many ways, deficient and deserve only patronizing treatment. Unlike good children with the potential for nurtured development, the elders are often treated punitively, like juvenile delinquents with a restricted future. This symbolic framework of demeaning labels such as "honey," "sweetie," or the undeserved use of the first name, creates a situation in which very little prospect exists for respectful relationships. Indeed, these labels foster a parent–child, rather than adult–adult relationship (Haney, 1992). As new caregivers are socialized into this symbolic arena, the negative results are reinforced by their peers, and the elders are caught in a debilitating negative cycle. One discovers, therefore, the need for a new set of symbols within which to work if improved relations are to occur.

The semantic orientation of the cross-cultural communication perspective helps address the problems of this confounding symbolism. The work of Benjamin Whorf and others accentuates the necessary mental conditioning by arguing that language is not merely a reproducing instrument for expressing ideas—rather, producing language plays a prominent role in actually molding the perceptual world of the people who use it (Carroll, 1956). For too long, the senior communities have been defined and labeled by outside, and often prejudiced, groups. Some have labeled elder-care facilities and communities as "senior warehouses" and likened them to ghettoes such as one might find in large cities. Although these metaphors and symbols do ignite interesting analyses of aging specific to the American culture, they encourage the broader foundation of a cross-cultural perspective for a solution. We must, therefore, train people once again to be sensitive of co-cultures and conscious of their own, as well as societal, misuse and abuse of symbols.

Confronting Stereotypes

Stereotyping combines the three semantic activities of labeling, metaphorizing, and mythmaking into a simplistic approach to everyday life. With stereotypes, one can reduce the complex semantic processes by short-circuiting the thought necessary. We simply take these semantic activities for granted, quickly accept the language provided, and presumptively apply the symbols involved. Unfortunately for us all, we begin to confuse reality with the symbols we use to organize and communicate about it. Thus, we lay the basic foundations for problems of human interaction.

This second category of illustrations, therefore, invites us to consider the oversimplifying stereotypes of both the elders as well as their caregivers. We recognize that stereotypes are not inherently bad; in fact, stereotyping entails the very human, normal process of categorization used to simplify and cope with our complex world. Some stereotypes, in fact, make very positive presumptions about their referents. When stereotypes become negative, unfounded, or debilitating for another culture, however, they need to be evaluated closely. Unfortunately, the stereotyping of elders has evolved into a counterproductive social norm with frightening implications. For the nursing home environment, the situation is perhaps at its worst because the physical and psychological illnesses make it even more difficult for the employees and others to manage, if not overcome, their negative stereotypes. Beyond the obvious challenges created by the stereotypes of elders are the further complicating negative stereotypes of the employee positions. Often, these jobs are perceived erroneously as being filled by people who "could not make it" as "real" nurses, who are "captured by circumstances in these inferior jobs," and who are saddled with the image of "bottom wipers." Even a casual application of the organizational communication literature classifies this demoralizing situation as one with little potential for job fulfillment or high morale (Conrad, 1994).

To approach the adverse stereotypes of elders, we need to work with several age groups and on dual levels. On one level, we simply need to make people of all ages aware of the false bases of their stereotypes and the negative consequences for elders and themselves. At another level, we hope to erode, especially for the younger participants, the tendencies to form false and potentially abusive stereotypes. The second set of adverse stereotypes involves the caregivers and their profession. Caregivers often cite a disheartening example of their situation: While helping a senior buy groceries, someone turns to them and mumbles under his or her breath, "I'd hate to have your job!" Any corrective action must help inoculate the caregivers against the negative consequences of such inappropriate behavior. By reconditioning and offering positive intergenerational experiences to the larger communities, the caregivers can receive positive reinforcements for their professional efforts and can learn how to cope with public expressions of negative stereotypes. Simultaneously, the elders receive more favorable attention which, in turn, can undermine negative stereotypes.

Interactional Anxiety and Uncertainty

The third category of illustrations involves the extensive uncertainty and anxiety that naturally emerge in senior living communities. Within the community are at least three interacting co-cultures, namely, the seniors or residents of the community, their staff caregivers and outside volunteers, and family members. The potential for uncertainty and anxiety in the interactions among these groups varies widely with the environment and understanding between and among the groups (Gudykunst & Kim, 1992). Uncertainty inversely corresponds with one's ability to predict and explain another person's feelings, attitudes, values, and behavior; less predictability leads to greater uncertainty. Although uncertainty is not necessarily negative and may serve as the spark for interactional challenge, it may also lead to frightening anxiety and complicated interactions. As with uncertainty, anxiety is not inherently negative; in fact, anxiety primarily serves to alert the system to become more active in adapting to one's situation, but anxiety also has a frightening downside if it becomes uncontrolled and weakens the ability of people to interact effectively. Counterproductive uncertainty and anxiety can adversely affect interactions between people; and the greater the difference between people, the greater the likelihood for adverse results. In nursing homes and retirement communities, the residents often become increasingly estranged, and the potential for counterproductive uncertainty and anxiety simultaneously grows.

The several reasons why seniors in nursing homes and retirement communities become estranged from the other co-cultures comprise a crucial part of the problem with their care and treatment. Unique to senior communities is that the resident, who is also the consumer in this situation, is made to feel like a stranger, an inversion of the social norm in which the consumer is treated as special. Further, the senior must often depend on the community, thereby reversing a lifetime of behavior designed to create independence. That many residents come from out of state, or at least out of the area, contributes even further to increasing estrangement among the residents. Staff members are often strangers, due to generational differences and the high level of turnover in a care facility; personal relations are difficult to develop with someone who may be gone tomorrow. Finally, families also become estranged in many cases because they are not present in the day-to-day life of the senior anymore. The caregiver also has more expertise than do the seniors' loved ones and thus may build a pattern of dependency with the resident that displaces the family. This may, in turn, create a pattern of avoidance wherein the family is reluctant to visit because the senior is increasingly different, and the caregiver may not take the time to personalize the interaction, thereby dehumanizing a resident or patient. The collective effect of this estrangement is increased uncertainty about the relationships and anxiety about interaction.

Caregivers in the nursing home often establish a self-defensive psychological distance from the elderly patients. This distance, in turn, creates uncertainty and anxiety. Because of its self-preservation, defensive value, the employees usually do not try to reduce uncertainty; instead, they are content to dehumanize the patients, treat them as objects rather than persons, and thereby obviate the need to reduce uncertainty. In distinct contrast to any defensive solace the distance provides employees, this treatment causes the patients to experience extreme anxiety from both their high uncertainty level and their "objective" treatment as "something" less than a person. The reaction by patients is remarkably predictable: some react passively, making no effort to respond; if they do respond at all, they do so with task-irrelevant behaviors. This passive response pattern, in turn, reinforces the propriety of the caregivers to sustain the objective dehumanization. Sometimes, the patients respond aggressively with an uninterrupted chain of complaints; this also reinforces employee disregard, and they reciprocate with aggression or avoidance behaviors. The aggressive response by patients is often a reaction against being ignored or otherwise taken for granted, but it can diminish the potential for any interactive resolution of the problems. The situation in the retirement community is not nearly as negative as in the nursing home, but this scenario of increasing estrangement, uncertainty, and anxiety is likely present to a lesser degree in any community that segregates elders and demands attention. Joint training for staff and family can provide critical interaction with the seniors as a way to help employees and other co-cultures to humanize their approach and residents or patients to develop a more viable strategy for addressing their situation.

Negotiating Social Reality

When members of two different cultural groups interact, they must create a shared ground on which they can interpret the ideas and behaviors of each other. In the cross-cultural communication literature, this common ground is sometimes identified as a "third culture," negotiated by members of the two interacting cultures (Useem, Useem, & Donoghue, 1963). In an ideal situation, each person contributes equally to this common ground as the parties involved negotiate a social reality sufficient for their interaction. When relations are unequal, the more powerful or manipulative party will control the construction of reality, often without realizing that reduced input from the other person can diminish the quality of the interaction and resulting relationship. A common situation in the nursing home and the retirement community unfortunately involves unequal power relationships in which the seniors have an insufficient role in the negotiation of their social reality, and the quality of interaction and relationships consequently diminishes. Ideally, the seniors themselves should make a major contribution to the negotiated reality of this third culture within which they will interact with the caregiving employees and visitors. Too often, the caregivers simply impose their views on the constructed culture, and the patients have very little input. Visits by outsiders, including family and friends, sometimes worsen rather than help the situation because their contribution is limited, and their interpretation of the situation is heavily dependent on the point of view of the caregiver. With a lack of complete information, the outsider tends to comply with caregiver instructions, becomes an unwitting contributor to the problem, and, therefore, has aggravating and inexplicable interaction with their relatives or friends. The fieldwork solution to this dimension of the problem has actually come from the empowerment of the residents themselves and reassertion of their rights and abilities as human beings.

Maintaining Progress

Finally, what we have learned about race relations in America has important implications for the nursing home environment. The central idea is that forced compliance can ultimately potentiate attitudinal change. The situation in some nursing homes for the elders is inhumane, with physical, as well as psychological, abuse. We simply cannot tolerate these quasicriminal patterns of containment. We must exert more municipal, state, and federal supervision to insure compliance with minimally tolerable patterns of behavior. On top of this, we recommend special education and training, perhaps provided by retired volunteers from local universities, to help the employees and patients better interact. Forced compliance alone will not insure a good environment, but it represents a good start. Education can help to enlighten the attitudes that may even spread outside the nursing home to influence a broader social awareness and improved treatment of our elders.

Beyond the more forceful efforts to address the problems in some nursing homes, we are still confronted with the task of sustaining our positive achievements in other, less extreme, situations. Unless checked, negative stereotypes, prejudice, and ageism lead to grim prognoses for our senior communities. Outside of current government regulations, social services, and human rights organizations, the solutions lie in continued vigilance and enhanced awareness. The problem is not, however, the sole responsibility of the institutions involved. The intergroup attitudes and problems we must confront are learned predispositions; as we continue to separate our elders in American society from the productive, respected mainstream, we continue to sustain these behaviors. We need to enlist the aid of elders in communicating an alternative message to society that elders have a significant contribution to make (Hutchison, 1991). We can easily introduce many seniors to work in volunteer programs and provide transportation to facilitate their involvement. This can permit them to live more rewarding and productive lives as well as communicate a valuable message to our society.

EDUCATIONAL AND TRAINING OPTIONS

Two consecutive field work opportunities totaling 6 years, plus countless years of experience from our other resources, have established the benefit of utilizing this multidimensional, cross-cultural communication perspective. Anecdotal evidence collected in a closed, poorly communicating care environment has been systematically applied to a "living community" in Colorado Springs, Colorado. After nearly 3 years, we have substantial evidence of the positive results we anticipated. The results were profound and immediate on all the co-cultures exposed to the training. Important to this success, however, was strong institutional support from the very top downward to create and perpetuate a constructive symbolic environment. The explicit practices and policies by the general manager of Winslow Court Retirement Community created a fertile ground for this cross-cultural communication perspective to succeed.

The purpose of this section is to elaborate the enlightened educational and training options as they are currently offered at Winslow Court Retirement Community. The following subsections are organized around the primary thrusts of their programs: intergenerational, community and caregivers, and primary culture and aging population. Within each of these three program categories are special exercises designed to adapt its ideas to varied audiences. Plans are constantly changing, alternatives are being developed, and new ideas are being sought. What follows is a description of an ongoing process with an invitation to any and all to expand and improve this conceptualization.

Stage One: Intergenerational Thrust

Designed to overcome the stereotypes developed between generations, this thrust builds on the ideas of improved awareness and interpersonal communication. Presently, this program relies primarily on an extensive exercise called "Aging Realities," which was developed by Bonnie jw Riley and which is followed by varied types of intergenerational social activities. The central exercise uses a four-piece photo display that depicts a person, currently in the senior years, at six different ages in his or her life, beginning with infancy and concluding at present age. This wide spread of ages helps the display to capture the attention of people at all ages, whether they are young children, teenagers, middle aged, or retired. The display is usually taken to a school or other group and presented by a caregiver and a senior, preferably the senior featured in the photographs. This activity allows the audience to view aging in a closer, more personal, and universal light.

Following preliminary work with the photo-display exercise, the program supervisor or speaker will organize an intergenerational day or activity to foster interaction among the various age groups. These supplemental activities focus on the interests and personalities of all individuals present rather than on the usual separation of generations by physical qualifiers and other generalities. This activity also highlights the vast range of interests and activities within one's own generation. In fact, a senior and a youth may often find a closer connection than a youth and peers who may have had significantly different life styles and experience. All parties leave the "Aging Realities" exercise and these supplementary activities with a more empathic understanding of aging's reality.

Winslow Court Retirement Community has developed two additional approaches to sensitize employees and the families of the elders. Also created by Bonnie jw Riley, the first is a program given to employees during the employment interview or orientation process. Appropriately entitled "People Against Growing Empty" (PAGE), this exercise helps employees experience the process of loss which most seniors will encounter. The employees begin by writing down everything that creates purpose in their life—in other words, their reasons for living. Through group discussion, they gradually cross off all items that a senior citizen in a worst-case scenario might encounter. Once family, career, health, and vocation are deleted, the potential staff member has acquired the viewpoint of the care receiver. Beyond these major purposes, they are asked further to delete incrementally the simple pleasures of the day. Once this negative visualization is complete, they are encouraged to imagine their potential position as creating an environment and atmosphere in which reasons to live can flourish. This serves as a strong sensitization as well as a very memorable lesson in empathy.

Another method of sensitization is directed toward family members. In addition to their own uncertainty and anxiety, family members also develop feelings of frustration, anger, and guilt. This exercise revolves around a monthly dinner for family and caregivers only. With some guidance and planning, this informal social event allows questions and advice to flow freely among differing families. Somewhat cathartic, this open expression helps everyone to realize that no one is alone in these feelings and invites some direct questions that one may not be able to pose directly to another family member. The dinner also permits the family to maintain contact and exposure to the living community, which can further reduce uncertainty and anxiety.

The results of these training efforts reflect profound alterations in negative stereotyping. Adults have come in for interviews saying, "My child is a friend of one of your seniors who visited her school." Such statements reflect changing relationships and the distinct advantages of confronting our stereotypes and interacting with the people we have stereotyped. As we have learned, coping with the aging process by elders is as widely diverse as the opinions of their youngers. "Aging Realities," the PAGE exercise, and the "cathartic dinners" can help most groups involved learn to understand and manage the aging process more effectively. Within these options, the participants in these training activities are invited to reassess what it means to age, whether they are now young or old.

Stage Two: Community and Caregiver Thrust

The central course in this stage is an all-day seminar targeted to children of seniors. Named "Adult Children of Aging Parents; A Caregiver's Education," it encompasses all aspects from financial to psychological effects of aging processes and encourages a proactive, informed approach rather than a reactive, emburdened route that involves unduly high physical and psychological expense. This course addresses the reduction of dysfunctional stereotypes of the elderly by their caregivers and the often confoundingly debilitating social beliefs of some elders. The goal is to develop positive, shared, cocreated relations and environments. Educating the family in their role as caregivers permits the extension of these educational benefits to the broader community outside.

The "Adult Children of Aging Parents" course has six primary topic areas: "Defining Your Role as a Caregiver" helps the participants define caregiving and understand the feelings associated with their role; "The Natural Aging Process" tries to dispel the myths of the aging process and helps to understand how lifestyle affects longevity; "Accessing the Aging Network" creates an awareness of the available services and housing options in the community and how to access other community networks; "Legal Issues and Interventions" provides insight to the legal dimensions and to know how and when to intervene; "Financial Considerations and Planning" provides an opportunity to ask questions of a panel of experts regarding one's financial concerns as a caregiver for a senior; and "Assessing Your Situation" helps the participants to assess the individual needs of their aging parents. Throughout the consideration of all these topics, experts provide their information and insights, but the participants are encouraged to individualize the questions and discussion. The final topic merely schedules this individualization.

In addition to the formal course, the employed caregivers are further sensitized through mandatory and confidential monthly educational meetings of all staff. This promotes shared meanings of symbols and experiences among the caregivers. A second approach designed to sustain sensitization is the offering to the staff of "The Pyrotechnology™ of Life Fulfillment" course (see the following section for details) which was designed primarily for residents of Winslow Court Retirement Community. The course involves life review and proactive lifestyles, both of which enhance positive symbol usage among employed caregivers in the work environment. By continued reinforcement of positive outward expressions, their attitudes seem to foster better interpersonal relations with the residents. Among those who have taken the life fulfillment and adult children of aging parents courses, trainers have observed a decrease in the use of negative self-fulfilling prophesies in regard to the senior community and a better understanding of aging developments.

Living communities such as Winslow Court Retirement Community provide cross-cultural communication education and reevaluation of stereotypes. Application and expansion of such programs can assist other homes and communities around the country. To paraphrase a frequent public remark of Pablo Picasso, we are each the age 50 we decide on. Let us strive to return the dignity to every age, that all might respect the age which we grow to be. To achieve this noble goal in America, society must change from the inside out. Cross-cultural communication has much to offer to equip that change, but it is the individual who must be persuaded to pick up the tools and begin.

Stage Three: Primary Culture Thrust, The Aging Populace

In several ways, the two component parts of this stage are the broadest and most significant. Encompassing the entire educational and training programs of Winslow Court Retirement Community is the University of Life conceptual programming. This expansive effort embraces all of the possible audiences. Of less scope, but of major importance for the residents, is perhaps one of the most innovative programs available, the course entitled "The Pyrotechnology™ of Life Fulfillment," designed and developed by James R. Ander. A variant of this course, entitled "The Pyrotechnology™ of Life Accomplishment," was developed to expand its audience to include caregivers and others.

Winslow Court Retirement Community operates with a distinctive philosophy: "To provide an environment that promotes education, recreation, creativity and opportunities within which residents can safely explore, recreate, enhance, enrich, and empower their lives in a multitude of areas." Within this philosophical orientation, their collective programs are captured under the label "University of Life." For purposes of illustration, the 1995 highlights of the University of Life included, among the other programs mentioned in this chapter, a large number of special, regular events to encourage the elders to assume a more active role in life and to share their abilities with others. Among these special activities are weekly opportunities to discuss current events; to participate with a licensed physical therapist in a combination of exercise and/or informational talks about health issues and programs; to work with a music therapist about singing, dancing, or song writing; and to work with inspirational or wellness groups. Other programs in the University of Life are designed primarily to stimulate discussion: "Mind Over Matter" incorporates mental puzzles and exercises to stimulate problem solving and perception, and "Residents Meeting—Life Celebration" is a monthly assembly and information exchange.

Central to all of these activities is the resident involvement in an Activity Council that helps to plan and implement activities and events. The Council was even involved in the selection process for their program director. A monthly meeting, which generally draws over half of the community, fosters discussion of issues and suggestions for every department. Resident volunteers also run the gift shop, and the "meet and greeters" is a resident-initiated welcome wagon. Other activities are also developed and executed by residents themselves; some of these involve the use of their lifelong skills and experiences rather than just games such as Bingo. All of this involvement increases resident ownership and preservation of their own lives and programming. In other words, through this empowerment, they become more active contributors to the negotiation of their social reality, their third culture.We must not forget that life is always and only valuable to those who have something to value.

The most intense course in the University of Life is "The Pyrotechnology™ of Life Fulfillment." Ander's trademarked label "pyrotechnology™," refers to the science and art of igniting and sustaining one's inner, self-propelling fire. The philosophy of this course is captured in the following introductory questions: "Do you really know how special and unique you are; and that there is always room for Growth, Improvement, and Fulfillment in your life?" This course teaches the participants how to identify and use more effectively their inner resources to realize an even greater sense of life fulfillment. Those who master the principles of "pyrotechnology™" may end up possessing and enjoying an inner strength and stability that helps them to become pillars of support and encouragement for many others. As they assume this new role, they also find that they are experiencing and relishing another dimension of life fulfillment.

This course of study takes an in-depth look at 24 factors and principles of "pyrotechnology.™" The 24 lessons are managed within the format of four modules:

Module I. The Foundation for Life Fulfillment
   Unit #1: An inside view of motivation
   Unit #2: Discovering your reasons for life
   Unit #3: Creating your life print
   Unit #4: Creating and maintaining a healthy mental attitude
   Unit #5: Till death do you part
   Unit #6: The awesome power of belief

Module II. The Framework for Life Fulfillment
   Unit #7: To build up—build down
   Unit #8: The self-fulfilling prophesy
   Unit #9: Conceptual preprogramming
   Unit #10: Games we all play
   Unit #11: Developing desirable desire
   Unit #12: Moving the immovable

Module III.   The Building Blocks of Life Fulfillment
   Unit #13:   Taking charge of the challenge
   Unit #14:   Rewards along the way
   Unit #15:   The great vehicle of persuasion
   Unit #16:   Fighting one more round
   Unit #17:   Your preventive maintenance program
   Unit #18:   The compensation factor

Module IV.   The Cornerstones of Life Fulfillment
   Unit #19:   Support the nucleus of success
   Unit #20:   The sanction for simplicity
   Unit #21:   Creative crisis management
   Unit #22:   The pioneering factor
   Unit #23:   There always is a way
   Unit #24:   When all else fails

This intensive, 24-week, life review and goal-setting workshop is largely constructed on the pragmatic, semantic foundations of the cross-cultural communication perspective. It begins with a quote attributed to Henry Ford, "Think you can, or think you can't, either way you are right," and students, whose average age in the pilot class was 86, are challenged repeatedly not to let outgroups, namely, their caregivers and society as a whole, define them.

To expand the potential impact of this special course, we attacked the stereotype of caregivers as "second best" and remote from some of their more emotionally or mentally challenged residents by simply opening up to all staff the premier course given for the seniors. This supported the development of a broader social environment and also equipped the caregivers with the identical terminology of those receiving care. Eventually, this class was opened to the community as a whole, again expanding the circle of awareness and symbol reconstruction for a profession so often misunderstood and separated from "normal" society. Newspaper coverage of graduation ceremonies and other intergenerational activities have also enhanced the potential for improved self-images of the caregivers; the outside communities now tend to acknowledge their efforts and profession. In fact, in writing about the elders, caregivers, and their work together, journalists have developed more positive labels and metaphors that emphasize respect rather than pity. During September and October 1995, special features regarding elders and their caregivers were prominent in major Sunday newspapers across the nation.

CONCLUSIONS, PROJECTIONS, AND REFINEMENTS

As this chapter attests, we discovered that the application of a cross-cultural communication perspective can be powerfully useful in categorizing the daily problems of elders in their care centers and in guiding the development of very practical solutions. To begin with, this study generated five categories for problem analysis: (a) Prevalent symbols used in the care centers for the elders inhibit constructive relationships; (b) dysfunctional stereotypes of elders and their caregivers confound relational development; (c) extensive uncertainty and anxiety result primarily from the estrangement of the seniors and inhibit positive relationships; (d) the elders contribute insufficiently to the negotiation of their social reality on which more effective interpersonal communication could develop; and (e) other co-cultural interactions can suggest directions for sustaining improvements.

Next, this study provided a foundation for the development of some very practical education and training prospects. Winslow Court Retirement Community has developed three primary thrusts for addressing the problem categories. An intergenerational thrust allows them to grapple with confounding symbols and the stereotypes that threaten relations among people from different generations. The second thrust is addressed primarily to the community and caregivers and tries to develop a more positive environment in which the elders can contribute more directly, and everyone can communicate more effectively. The third and most comprehensive thrust is directed toward the broader personal and cultural changes that must ultimately occur.

Throughout all of the corrective approaches to the problems identified, we acknowledged one central theme and challenge: How can we build sufficient understanding and skills for the primary groups or co-cultures involved to negotiate a social reality conducive to the communication and developmental needs of the elders? To meet this challenge, we had to educate and/or train at least four different groups, namely, the elders, the employed caregivers, the administrators, and the families and friends who are also caregivers in an extended sense of that word. As we tried to address the central challenge, we reinforced the primary theme of the cross-cultural communication perspective. Through the examination of symbolic activities, especially the interpersonal communication among the co-cultures involved, we can better understand and resolve many of the problems confounding the treatment of elders in American society.

The primary question remaining for this final section is, Where do we go from here? In many ways, the present study was exploratory. One thing we must now address is further refinement of the concepts and ideas. Can we, for example, better define the cultural characteristics of the primary groups involved? Can we then identify the patterns of cultural evolution that lead to these characteristics? In other words, can we specify how the co-cultures differ from each other, how these differences evolved, and what are the deleterious effects of these developments? One possible operationalization of this concern is how do elders become estranged and co-culturalized? Are there positive and negative aspects of this enculturation? If so, how do we enhance the positive so that the consequent differences are not over time counterproductive? How do we monitor the development of the negative aspects in order to control the tendencies for negative stereotyping? For those who enjoy more microanalytic studies, we need to systematize the symbols, metaphors, and myths that pervade the aging process and treatment centers for elders. Awareness is the forerunner of solutions, and the more we can tease out the vestiges of unfounded prejudice, the better we can attack them. For those who enjoy more macroanalytic studies, we need to examine the political and economic ramifications of our efforts to improve the care and treatment of elders. No socially significant program lacks political and economic implications. To anticipate these nuances can help us locate the motivating forces that sometimes lead us to the cycles of counterproductive symbolic behaviors.

More specific questions emerge as one looks at any part of the cross-cultural communication perspective. From sociolinguistics comes a raft of concepts and principles that are readily adaptable for this line of investigation. From psycholinguistics comes possible answers to the ways the symbols suppress the realization of elders' potential and establish their most debilitating social cycle of doubt about themselves and their value. From anthropology comes the revealing ethnographies that enrich our understanding of the symbolic environment of the care centers. From communication comes that overarching and very practical concern for the development, transmission, and adaptation of messages. Perhaps one of the most significant outcomes of the cross-cultural communication approach is a set of questions that other cultures have long asked about our treatment of elders. What does our current approach to elders say about our culture? What are we doing that reflects so badly on our way of life? What can we do to help us better understand the pitfalls of our behavior? Can we learn from other cultures some principles that might help us overcome the shortsightedness of our behavior? One primary principle of cross-cultural relations deserves restatement as a closing thought: If a major reason to study other cultures is to learn from them for the betterment of humanity, then why will we not learn about the treatment of our elders? We can return value to those golden years.

ACKNOWLEDGMENTS

The authors wish to express their deep appreciation to two administrators whose assistance was indispensable in making this chapter possible: Ms. Bonnie jw Riley, General Manager, Winslow Court Retirement Community, Colorado Springs, CO, and Mr. James R. Ander, President, Creative Profit Systems, Incorporated, Colorado Springs, CO.

REFERENCES

Carroll, J. (Ed.). (1956). *Language, thought, and reality: Selected Writings of Benjamin Lee Whorf.* New York: Wiley.

Conrad, C. (1994). *Strategic organizational communication* (3rd ed.). New York: Harcourt Brace.

Cupach, W., Grooters, C., Hill, L., Long, L., & Long, P. (1992, November). *Social treatment of the elderly: Perspectives from intercultural communication.* Paper presented at the annual convention of the Speech Communication Association, Chicago, IL.

Gudykunst, W., & Kim, Y. (1992). *Communicating with strangers* (2nd ed.). New York: McGraw-Hill.

Haney, W. (1992). *Communication and interpersonal relations* (6th ed.). Boston: Irwin.

Hutchison, F. (1991). *Aging comes of age: Older people finding themselves.* Louisville, KY: Westminster John Knox.

Kennan, W., & Hill, L. (1979). Mythmaking as social process: Directions for myth analysis and cross-cultural communication research. In W. Davey (Ed.), *Intercultural theory and practice: Perspectives on education, training, and research* (pp. 44–67). Washington, DC: SIETAR, Georgetown University.

Useem, J., Useem, R., & Donoghue, J. (1963). Men in the middle of the third culture. *Human Organization, 22,* 169–179.

9

The Dilemma of Oklahoma Native American Women Elders: Traditional Roles and Sociocultural Roles

Lynda Dixon Shaver
Bowling Green State University

Grandmother
SHE walks in life that is not always Beauty.
   SHE speaks in tones not always Dulcet.
      SHE is daughter, niece, granddaughter, sister, aunt, wife, mother, grandmother.

SHE is girl, woman, lady.
   SHE is Native, Cherokee, Deer Clan.
      SHE is family, healer.
      SHE is LIFE.

—Reed Woman

Oklahoma Native American women elders face a dilemma that results from a conflict between their perspectives of their roles and social perspectives of their roles in life. The conflict is between Native American perspectives and mainstream social perspectives.

Oklahoma Native American women's presence in Oklahoma today is the result of government ordered death marches of the 19th century. Although thousands died on the marches to Oklahoma from all parts of the continental United States, more suffering awaited the nations on their arrival (Deloria, 1974; Strickland, 1980; Woodward, 1963). Contrary to government promises, Native Americans found poor living conditions and an inhospitable land in what was known as Indian Territory (Filler & Guttmann, 1962;

161

Strickland, 1977, 1980; Wardell, 1977; Washburn, 1979; Woodward, 1963; Wright, 1986). The nations lost their elder women, their lands, and their ways of living. These losses created social and health problems that Oklahoma Native Americans still experience.

The elder women were the first to die on the long marches to Oklahoma. The Indian nations lost a generation of women elders whose roles as advisors, healers, and nurturers were vital to the tribes (Rader, 1978). In their absence, the U.S. government provided a "fort-Indian" approach to health care by handing out blankets and a few medicines. The Bureau of Indian Affairs (BIA) and the Department of the Interior (Glenn, 1990/1991) have at various times through this century attempted to provide health care for Native Americans, with generally unsatisfactory results (Glenn, 1991/1990; Popple & Leighninger, 1993; Rader, 1978).

Prior to the marches, the various Native American nations who are now in Oklahoma respected and revered women elders. They had been loved by their people as healers, caregivers, mothers, guardians, nurturers, family counselors, providers, and sources of wisdom and knowledge to their tribes. Many factors, historical and current, among Native people and mainstream society have been involved in the changing perspectives of the roles of Native American women elders.

Understanding the historical circumstances of Oklahoma Native Americans is vital to understanding the current dilemma of Oklahoma Native American women elders. Three factors have lead to the dilemmas of Oklahoma Native American women: (a) cultural deprivation because of prejudice shown by Euro-American mainstream populations (Shaver, in press); (b) forced restrictions in traditionalism from governmental and societal pressures (Mankiller, 1994), with the loss of tribal lands (Deloria, 1974; Lujan & Glenn, 1989); and (c) federal bureaucratic health care from Indian Health Service (Glenn, 1990/1991; Indian Health Service/Tribal Residual Workgroup, 1995).

The purpose of this chapter is to analyze the language culture of Native American women in Oklahoma to study the dilemmatic elements of the conflict between the women and society's negative perspectives of women elders' life roles.

Indian Health Service

Indian Health Service (IHS) is a public health federal bureaucracy. The Department of Public Health was given the charge of Native American health care in the 1970s and created IHS, a federally funded bureaucratic health care delivery system (Glenn, 1990/1991; Perrone, Stockel, & Krueger, 1989). For almost 25 years, IHS has provided the only health care for the majority of poverty-line Native Americans and many who are working and/or middle class. Women, in particular Native American elders, constitute the primary patients at IHS centers (Indian Health Service, 1989, 1993). The irony is that although health care is essential for many Native American people, including women elders, IHS by its very nature assists in the erosion of the traditional roles of Native American women elders and encourages behavior that is not positive toward women.

Glenn (1990/1991) described IHS in an ethnographic health communication study. The system can be characterized as the following: a federal bureaucracy; a rationed health plan; an aggregate health care program providing care that appears to be, but is not, individual care; a training center for primarily Euro-American middle-class doctors (over 90% are male) who are repaying government educational loans; a training center for hospital administrators, public health workers, nursing students, allied health students, and other health providers who are giving service for student loans; and a pork-barrel commodity for politicians who place IHS facilities in politically expedient locations.

METHOD

The study explores the dilemmatic elements of the conflict between Native American more positive perspectives about elder women and society's negative perspectives of their roles in life through perspectival rhetorical analysis. This methodology is grounded in interpretive theory and informed by rhetorical theory (Burke, 1966) and semiotics (Eco, 1990). This methodology has been used to analyze human interaction as displayed in communication through many channels, such as letters, interviews, surveys, published oral histories, media messages, public presentations, public records, architecture, and posted public signs (Shaver, 1991; Shaver & Shaver, 1995; Shaver & Shaver, 1992a, 1992b, in press).

Language culture (Shaver, 1991; Shaver, 1993) is defined as the perspective of people as revealed through their discourse. Potter and Wetherell (1987) defined *discourse* in the broadest sense as encompassing verbal and nonverbal communication.

Eco (1990) discussed the interpretation of language from the view that there are not unlimited interpretations due to the common knowledge of like people, the ethnographic data of language, and the responsiveness of readers/listeners to the shared interpretation. Burke's (1966) discussion regarding the symbolic nature of language and Billig et al.'s (1987) presentation of social dilemmas contributed to the insight that conflict can be analyzed through interactants' discourse. The sites of conflict (Shaver & Shaver, 1992a) emerge from the discourse (i.e., the language culture) and reveal the perspectives of the interactants.

The analysis of their language culture allows researchers to analyze the sites of conflicts that emerge from the women's discourse.

Procedure

For this study, two data sets are used. First, one data set is field notes of interviews with 32 Oklahoma Native American women from the late 1980s through 1995. The women are 21 to 97 years of age. Second, Native American women and health provider interactions from the same IHS clinic were recorded on 41 audiotapes with verbatim transcriptions (Glenn, 1991/1990). The women's ages are between 41 and 67 years. The interactions are between these Native American women and (a) a Euro-American male physician at an IHS clinic; (b) two female screening Native American nurses (one is a Native American registered nurse, and the other is a licensed practical nurse), and (c) a female Native American physician's assistant. All of the health providers were in their 30s.

All the women in this study are Native American women who are legally affiliated with one of 34 federally recognized tribes in Oklahoma. The women are residents of Oklahoma, although some have lived in other parts of the United States.

ANALYSIS

The current sociocultural perspectives about aging Native American women are negative. The change from positive, traditional perspectives of the roles of women elders to negative perspectives has been the source of many problems for Native American women elders in Oklahoma. The interviews reveal elder women's awareness of the negative trends that include the unmet expectations of traditional respected roles for the women. The IHS audiotaped interactions show the continued erosion of respect for Native American women elders and their diminishing roles as caregivers and nurturers.

Informal Interviews

The informal interviews (see Appendix) with Native American women included young and old women. However, our focus is on aging issues for women who are 55 years of age or older. The perspectives of the young women on women elders informed the analyst about elder issues. The interviewed women can be characterized on a continuum from very traditional to nontraditional Native Americans. The interview settings were diverse, including family reunions, grocery stores, service stations, retail stores, health clinics, public schools, universities, town festivals, and private homes. The interviews lasted from 15 minutes to one hour. The women spoke of their great respect for their mothers, grandmothers, and great grandmothers. Interviewees talked about how different society is today and how their lives are unlike their mothers' and grandmothers' lives.

Responding to open-ended relational questions and ingroup regional and Native American topics, the women's stories included facts and themes about their families, regardless of tribe or location in Oklahoma. These facts and themes are: identification of tribal language speakers; knowledge about the practice of medicinal care that previous generations had used did not hand down; personal habits of grandmothers and mothers that were tribal; startling family stories of wrongs by Euro-Americans (e.g., murders, crimes, and harassment) that were not told until the storyteller was of a great age; explanations about family members who were known to have existed but about whom information was not available because of fear of an unfair legal system; the respect and the obedience of family members to the rules of elder women; and mothers and grandmothers who took care of family members in financial or health crises. Thus, the women recounted family stories that explicitly and implicitly revealed the diminishing respect for women elders from one generation to the next as the traditional roles change with the loss of their families' native culture.

Traditional Roles

Various writers and Native American women discuss the traditional roles of women elders as life-givers, healers, caregivers, mothers, guardians, nurturers, family counselors, providers, and sources of wisdom and knowledge to their nations, including council decisions and participation in battle. Unlike contemporary society, their contributions and their tribal value increased as they aged (Balmer, 1994; Brown, 1994; Carmody & Carmody, 1993; Harjo, 1990, 1992; Hawley, 1994; Mankiller, 1994; Perrone, Stockel, & Krueger, 1989; Wall, 1993; *The Woman's Way*, 1995). There were living symbols of the harmony between people and nature (Wall; Wilder, 1994; *The Woman's Way*, 1995).

Today's traditional women elders are consciously disappointed with the lack of respect that they experience from society and some family members. Their younger counterparts are aware of the changes by generations. Because culture is both conscious and unconscious, many nontraditional Native American women,unconsciously have the same expectations of beliefs about and appropriate behaviors for themselves, as well as beliefs about and behaviors toward them from family and society. Therefore, nontraditional women reveal their disappointment in their roles through their language, demonstrating that their dissatisfaction is conscious but that the source of the dissatisfaction is unknown.

Traditional and nontraditional women find issues of self-identification as Native Americans are difficult. Self-identification as a Native American is a sensitive and complicated issue because of the federal government's monetary and political intrusions into tribal traditions of Indianness (Deloria & Lytle, 1983; Glenn, 1990/1991; Pratt, 1985). Traditional women know about the historical events that have negatively affected their mothers by stealing their traditional roles and culture (Shaver, in press). As they age, nontraditional women often begin to question the past and the practices of their mothers and grandmothers. Many of their mothers, grandmothers, and great-grandmothers were compelled to assimilate to mainstream culture. Successive generations of women elders have been deprived of their cultural birthright (Harjo, 1990, 1992; Shaver, 1993, in press) by historical and sociocultural events.

Four factors are discussed regarding the issues of identification of self and the loss of culture. First, identification as a Native American was made a legal procedure demanded of the federal government. These demands are the result of efforts to control Native population by census-taking, disbanding of tribes, stealing of tribal lands, and restricting tribal government activities (Deloria, 1974; General Allotment Act, 24-388, 1887; Harjo, 1992; Lujan & Glenn, 1989).

Second, the women's children and their children's rights were vulnerable to the whims of court-appointed non-Native American guardians for children identified in the census as one-fourth Native American or more (e.g., General Allotment Act, 1987).

Third, many women married Euro-American men who were desirous of Native women who acted Euro-American. In a time of patriarchy among the Euro-American fundamentalist Bible Belt society that characterizes Oklahoma (Balmer, 1994; Brown, 1994; Hawley, 1994; Perrone, Stockel, & Krueger, 1989), women, in obedience to their husbands and their Euro-American in-laws, were forced to shun Native friends and family. Mothers forbade their children to speak their Native language, and few of the traditional medicine or beliefs were taught to succeeding generations. These assimilation behaviors were to protect their children from the violent and active bias of the times and to satisfy the wishes of the heads of their households. Even outside of the family, children were forced to reject their culture. From the turn of the century until the 1950s, Native children who went to boarding schools, some by force, were physically punished for traditional practices (Coleman, 1993).

Fourth, the law made it desirable, profitable, and safe to be more Euro-American than Native American. Berkhoffer (1978) and Rader (1978) discussed both historical and current bias and prejudice toward Native Americans in Oklahoma. Rader further noted that in McIntosh County, a Creek and Cherokee area in old Indian territory, the current have-nots and the disenfranchised are African Americans and Native Americans.

The stories told by the women about their families and these events demonstrate the historical and sociocultural pressures that made traditional roles for Native American women elders less and less possible.

Current Sociocultural Perspectives. Today's Oklahoma Native American women elders and their expectations of respect are far different from earlier generations and more negative than the expectations of their mothers and grandmothers. Mainstream U.S. culture presents many problems for all aging women: bias against the nonyoung; pressures on women to be unnaturally thin, young, and mainstream attractive; prejudice against physically different women; and negative perceptions of women who are culturally different from mainstream society. All aging women face these difficulties; however, Oklahoma Native American women elders face these problems and others that are directly related to their loss of culture.

The contrast between traditional roles of Native American women elders and the sociocultural roles of today's society is stark. Women elders, regardless of cultural differences, are expected to assume the role of the mainstream expectations of worth in society. They are judged by their career success, their contributions to society, and their physical appearance (which includes mainstream, Euro-American attractiveness and youthfulness). Additionally, stereotyping in the media of young Native American women as beautiful slim princesses (e.g., the Disney movie *Pocahontas* in 1995) and older Native American women as unattractive, overweight squaws (Stedman, 1982) contributes to the negative reactions to Native American women elders.

Economics and Socioculture in Oklahoma.   Oklahoma has not recovered from economic crises of the 1980s, and newspapers report many counties with double-digit unemployment figures. In addition to Oklahoma's unique problems, Popple and Leighninger (1993) noted that 65% of Native American women and men elders live below the poverty level. Because women account for three fourths of the poor, Native American women are disproportionately represented in these statistics. Gordon-Bradshaw (1988) noted that among Native Americans in the U.S. 1985 workforce, women were heads of households in 25% of the families, made a median income of $15,000, were unemployed at a rate of 13%, and were listed as 48% of the workforce, with 31% having finished secondary education and only 7% having completed a college degree.

Women elders face many challenges because of sociocultural perspectives that are negative about them, and the continued economic problems as women and minorities in Oklahoma contribute to their problems.

Audiotaped Transcriptions from an IHS Clinic

IHS has made elder women's traditional roles more difficult. As an inflexible health care delivery system, IHS contributes to the dilemma of individual Native American women elders who are still attempting to take care of their children, grandchildren, great-grandchildren, spouse, parents, other family members, and, lastly, self.

As aging Native American women reach their 50s, they often have continued their mothers' and grandmothers' attempts to assume the role of family and tribal caregiver. However, they make these efforts without the cultural respect, support, or resources of their maternal predecessors.

In the recordings, the topics and ways of speaking reveal the women's dilemmas of time, needs, respect, and health issues. These dilemmas merge together as multiple problems. They are not discrete categories, but they allow for discussion because they are the sites of conflict for women elders.

Time.   The federal bureaucracy allots time and resources for 8 to 12 patients per clinic session. Sanctions are placed against people who miss appointments, who bring their children, who are late, or who expect to be seen without an appointment. Posted signs announce that if they miss appointments, they will not be able to return to the clinic for one year.

The issue of time is different for a federal organization than for an aging woman. Many of these women are responsible for their grandchildren and have no child-care resources. The clinic will not allow people to bring children into examination rooms with patients, and unattended children are not allowed in the waiting room. Some of these women have only Social Security as an income. However, many of these women are not retired; they often have low-paying jobs that do not include paid sick leave. They often do not have private or group insurance. They do not have reliable transportation. "My sister has a stick shift but the clutch is out," says an unemployed woman in her 50s who is seriously ill because she ran out of medicine and had no car. Time and its orderly use is an economic luxury for most aging Native American women.

Bad patients miss appointments, are late to appointments, do not return in a timely manner, are not compliant in taking medication, and so on. Each of these bad patient behaviors is generated by time differences between poor women elders and a machine-like federal organization.

Needs.   The physician does not seem to understand that few women in their 50s and older have come to the clinic just for their own health needs. They have "saved up" for this visit by putting off their own health needs until they have medication to be filled for themselves, husband, children, grandchildren, and parents; they have multiple health questions or problems; and they can no longer tolerate or ignore their health problems.

In tape after tape, the issues that surfaced included missed appointments, failure to comply with required repeat or follow-up visits, and failure to take medication. Women were questioned or chastised for not complying with the demands of the clinic or of the doctor. "What am I going to do with you, Rowena?" says the thirty-year-old doctor in a pretend fatherly tone to a 46-year-old woman. "You've pushed yourself too far this time," he says to a 47-year-old woman who has just explained that she is helping her son raise his three children and that the son lives with her. In telling a 51-year-old woman that she should have returned earlier, he does not appear to hear her when she says that she does not have a telephone; the telephone—at the corner market is often in use, and the single line to the clinic is busy when she can get to use the telephone. The physician's manner suggests that women in their 50s and older should have financial resources and not have these types of family responsibilities

Family health needs and personal health needs of patients are combined in the patients' discourse. This confounds the physician or physician's assistant, who continues to ask questions of the patient to elicit one aliment or one problem. Rarely does an elder woman go to a clinic for one problem; she takes her family's needs with her. The conflict is inevitable when the physician has been trained to treat only one problem per patient per visit.

When caregivers ask for the patient's ailments, the patient responds in an unexpected fashion. The doctor in this study is confronted with patients who present their families needs and their own needs in nondirective and nonlinear ways so that they can maintain the goodwill of the clinic and still meet their families multiple needs.

One patient explained that her aunt died, her son has leukemia, she has raised five children, and she is raising her son's children. In soft tones and in nondirective ways, she gently complains about the problems in getting in to see a doctor. He defends his clinic by adding more bad news that the resources have been cut, "The total number to be seen is dropping from 12 to 8. Her response is, "[I'm] sole provider for my whole bunch, you know, chauffeur [laughter] you name it" [followed by her nervous and uneasy laughter].

The stress is great on aging women, and it increases as they age and as they try to be caregivers to their families. One grandmother talks to the Native American licensed practical nurse (LPN), who is screening the patient (P) and taking vital signs:

P: I want to show you something.
LPN: Oh, a baby.
P: Uhnhuh.
LPN: Oh cute.
P: Uhnhun. It's been 2 weeks tomorrow. They got his hair parted now.
[laughter between LPN and patient.]
LPN: He's cute.
P: He just weighed 8 lb 4 oz.
LPN: Boy! that's big.
P: His daddy [her son] was 10 lbs.
[a few seconds' interruption when LPN is asked questions by another caregiver]
P: You don't want to get babies too big.
LPN: No when they are born they have problems.
P: Yeah. this is a good size. That's a good size baby.

The patient reveals that this is her grandson, her son's child. He, his wife, this child, and his other children are living with her, her husband, and her aunt. As the elder woman, she is responsible for them. Her health is at risk because she has waited to come because she could not afford to lose part of her pay.

When another woman tells the physician, "I got problems, you know?" She had talked about her son and his children living with her and her chronic illness. The physician is still expecting a one-problem agenda. He perceives her to be a noncompliant patient, or a "bad patient," who, in her 50s, should have only her own health to consider. He hears what she says about her family, but he still expects her to put her health considerations as a primary concern. His expectations are based on the Euro-American model of aging women who are of little social value and who display behavior appropriate to individualism. Rather than conforming to the doctor's sociocultural perspectives for aging women, the patient persists in her attempts to fulfill tribal traditions for aging women by being caregiver to her grandchild, nurturer to her daughter-in-law, and the source of wisdom for her family. The IHS clinic and its organizational perspectives as displayed by the employees do not support her attempts. Rather than reward her attempts, she is penalized by a bureaucratic health care delivery system.

Respect. The respect of traditional tribal people toward the aged is vital to understanding the disrespectful way that women elders are treated at IHS clinics. In particular, physicians have very little training in the culture of their patients. In fact, the American Medical Association's (AMA) biomedical model of health and health care promotes and reinforces the negative mainstream sociocultural perceptions of older women in general and Native American women elders in particular.

To pry into Native American women's tribal affiliations, to quiz them about the cultural artifacts in their lives, or to tease using stereotypes causes pain to Native American women. These behaviors would not be tolerated in private discourse. However, when a higher status physician, who is male, middle class, and Euro-American, behaves in these ways, the Native American woman patient is further victimized by the one person who is supposed to consider her welfare. IHS employees show their disrespect through their language and culture.

The doctor asks a 60-year-old Ponca woman to lift her arms for a breast check and queries, "OK, what tribe are you?" This is an impolite question in regular social settings among Native Americans. She responds that she is a Ponca; he replies with laughter, "Ponca? ... I know how those Ponca girls are ... . Isn't that right, Lora?" Lora is a Ponca LPN. She does not answer. Later, he (D) asks the patient (P):

D: "Do you speak the language?"
P: Ah, — a little.

D: Do you speak any Ponca, Lora [the Native American nurse]?
N: Mom can.

Again, the questions are intrusive because the answers are embarrassing to the women. "Mom can" illustrates the loss of another critical part of culture for that particular family.

The doctor extends the conversation by saying to the nurse that he stood by the nurse's mother at a powwow. He says, "Your mom looked nice the other night." The doctor continues, "I was standing next to her the whole time." The elder woman chose not to speak to him. He believes that it is because she did not identify him. Another interpretation is that she chose not to recognize him because he was a male visitor with higher status. She would defer to his timing. His interpretation is that her lack of obvious recognition was proof of her incompetence in a social setting.

When the physician interacts with elder women, he displays the following behavior: his voice becomes more highly pitched, he uses a sing-song voice that is used with small children, he calls the women by their first name ("Hellooooo, Gladys!"), he refers to them with terms of endearment that a close relative might use ("dear," "babe," and "sweet-heart"), he makes personal comments about their hair or clothing, and he teases them about their behavior or their activities. The behaviors were intensified and multiplied as the age of the patient increased. The physician asks in a sing-song, high-pitched voice, "How are you today, young lady?" He then says, "All dressed up again today? Your sugar is 157 today."

A 67-year-old woman's husband talks for her because she is too ill to speak. She has delayed this trip until she could no longer tolerate her pain. She cannot answer the doctor who recommends that they go to the larger IHS hospital emergency room because the regular clinic will not accept them for 2 weeks. The doctor calls her "young lady" and makes a comment about her hair. Many traditional Native American women from several nations are noted for their reticence, their modesty, their quietness with strangers, and their formal language and behavior with strangers. The physician showed a lack of respect for the women, but because he represents their only health care source, they responded to him mildly, without visible offense.

Several of the women elders bring in their handmade crafts. The doctor occasional bought some of these and complimented the women for their work. An exchange follows that negates previous compliments and establishes a trivial evaluation of their efforts:

D: That's awful pretty ... Did you make that?
P: Yeah.
D: All these talented people making all these things. Actually, I did a lot of that stuff myself.
P: You do?
D: I do—I used to crochet a lot and make my shirts and things like that.
P: [she finally realizes that he is kidding.] Oh, Yeah?

An elder woman is told that she must have surgery in the following exchange. The doctor asks who she has used for her other operations:

P: Well, Dr. Smith who usually does all my surgery died so I don't know who to go to now.
D: OK, ah ...
P: He's done all of my surgery. See, I've had tumor removed from my breast and that's where I had that hysterectomy and a tumor from my uterus, a total hysterectomy.
D: Did you go get a mammogram done, by the way?

He ignores the poignant problem that she has outlived her only physician and surgeon. The change of subject and the lack of empathetic response is an evaluation that her loss and her fears are unimportant.

Health.   The health of Native American women elders becomes an issue in IHS because of the assumption of common goals and shared lifestyles. Whereas the statistics of health reveal that Native Americans are not living longer, nor are they living better, women elders are forced by poverty to continue to use a health care system that is not compatible with their traditional needs, their current socioeconomic status, nor their resources.

One woman discusses her grief since the death of her brother from liver disease, tension between daughter and stepfather, the stress of her marriage falling apart, and her health problems from menopausal symptoms and stress. Her request is just for two medicines. She wants help to sleep and help to stop her nausea so she can work. Her goal is not to be well; her goal is to continue to work so that she can support her family and take care of her family.

Another patient is seriously ill with bronchitis and is told not to work. She asks the doctor for a note and repeats the request out of fear that it will not be persuasive enough for her to keep her job. The doctor responds:

D: Your son lives with you, doesn't he?
P: Yeah, uh huh.
D: Well, let them [the son, his children, and his wife] take care of
        you for the next couple of days.

The idea that she remains the family caregiver even when she is ill is not
considered by the doctor.

The same bureaucracy that requires lengthy self-identification further
erodes the women's self-worth by the complicated methods of receiving
medicine. There is a list of specific medicines for ailments that is not
all-inclusive. Its restrictive criteria excludes newer and more expensive
medicine. For chronically ill patients, the attending physician must write
letters to justify his choice and amount of prescription. A panel then
determines if it will approve the medication. A woman carefully explained
with self-deprecating humor that a previous letter from the doctor requested
a medicine that was not on the approved list and that she was having trouble
getting her medicine: "Yeah, they don't trust sending money to me [nervous
laughter]; they send it to that prescription shop and I just get it until the
money plays out. It'll last me almost a year."

Time, needs, respect, and health issues reveal the dilemma—the conflict
between the traditional roles of Native American women elders and the
current sociocultural roles placed on them.

CONCLUSION

Through the interviews with Oklahoma Native American women and the
audiotaped interactions at an IHS clinic, the discourse of the
women—young and old—reveals the dilemma of women elders. Their
traditional roles have been lost through historical events and current
sociocultural and economic circumstances. Conscious expectations of
traditional Native women elders and the unconscious expectations of less
traditional women elders are not being met in a society that does not
value women elders. Time, needs, respect, and health conflicts at IHS
reinforce negative images of women elders. They must make accommo-
dations for health care for themselves and their families with an inflexible bureaucratic health care delivery system that reveals its lack of
respect for women elders by a disregard of their time and needs, by a
lack of respect for the women elders, and by a dearth of understanding
of their health needs.

Since 1992, several nations have made application to assume responsibility for the federal clinics and hospitals that serve their people. These arrangements have been made on a temporary basis and, unfortunately, with reductions in health care spending from the federal government (*Health Signals*, 1995a, 1995b). IHS is in a state of flux and transition. Although some innovations are hopeful signs of positive change, they contribute to a negative climate within the various clinics and hospitals as Native Americans are unsure of continued health care. Native American newsletters such as *Health Signals* (1995a, 1995b), produced by the Cherokee Nation, reveal ongoing reorganization within IHS and the efforts of various nations to take charge of their health care delivery system.

Although sociocultural perspectives are difficult to change, active involvement of individual Native American nations in IHS may lead to more positive perspectives of women elders through the primary health care delivery system for Native American women elders. The continued questioning by women of women elders' roles in many tribes may lead to attitudes and behaviors that show respect for the valued and necessary roles of Native American women elders in their family, in their clan, and in their nation.

REFERENCES

Balmer, R. (1994). American Fundamentalism: The ideal of femininity. In J. S. Hawley (Ed.), *American fundamentalism and gender* (pp. 47–62). London: Oxford University Press.

Berkhoffer, R., Jr. (1978). *The White man's Indian: Images of the American Indian from Columbus to the present.* New York: Vintage.

Billig, M., Condo, S., Edwards, D., Gane, M., Middleton, D., & Radley, A. (1987). *Ideological dilemmas: A social psychology of everyday thinking.* Newbury Park, CA: Sage.

Brown, K. (1994). Fundamentalism and the control of women. In J. S. Hawley (Ed.), *American fundamentalism and gender* (pp. 175–202). London: Oxford University Press.

Burke, K. (1966). *Language as symbolic action.* Berkeley, CA: University of California Press.

Carmody, D., & Carmody, J. (1993). *Native American religions.* New York: Paulist Press.

Coleman, M. (1993). *American Indian children at school, 1850–1930.* Jackson, MI: University Press of Mississippi.

Deloria, V. (1974). *Behind the trail of broken treaties: An Indian declaration of independence.* Austin, TX: University of Texas Press.

Deloria, Jr., V., & Lytle, C. (1983). *American Indians, American justice.* Austin, TX: University of Texas Press.

Eco, U. (1990). *The limits of interpretation.* Bloomington, IN: Indiana University Press.

Filler, L., & Guttmann, A. (Eds.). (1962). *The removal of the Cherokee nation: Manifest Destiny or national dishonor?* Lexington, MA: Heath.

Glenn, L. D. (1990/1991). Health care communication between American Indian women and a White male doctor: A study of interaction at a public health care facility (Doctoral dissertation, University of Oklahoma, 1990). *Dissertation Abstracts International, 51,* 2722B.

Gordon-Bradshaw, R. (1988). A social essay on special issues facing poor women of color. In C. Perales & L. Young (Eds.), *Dealing with the health needs of women in poverty: Too little, too late* (pp. 243–259). New York: Harrington Park Press.

Harjo, J. (1990). *In mad love and war.* Hanover, NH: Wesleyan University Press.

Harjo, J. (1992). Reinventing the enemy's language. *Common Ground, 6,* 28–33.

Hawley, J. (Ed.). (1994). *Fundamentalism and gender.* New York: Oxford University Press.

Health Signals. (1995a, July). Tahlequah, OK: Cherokee National Health Services.

Health Signals. (1995b, October). Tahlequah, OK: Cherokee National Health Services.

Indian Health Service of Oklahoma. (1989). *Indian Health Service Report FY 1989.* Oklahoma City, OK: Author.

Indian Health Service of Oklahoma. (1993). *Indian Health Service Report FY 1993.* Oklahoma City, OK: Author.

Indian Health Service/Tribal Residual Workgroup. (1995). *Final Report of Indian Health Service/Tribal Residual Workgroup.* Washington, DC: Author.

Lujan, P., & Glenn, L. (1989). *History of the Indians in Oklahoma.* Unpublished manuscript, University of Oklahoma, Norman, OK.

Mankiller, W. (1994). *A chief and her people.* New York: St. Martin's Press.

Perrone, B., Stockel, H., & Krueger, V. (1989). *Medicine women, "curanaderas," and women doctors.* Norman, OK: University of Oklahoma Press.

Popple, P., & Leighninger, L. (1993). *Social work, social welfare, and American society* (2nd ed.). Boston: Allyn & Bacon.

Potter, J., & Wetherell, M. (1987). *Discourse and social psychology: Beyond attitudes and behavior.* Newbury Park, CA: Sage.

Pratt, S. (1985). Being an Indian among Indians. (Doctoral dissertation, University of Oklahoma). *Dissertation Abstracts International, 46,* 1277A.

Rader, B. (1978). *The political outsiders: Blacks and Indians in a rural Oklahoma county.* San Francisco: R & E Research.

Shaver, L. (in press). The cultural deprivation of an Oklahoma Cherokee family. In D. Tanno & A. Gonzalez (Eds.), *International and Intercultural Communication Annual 22.* Thousand Oaks, CA: Sage.

Shaver, L. (1993). The relationship between language culture and recidivism among women offenders. In B. Fletcher, L. Shaver & D. Moon (Eds.), *Women prisoners: A forgotten population.* (Pp. 119–139) West Port, CT: Praeger.

Shaver, L., & Shaver, P. (1995). Caregivers in communication with HIV patients: A perspectival rhetorical analysis of health discourse. In L. Fuller & L. Shilling (Eds.), *Communicating about communicable diseases* (pp. 261–276). Amherst, MA: HRD Press.

Shaver, P. (1991). An analysis of political discourse elements supportive of the mass communication process in the United States with specific reference to arguments utilizing First Amendment principles. (Doctoral dissertation, University of Oklahoma). *Dissertation Abstracts International, 52,* 3477A.

Shaver, P., & Shaver, L. (1992a). The chromosomal bivalency model: Applying perspectival rhetorical analysis in intercultural consulting. *Intercultural Communication Studies, 2,* 1–22.

Shaver, P., & Shaver, L. (in press) "Icons" of bureaucratic therapy: An application of Eco's semiotic method. *Intercultural Communication Studies.*

Shaver, P., & Shaver, L. (1992b). *Signs in the organization: Architectural changes as organizational rhetoric in a public health facility.* Paper presented to Western Speech Communication Association, Boise, ID.

Stedman, R. (1982). *Shadows of the Indian: Stereotypes in American culture.* Norman, OK: University of Oklahoma Press.

Strickland, R. (1977). In search of Cherokee history: A bibliographical foreword to the second printing. In M. Wardell (Ed.), *A political history of the Cherokee nation 1838–1907* (pp. 1–18). Norman, OK: University of Oklahoma Press.

Strickland, R. (1980). *The Indians in Oklahoma.* Norman, OK: University of Oklahoma Press.

Wall, S. (1993). *Wisdom's daughters: Conversations with women elders of Native America.* New York: Harper Collins.

Wardell, M. (1977). *A political history of the Cherokee nation 1838–1907.* Norman: University of Oklahoma Press (original work published 1938)

Washburn, W. (1979). *Red man's land/White man's law: A study of the past and present status of the American Indian.* New York: Scribner's.

Wilder, K. (Ed.). (1994). *Woman writers of the Southwest: Walking the twilight.* Flagstaff, AZ: Northland. *The Woman's Way.* (1995). Richmond, VA: Time-Life.

Woodward, G. (1963). *The Cherokees.* Norman, OK: University of Oklahoma Press.
Wright, M. (1986). *Indians of Oklahoma.* Norman, OK: University of Oklahoma Press.

APPENDIX
DESCRIPTION OF THE INTERVIEWS
WITH OKLAHOMA NATIVE AMERICAN WOMEN

The open-interview process consisted of using referrals through networks of family, friends, and colleagues. The interviews often took place in public settings such as reunions, centers for community gatherings, city and county festivals, holidays, and retail stores.

The interviews began with relational talk about what was happening in the interviewee's and the interviewer's lives. Rather than ask questions that were directive, the interviewer would ask questions such as the following:

1. "How is your family?"

[After responding with appropriate questions and empathetic responses, the interviewer would follow any new topics or continue with the following. Depending on whether the person's mother was still living or not, the question would involve some known fact about the person's mother, such as longevity, humor, good works, health problems, and so forth.]

2. "Your mother was remarkable. I know that she never missed a day of church while she was able to go."

[Another question was to ask about grandmothers, using similar questions, or to ask a more evaluative question such as the following.]

3. "Do you think our grandmother [or mothers] had more problems than we do?"

4. "Is it easier to age now than when our mothers [or grandmothers] were living?"

Because of the informal nature of the settings, the explanation that some of the information would be used in the interviewer's professional work, and the social connections of the interviewer to the interviewees and/or to their acquaintances, the broad questions resulted in answers that were both specific and general about the topic of Native American women elders.

IV

POPULAR CULTURE AND AGING

INTRODUCTION

Part IV analyzes the portrayals of elders in popular culture in American society. A sample of the popular media is included in this section. Chapter 10 investigates the images of older adults in folktales and fairy tales while focusing on verbal descriptions that may have shaped and influenced our perceptions of this influential segment of the population. Chapter 11 examines a sample of the self-help literature published since 1990 that addresses aging and longevity and the extent to which the cultural models contained therein further a negative or facilitative view of aging. Chapter 12 explores the portrayal of older people across ethnic lines on television soap operas and is derived from years of researching this art form on daytime television drama. Considering the new grey market, chapter 13 takes a look at television commercials run during the day to ascertain if the portrayal of aging is fairing better nowadays.

The theme of this section is to show the role of selective popular media in portraying our elders. Too often, the portrayal tends to be less than complimentary, with a negative spillover effect on perceptions. Because Americans rely heavily on the media, their mediated perceptions can have a profound impact on one's attitudes toward elders. Such research can hopefully assuage the bad rap that elders receive in popular media.

10

Images of Elders in Traditional Literature

Carole E. Tallant
University of North Carolina at Wilmington

An important yet unfamiliar tale recorded by the brothers Grimm in 1840 offers a penetrating commentary on human perceptions of aging. The story, *The Life Span* (Zipes, 1987) affords a fanciful look at how God decides the life span of humans and animals. In the story, after God creates the world, He calls each living creature to Him to assign its life span. The ass, the dog, and the monkey all complain and grumble that their assigned spans of 30 years are far too long, given the horrendous living conditions they must endure. Patiently, the Lord hears their protests and wisely deducts 18, 12, and 10 years from the allotted life spans of the ass, the dog, and the monkey, respectively.

Then man appears and disputes his allocated 30 years as far too short. Compassion prevails and the Lord bestows on man the 18 years taken from the ass. Man implores God for even more time, so God grants him the 12 years retrieved from the dog. Man repudiates the life span once again, so the Lord finally assigns him an additional 10 years subtracted from the monkey, bringing his total to 70 years. Man reluctantly departs, still unsatisfied, and the tale ends with a compelling assessment of human life:

> So man lives seventy years. The first thirty are his human years, which pass by rapidly. This is the time when he is healthy and cheerful, works with pleasure and is glad to be alive. After this period come the eighteen years of the ass, when one burden after the next is laid upon him. He must carry the grain that nourishes others, and he receives blows and kicks as reward for his faithful service. Then comes the twelve years of the dog, when he lies in the corner, growls, and has no more teeth with which to bite. And when this period is over, the ten years of the monkey round out his life. Then man becomes soft in the head and foolish, does silly things, and becomes the laughingstock of children. (Zipes, 1987, p. 557)

This wonderfully wise yet simple folktale embodies one of society's prevailing views of aging: Youth is a glorious time of unbridled pleasure and vibrant health, middle age is an oppressive period of travail and labor, old age is a harbinger of decline, and extreme old age is a time of decay and unremitting impotence. This traditional tale, one of thousands transmitted orally from one generation to the next, offers but one example of commonly communicated images of aging adults depicted in a wide variety of folktales and fairy tales. Although we may think of traditional tales such as *Cinderella* and *Jack and the Beanstalk* as mere nursery trifles, this substantial body of oral literature records powerful symbols of humans' deeper needs and concerns. As such, they provide important insights into both ancient and contemporary perceptions of older individuals. Such tales are "reality made evident" portraying aging beings that have striking resonance even in today's society (Opie & Opie, 1974, p. 11). We find grumpy, old curmudgeons with beards as white as snow; ugly old crones who require support from crutches; physically impotent men who must rely on the strength and physical prowess of invigorated youth; and spiteful, jealous, old fairies who consign baby girls to centuries of sleep. These negative images anticipate some of the contemporary stereotypical perceptions of the aged. More significant, however, are positive portrayals of men and women that appear in traditional stories, in particular, wise old women characters (Barchers, 1990). These characters abound in traditional literature and function as tradition-bearers and custodians of knowledge, heritage, and culture. Further, they frequently possess formidable power that they willingly pass on to younger, respectful characters who prove worthy of this transfer of power. Such depictions support a more balanced view of the aged as significant contributors to society.

This chapter examines commonly constituted images of older men and women in a wide variety of folktales and fairy tales. It focuses on the verbal descriptions that may have shaped and influenced our perceptions of this influential segment of the population. By examining the stock characters so often found in traditional tales, we can deepen our understanding of the roots of our modern day perceptions of aged adults.

PERSPECTIVES ON AGING

A pervading societal attitude about aging concerns usefulness and productivity. For example, when adults become too old to produce or achieve, they frequently disengage from society. Whether through forced retirement or self-imposed withdrawal, humans who feel unneeded may disengage from typical achievement-oriented activity that often gives life resonance and meaning. Disengagement theory, prominent in the 1960s, asserts that normal aging brings about a mutual withdrawal or disengagement by elders from others in their social group, usually a withdrawal initiated by the elders themselves or by others in the system (Cumming, 1964; Mullen, 1992). More significant is what I designate "forced" disengagement, a deterrent to successful aging.

The traditional tale, *The Bremen Town Musicians* (Zipes, 1987) highlights this notion of forced disengagement and devaluation of the aged. Typical of the folktales that feature animals as protagonists, this tale provides clear examples of beings that have apparently outlived their usefulness in society. We learn that four aged animals, a donkey, a cat, a dog, and a rooster, have for years diligently performed their jobs but are now deemed valueless by their masters. Because the donkey's strength has failed, his owner thinks it best to save food and "dispense with him" (p. 105). The aged cat, once a prime mouser, now has dulled teeth and would rather sit by the fire than chase rodents; she faces drowning. The old hunting dog, now too weak to continue his livelihood, also faces execution. We learn that the rooster will become tomorrow's stew if he stays with his master. The animals, however, learn of the fate that awaits them and refuse to be intimidated by their perilous situations. They, instead, remain optimistic and run away to Bremen, assured that they can find meaningful employment as musicians. During their journey, they encounter dangerous adversaries, but with determination, group effort, and brain power, they overcome all obstacles.

This tale suggests themes that resonate in contemporary society. Although our society may not literally put people to death as they age, it does, in some cases, force retirement on them. When older people resist disengagement because of a desire to remain active members of their social sphere, forced disengagement may brutally assault their self-concept. When forced to abandon activities performed most of their lives, aged individuals may suffer egregious identity crises. After all, occupational achievements provide a major source of esteem and sense of gratification for humans (Kaufman, 1986). In fact, the self of the present uses the past as a basis for identity (Mullen, 1992), and retirement may cause grave discontinuity for the elderly (Manney, 1975; Mullen).

When the young usurp their elders' roles as productive contributors to society, they may instigate stigmas that derogate and devalue their aged predecessors. Even though the more vigorous youth are empowered as they assume the mantle of power, position, and prestige, the once-valued adults are now "sidelined," divested of their former status, self-esteem, and even identity (Cockerham, 1991). *The Bremen Town Musicians,* and other traditional tales remind us that many elders deemed worthless by society want desperately to remain in contact with ongoing life. Further, many retain the resourcefulness, ingenuity, and competence to do so.

Western culture supports particularly negative and naive ideas about aging (Cockerham, 1991). Older adults are characterized as frail, incompetent, eccentric, abrupt, abrasive, and doddering (Hummert, Wiemann, & Nussbaum, 1994). We associate advanced age with diminished attractiveness, declining productivity, and attenuated performance (White, 1988). In short, we perceive old age as a time relegated to stagnation of the human spirit and passive spectatorship of life.

The United States, in particular, lionizes and venerates youth, and most of us dream of avoiding growing old because it signifies not only oncoming death but also loss of looks and declining health (Cockerham, 1991). Klemmack and Roff (1984) suggested that even elders fear continued aging because of the unavoidable outcome. To combat such reminders, the young often avoid older people and find ways to devalue them. In this way, they symbolically deny their own approach toward old age. Haber (1983) maintained that the general devaluation of the aged evolved from strong associations with poverty and dependence. To many, to become old is to become poor and useless. Ageism arises not only because of associations with poverty but also because of associations with declining physical attractiveness (Cockerham, 1991). Our stereotypical images of feeble, drooling old people is what we fear awaits all those who live long enough.

The Grimms' tale *The Old Man and his Grandson,* collected in Zipes (1987), offers a poignant view of old age from the perspective of the young. The story unfolds with a precise description of a grandfather who exemplifies many current stereotypical images of old age: He has weakened eyesight, poor hearing, and muscular palsy. His son and daughter-in-law find him so disgusting as he spills his soup that they isolate him in a corner behind the stove and coerce him to eat from a bowl, an action not too remote from our contemporary practice of institutionalizing our eldest citizens. Eventually, the tremor in the old man's hands becomes so pronounced that he is unable to hold his food bowl. His hard-hearted daughter-in-law scolds him when he accidentally breaks his bowl and she replaces it with an old wooden bowl. During this time, the innocent yet perceptive grandson watches. When he one day pieces together a crude wooden trough, his parents inquire what he is doing: "'I'm making a little trough,' answered the child. 'My mother and father shall eat out of it when I grow up'" (Zipes, 1987, p. 289). The moment has a profound effect on the parents as they realize that they, too, will one day be old and perhaps have children who will treat them the way they have treated the old man. The child's simple yet telling action causes them to bring the grandfather back to the table and back to society to live his final days in dignity, surrounded by loving, supportive relatives.

ELDER CHARACTERS IN TRADITIONAL LITERATURE

Examination of traditional stories reveals descriptions of elders ranging from the barest sketch to richly developed portraits. Of the 396 tales that I read for this study, numerous depictions of older people emerged that will be discussed later. I focused on the complete collection of the brothers Grimm because it provided the 25 most widely anthologized stories as well as many lesser known but equally significant tales. Of the 242 Grimm's tales, 38% ($n = 92$) had explicit depictions of the elderly. Of those, 32% were overwhelmingly positive portrayals, and only 13% were negative. The remaining stories merely offered neutral (neither positive or negative) depictions.

A common core of characteristics about older adults emerged from these stories. Generally, these "liminal beings" are caught between two worlds (Stern and Henderson, 1993, p. 45). They often assume positions of authority and power by virtue of their position or age, but they may be viewed with revulsion or suspicion. Other characters alternately admire or fear them for their toughness, resiliency, fearlessness, creativity, resourcefulness, and even their idiosyncratic behavior. Some appear as physically impotent, unattractive, cruel, poor, grumpy, and feeble beings. Often, they inhabit cottages or hovels in the woods or in forests. They congregate around wells (the meeting place of preindustrial communities) or dwell below the ground. They may appear wise and sage in their advice-giving, and they may be the caretakers of important cultural and historical information that is lost to the young (Livo & Rietz, 1986). Frequently, they safeguard powerful magical objects that they will relinquish only to respectful, deserving young heroes and heroines. They regularly display compassion and kindness to unfortunate creatures and are willing to reward greatly those who are generous of spirit and respectful to less fortunate beings. If crossed, they can resort to unmerciful cruelty and vengeance. More often than not, they determine the protagonist's destiny. In short, whereas some tales confirm negative images of decline in old age, many of them offer strong affirmations of the power, wisdom, and value of old age.

A comparison of young and old characters in traditional tales also yields important general information. Whereas the youthful protagonists that inhabit these tales are characterized by exuberance, boldness, and beauty, their aged counterparts are often depicted as patient, passive, and physically unattractive. The young often involve themselves in risky behavior, whereas the old cloister themselves in relative safety. Rarely do young female protagonists possess physical or mental defects, whereas young male heroes may appear physically unblemished but possess major personality flaws such as laziness or gullibility. In contrast, the old, whether men or women, display outward physical imperfections, but inner beauty and fortitude that transcend their outward appearance. Although we rarely see young villains, elders comprise the vast majority of villainous creatures in traditional literature. Even the evil queen so obsessed with her mirror is considerably older than Snow White. Most of these aged villains are magical beings such as witches, gnomes, and dwarfs. In general, the young are judged by their actions or birthright, whereas older characters are judged by their information or power. Both sets of characters receive strong judgment because of their appearance. Invariably, the young are the focal characters in such tales, whereas old people function as their supporting cast.

Often, the actions and knowledge of older characters bring about pivotal changes in the young protagonists' lives. For example, Grimm's tale *The Twelve Brothers* (Zipes, 1987) shows how the protagonist's fortune is altered as a result of a chance encounter with an elder; although aged characters may appear only within the space of a few lines, they function to create a more diverse story world. In other words, the fictional world has more verisimilitude as a result of its being inhabited by both the old and young. Further, elders often hold the rights to important lore or information that precipitates pivotal changes in the lives of other characters. Also important to this study, however, is the fact that their supporting status within the stories reflects the marginalization that elders often experience in society.

Positive Images of Elder Characters

Some stories, however, actually feature older characters. These major characters function both on surface as well as deeper symbolic levels. They communicate truths and realities deeply revered within the different societies from which the stories originated. In these stories, we find a wide variety of characters, including wise old women who reward generosity and kindness; sage old men who offer advice and information; clever, resourceful old animals who represent human characteristics; aging parents who may demean or support their children; kind or wicked old mothers-in-law; kind or brutal old gnomes and dwarves; ignorant or kindly old fathers; wise old kings; poor old women; generous old foster parents; and heroic old soldiers.

A less familiar but significant story that features the concepts of marginalization of elders is the Mongolian tale *The Golden Pitcher* (DeSpain, 1994) in which an old man's wisdom saves his people. The story suggests that aged adults often are the tradition-bearers of a culture as well as the repositories of a society's history and knowledge. Primitive cultures, in fact, designated one revered person as the preserver of the tribe's entire history. They are frequently more than mere "custodians of heritage" (Kirshenblatt-Gimblett, 1989a, p. 138). Though they have witnessed past events, they are also experts on current life cycles. Their age, experience, and accrued wisdom make them especially proficient at preserving wisdom from antiquity, settling current disputes, and seeing events from a uniquely qualified position. In short, they speak the society's very culture (Mullen, 1992). Without the linkage elders provide to the past, people of the present would have far less success in discovering their roots and identities.

Negative Images of Elder Characters

Traditional literature also portrays older people in a negative manner. Usually, these characters are portrayed as stupid, easily duped, or untrusting, often a parent. In these stories, if the parents realize their mistakes, they live happily ever after. In the case of unrepentant misdoing, the old person invariably suffers a dreadful fate. Often, they are duped into pronouncing their own death sentences. We find examples in *Hans the Hedgehog, The Expert Huntsman*, and *The Water of Life* (Zipes, 1987).

Other elderly characters include old witches and sorceresses whose ulterior motives prove to be their undoing, for instance, *The Blue Light*, *Jorinda and Joringel*, and *Hansel and Gretel* (Zipes, 1987). Other less complimentary portraits of elderly characters include old dwarfs in *Snow White and Rose Red*, old cooks in *The Pink Flower*, and untrustworthy people in *The Tailor in Heaven* (Zipes, 1987). Interestingly enough, rarely do we find exceptionally negative portrayals of older humans. Instead, the core of such portraits is limited to magical creatures.

WISE OLD WOMEN CHARACTERS

One prominent figure in traditional literature is the wise old woman character. Folklore is replete with examples of her. In some stories, she appears as an old woman advisor who aids protagonists in overcoming obstacles and achieving their goals. Usually an unnamed woman who may be referred to as "grandmother" or "granny," or even "mother," this ancient matron invariably counsels the protagonist as to how to combat foes successfully. She may also tender advice for escaping dangerous situations or knowing which path to travel, and how to retrieve loved ones who have been ensnared by evil nixies, dwarfs, gnomes, or sorceresses.

This woman may appear only briefly in tales, sometimes within the space of a few lines, but her import to the outcome of the story is crucial. Rarely does she possess unlimited power, and even fairy godmothers (one type of wise old woman) cannot alter a wicked heart or completely undo a loathsome magical spell. Often, the wise woman merely alleviates the ill effects of a curse or assists the hero or heroine in breaking a spell (Opie & Opie, 1974). In this way, she retains a striking humanness, even against the magical backdrop of the tale.

Generally, these characters are very old, white-haired beings who hobble about on crutches. Illustrations that accompany such tales invariably magnify the stereotypic notions of their physical appearance by depicting them as hunched over, with long noses, deeply wrinkled skin, crooked fingers, and sunken eyes. Their attire resembles old peasant garb, tattered and disheveled. Unquestionably, these figures epitomize unattractiveness as a central part of old age. What exonerates them, however, is their inner spirit and beauty. Their actions, kindness, wisdom, and concern for deserving creatures make them deeply attractive characters. It is as if their aged bodies merely reflect outward trappings and disguise what is valuable and beautiful within. They possess tremendous worth and power apart from their outward appearances. In so many fairy tales, the real magic lies in "people and creatures being shown to be what they really are" (Opie & Opie, 1974, p. 14). Also, according to Opie and Opie, the happy endings occur only when poverty is finally seen as inconsequential or when loathsome aged crones are accepted for their inner beauty.

Although many stories include her, two traditional tales in particular feature the wise old woman character: *The Goose Girl at the Spring* and *The Nixie in the Pond* (Zipes, 1987). The former story, in fact, includes one of the richest, most detailed depictions of this character. The story provides an important example of especially positive images of older women, because the character's actions and language choices suggest far greater complexity than we see in more superficially drawn characters. These stories warrant a detailed discussion because of the information they yield about wise old women.

The Goose Girl at the Spring begins with a vivid description of "a very old woman who lived with a flock of geese in a lonely place on a mountain" (p. 562) who appears quite energetic and vigorously pursues the activities of a much younger person . As she goes about her workaday chores, she greets passersby in a friendly manner, yet people are suspicious of her vigor and sociability and assume she must be a cunning witch. One day, a handsome young count chances upon the woman and generously offers to carry her heavy baskets of grass and fruit. After they arrive at her cottage, he spies a goose girl, presumably the old woman's daughter, whom he perceives as "big and strong, but ugly as sin" (p. 565). As a reward for his kindness, the old woman presents the count with a little box carved from a single emerald that she claims will bring him luck. This tale follows the formula in which the wise old woman rewards the protagonist with a powerful object and sage advice. Indeed, the box bears him fortune, for he later meets the true parents of the goose girl, a king and queen who are grief-stricken over her disappearance. We learn that the hideous goose girl is, in reality, their youngest and most beautiful child. She cries not mere tears but "pearls and jewels" (p. 566). Three years before, the father disowned his daughter when she refused to engage in meaningless flattery. The now remorseful king wishes to find his beloved daughter, and the king and queen convince the young count to take them to the wise old woman. After their arrival, the goose girl transforms into her true self, and the count is instantly smitten with love. The wise old woman rewards the goose girl for her three years of service with a gift of all of the priceless pearls she previously shed as tears. The story ends in an unusual manner when the storyteller corroborates that the old woman was not a witch but "a wise old woman who meant well" (p. 570). In fact, the storyteller asserts, she was probably the one who "at the birth of the princess gave her the gift of weeping pearls instead of tears" (p. 570).

This traditional tale serves as a consummate testament to the power that allows people to see beyond the outward trappings of old age. We learn from the story that though we may fear the outward manifestations of old age, it is a necessary stage that can move us to a higher sphere of understanding, compassion, and power.

Whereas the previous story features a wise old woman as a central character, *The Nixie in the Pond* (Zipes, 1987) reflects a more customary approach by incorporating her as a supporting character. In this story, a miller unknowingly promises his newborn son to a magical, evil nixie in exchange for prosperity. Only after years have passed and the son is happily married is the promise realized. The son's wife must now rescue her husband from the wicked grip of the venal nixie. She receives aid from a wise old woman. Three times the friendly, white-haired old dame comes to her assistance, each time offering sage advice along with a magical object. Even after the rescue, the young woman must rely on the old woman in order to escape the vengeance of the nixie. This story and many others are rife with examples of older women and the valuable contributions they make to society. In some of the stories, a stepchild or youngest child receives information and magical objects as rewards for kindheartedness. Other stories that offer similar portraits of older adults include *The Water of Life* (Zipes, 1987), *Frau Holle* or *Mother Holle* (Zipes, 1987), and *Toads and Diamonds* (DeSpain, 1994). In many of these tales, the older women may make only brief appearances, but they all perform crucial acts of wisdom and generosity that allow the protagonists to overcome insurmountable obstacles and attain their destiny.

In some stories, the old women appear as all-knowing individuals who provide enchanted objects that supply endless food to poor but deserving characters. In *The Sweet Porridge* (Zipes, 1987), for instance, an old woman presents a starving child with a bewitched pot that produces life-giving porridge. In *One-Eye, Two Eyes, Three Eyes* (Zipes, 1987), the protagonist receives a food-supplying table from the wise old woman. In some cases, the wise old woman offers advice of incalculable import. In *The Three Little Birds* (Zipes, 1987) a wise old woman gives a king's son information that helps him traverse an uncrossable river and assists him in finding his long lost father. She later accommodates his sister in a similar manner. In some stories, such as *Sweetheart Roland* (Zipes, 1987) the wise old woman advises and provides magical assistance that ensures the deserving young maiden will win back her true love from a false bride.

In other stories, the ancient women function as caretakers of robbers, ogres, or devils. A surface textual reading might suggest that the stronger, younger, evil characters take advantage of the old women's frailty, but in fact, the old women generally outwit their adversaries with quick thinking, cunning, and daring ploys. For instance, in *The Robber Bridegroom*, a palsied woman "whose head was constantly bobbing" (Zipes, 1987, p. 154) appears to be completely controlled by a band of robbers. However, she takes the initiative and executes a bold escape that frees herself and a young bride who would surely die without her assistance. In *The Devil and his*

Grandmother and *The Devil with the Three Golden Hairs* (Zipes, 1987) the protagonists receive help from crafty grandmothers who hoodwink their own grandsons into answering important riddles. In so doing, they ensure that three soldiers will escape the bonds of eternal damnation and that a young hero will foil death and wed a princess. As testament to the import of the wise woman, at least one entire volume is devoted to tales that feature her (Barchers, 1990).

AGED MEN IN TRADITIONAL STORIES

Traditional literature portrays a wide variety of aged men in both positive and negative ways. Often, old men are the sole bearers of important ancient lore that greatly benefits younger, less knowledgeable characters. In *The Water of Life* (Zipes, 1987), for example, a wise old man knows of an ancient remedy that will save the king's three sons. Sometimes, in stories, the old man parallels the wise old woman's function as an adviser and provider of magical objects to those who show respect and courtesy. Examples include *How Some Children Played at Slaughtering*, *The Wild Men*, *The Long Nose*, and *The Robber and His Sons* (Zipes, 1987).

The tale *The King of Colchester's Daughter* or *The Three Heads in the Well* (Opie & Opie, 1974) offers a detailed portrait of wise old men. The daughter of a king receives undeserved and unfair treatment by her step-mother. The cruel woman sends the girl on an impossible task in which she encounters a wise old man. She shares her meager lunch with the "aged father" who is so moved by her generosity that he gives her detailed advice about an enchanted hedge and three old men's heads that will appear (Opie & Opie, 1974, p. 208). The girl follows his advice and treats the three fearsome heads with kindness. In gratitude, the three heads each reward her with gifts of unimaginable beauty, sweet-smelling breath, and marriage to a prince. When the girl returns home, the surprised stepmother covets the same gifts for her own undeserving daughter. When that daughter refuses to share her lunch or treat the three heads with charity, she is punished with leprosy of the face, foul-smelling breath, and betrothal to a poor country cobbler. Here, we see the theme emerge in which an unattractive yet powerful elder willingly bestows his power only to a deserving character.

Although there exists some wise old men parallels to wise old women, many depictions of older man vary in one important way. Often we find older men who possess no magical powers. Instead, they live or die by their wits, bravery, resourcefulness, or luck. Perhaps because women, not men, were the tellers of tales in traditional cultures, we find more power of the magical variety imbued within women characters.

One story, *The Shoemaker's Dream* (DeSpain, Vol. 2, 1994) tells of a poor old shoemaker who has a dream of a visit from an angel who promises him great wealth if he follows her advice. Scoffed at by his wife and friends, he struggles to make the long and difficult journey to a bridge in Amsterdam to locate his promised fortune. The ironic ending brings him wealth beyond his wildest dreams and the respect of his wife. Perseverance, not magic, provides his reward.

Perseverance as well as quick thinking and resoluteness figure prominently in the portrayal of the old man in the Japanese tale *The Burning of the Rice Fields* (DeSpain, 1994). In this classic tale, a grandfather realizes his village is about to be decimated by a giant tidal wave and courageously sets the rice fields on fire in order to save the sleeping villagers.

In some instances, old men are rewarded for obedience to higher powers. In *The Old Man with a Wart* (DeSpain, 1994) two old men each have large, disfiguring warts that resemble peaches on their faces. On two different occasions, each encounters powerful Storm Spirits who demand that the old men dance as the spirits sing. The first old man dances with wild abandon and is rewarded for his compliance with the spirits' demands; the spirits remove his wart. The second old man refuses to dance and is punished by being saddled with not only his own wart but also the wart of the first old man. Similar themes of obedience, bravery, and good fortune figure prominently in the depictions of mortal older men in this way.

In some stories, the older man literally blunders his way into good fortune. In the Persian tale *The Astrologer and the Forty Thieves* (DeSpain, 1994), an old astrologer knows that 40 thieves have absconded with the royal treasure and requests "40 days to consult the stars" (p. 59) as to their whereabouts. Jamal, the astrologer, places 40 figs in a jar and plans to remove one each night in order to keep an accurate count of the passing days. On each of the 40 nights, one of the thieves arrives in time to hear Jamal remove a fig and proclaim, "Ah, there is one of forty" (DeSpain, p. 60). Quite by accident he solves the case, and the awestruck thieves voluntarily return the treasure. Here, we see an old man who is empowered not through magic but by ordinary luck.

These and other stories like them feature important cultural insights. Unlike the wise old women who exist as supporting yet significant characters, the elder men often are the protagonists or major characters. However, they possess no extraordinary powers, unlike wise old women, but only qualities available to any mortal.

Other similar stories offer glimpses into positive qualities associated with old age, qualities such as knowledge in *Briar Rose*; love of children in *Faithful Johannes, The Two Brothers; The Donkey* (Zipes, 1987). Frequently, we see characters who give wise counsel, as in *The Three Sons of Fortune*, or insight into the true value of things in *Bearskin* and *The Four Skillful Brothers* (Zipes, 1987). Kindness may be a prominent characteristic of an elder as in *The Three Little Birds* or concern for the well-being of servants in *The Poor Miller's Apprentice and the Cat* (Zipes, 1987).

WOMEN AND MEN ELDERS IN TRADITIONAL STORIES: COMPARISON AND CONTRAST

Comparing and contrasting wise old women and aged men characters yields important similarities and differences in their function and value in traditional stories.

Similarities

Traditional stories describe the physical appearance of elder men and women in a parallel manner. Both have hobbled, bent over postures, and are usually in need of a crutch or some means of support. They have markedly aged faces lined with many wrinkles. Their skin is craggy and crinkled, and their hair is thinning and white. Men, of course, frequently have long beards. Both men and women appear bent over, feeble, and physically unattractive—even repulsive. However, in many instances, both men and women's outward physical countenance merely conceals an inner beauty that is compelling and irresistible to the onlooker who has the willingness to see beyond the obvious.

Further, male and female elders often exist as supporting characters who bring about a significant change in the life of the protagonist. However, men, more often than women elders, also function as major characters in some stories. That key difference will be explored later.

Both aged men and wise old women are often found to function as advisors of some kind; in other words, as elders, they benefit from their age and experience and can pass along sage recommendations and meaningful information to the young protagonists who inhabit the stories. Further, they, like many characters in traditional literature, remain unnamed throughout the story, particularly if they function as supporting rather than major characters. Significantly, however, they are often referred to as "Granny,"

"Mother," or "Daddy," all labels that designate relations or kinfolk. Perhaps the fact that they are sometimes referred to by terms that are reserved for family members suggests that the younger characters pay a kind of homage to the elders. Certainly, in primitive cultures, elders, particularly family elders, were considered influential and important people in society.

Elder men and women are also the sole bearers of potent magical objects and charms. Significant, too, is the fact that they voluntarily confer those objects and talismans only to worthy younger characters, characters who possess traits such as kindness, loyalty, generosity, and bravery. Some stories contain elder characters who are quick to dole out harsh punishments to young characters who display temperaments that reflect rudeness, impatience, indifference, and unwillingness to listen to the wise words of their elders.

Differences

One key difference between aged men and wise old women in traditional literature is that more stories feature wise old women. Perhaps this disparity exists because, for so long, storytelling and stories were relegated to the exclusive domain of women in ancient cultures. While men worked the fields and went to war, women tended the hearth and home and passed on their lore to daughters and children through stories. As a result, stories tended to reflect the wisdom of the female elders in story characters who possessed similar qualities.

However, we do find that stories more often feature old men as protagonists than old women. Perhaps in male-dominated cultures, when men began to take over the role of culture bearers and storytellers from women, stories began to reflect this shift. In these stories, though, the older male protagonist is not a being possessed of extraordinary powers or wizardry. Instead, in some of the stories discussed previously, we find elder men who seem remarkably human because of their stupidity or serendipitous reliance on luck.

Old peasant fathers and even kings regularly present traits of weakness, obtuseness, and lack of insight into proper parenting. They often tend to be dominated by women, either new wives or stepmothers. Further, these men, unlike wise old women, have an absence of magical powers. Instead, they survive and gain influence through more human traits such as cleverness, bravery, or good fortune. Additionally, in order to succeed, some of these men must rely on the help of a grandchild or other very young person.

CONCLUSION

One means of dispelling unfavorable perceptions of older adults may exist in our traditional literature. These minimal narratives employing both uncomplicated or complex plots, flat characters, and compelling rhetorical devices have long engaged readers in a way that makes them an important part of the fabric of our folklore and reflectors of our cultural values. They contain universal themes that transcend their countries of origin and "create universal bonds of understanding" (Zipes, 1987, p. xxxiv). One scholar suggests that fairy tales may serve as training manuals for contemporary behavior and attitudes (Lieberman, 1972). Evolving from the human need to communicate life's surface and inner experiences to others, these tales reflect humans' intense desires to preserve the actions of ancestors, encode revered norms of society, and entertain (Pellowski, 1990; Sawyer, 1970). In one sense, traditional literature offers a means of preserving the cultural heritage of elders. As a result, they provide one channel to a deepened understanding of the aged. Noted psychologists Hillman (1979) and Bettel-heim (1976) championed the notions that exposure to the great body of traditional literature can improve our ability to project ourselves and our experience into the tales, and thereby, ensure a critical path to well being. As a society, we need to discover and embrace the underlying values of different co-cultures, including the aged. The richness and complexity of our cultures lie in our variant multicultural makeup (Cooper, 1994). Traditional literature gives artistic expression to the experiences of elders of the past and provides insight into current social perceptions of old age.

Young children comprise the largest audience for traditional stories. Depending on which stories they hear and read, impressionable youth may discern profoundly different images of older adults. Children have unparalleled abilities to immerse themselves in the fiction of stories and embody the psychic feelings of characters. I have seen this happen on countless occasions with my own child and other children I have told stories to. Their ripening imaginations provide an eager willingness to embrace the characters and situations embodied within traditional stories. Clearly, the tales' impact on children could be far-reaching. Children, who grow into adults and embody future perceptions and attitudes about aging, might be positively influenced by these stories if they are presented wisely. Silent and oral reading of these stories might inculcate changed attitudes about what it means to be old in a society that reveres youth. Traditional storytelling could certainly offer a profitable approach in presenting these stories to the young. Preliminary studies show little marginalization and devaluation of elders among children (Seltzer & Atchley, 1971). Thomas and Yamamoto (1975) found that young children tended to perceive older adults as both good and wise. Only as they grow into adolescence do children's attitudes become less positive.

In order to discover the extent of the power and influence of these stories, it is essential to examine the long-term effect of such stories on children. If we listen to the wise voices that emerge from these stories, they might herald a deeper, more balanced understanding of what it means to be old. They provide powerful insights into both negative and positive stereotypes we continue to cling to, even in contemporary society. Many of the stories champion the notion of wisdom, power, and inner beauty that accompany old age. As a body of literature, they anticipate the realization that old age may bring about changes in our outward appearance, but our inner self remains as vibrant and resourceful as ever. Perhaps these tales and others like them will dispel the notion that we are all destined to become, as the opening story suggests, "soft in the head and foolish . . . the laughingstock of children" (Zipes, 1987, p. 557). Further, they might help to banish our society's proclivity to treat older adults as if they "belonged to another species" (Beauvoir, 1972, p. 806). Perhaps they can help promote a view of old age as a "ripening toward death in a fruitful way" (Waxman, 1990, p. 2) rather than a time of mere decay.

REFERENCES

Barchers, S. I. (1990). *Wise women: Folk and fairy tales from around the world.* Englewood, CO: Libraries Unlimited.

Beauvoir, S. (1972). *The coming of age* (P. O'Brien, Trans.). New York: Warner Books.

Bettelheim, B. (1976). *The uses of enchantment: The meaning and importance of fairy tales.* New York: Knopf.

Cockerham, W. C. (1991). *This aging society.* Englewood Cliffs, NJ: Prentice-Hall.

Cooper, C. S. (1994, November). *Storytelling in the basic course for the promotion of cultural diversity.* Paper presented at the convention of the Speech Communication Association, New Orleans, LA.

Cumming, M. E. (1964). New thoughts on the theory of disengagement. In R. Kastenbaum (Ed.), *New thoughts on old age* (pp. 3–18). New York: Springer.

DeSpain, P. (1994). *Twenty-two splendid tales to tell from around the world* (Vols. 1-2). Little Rock, AR: August House.

Haber, C. (1983). *Beyond sixty-five.* Cambridge, UK: Cambridge University Press.

Hillman, J. (1979). A note on 'story.' *Parabola, 4,* 43–45.

Hummert, M. L., Wiemann, J. M., & Nussbaum, J. F. (1994). *Interpersonal communication in older adulthood: Interdisciplinary theory and research.* Thousand Oaks, CA: Sage.

Kaufman, S. R. (1986). *The ageless self: Sources of meaning in late life.* Madison, WI: University of Wisconsin Press.

Kirshenblatt-Gimblett, B. (1989a). Authoring lives. *Journal of Folklore Research, 26,* 123–149.

Klemmack, D. L., & Roff, L. L. (1984). Fear of personal aging and subjective well-being in late life. *Journal of Gerontology, 39,* 756–758.

Lieberman, M. (1972, December). Some day my prince will come. *College English,* 383–395.

Livo, N. J., & Rietz, S. A. (1986). *Storytelling: Process and practice.* Littleton, CO: Libraries Unlimited.

Manney, J. D., Jr. (1975). *Aging in American society: An examination of concepts and issues.* Ann Arbor, MI: Institute of Gerontology.

Mullen, P. B. (1992). *Listening to old voices: Folklore, life stories, and the elderly.* Urbana, IL: University of Illinois Press.

Opie, I., & Opie, P. (1974). *The classic fairy tales.* New York: Oxford University Press.

Pellowski, A. (1990). *The world of storytelling, expanded and revised.* New York: Wilson.

Sawyer. R. (1970). *The way of the storyteller.* New York: Penguin.

Seltzer, M. M., & Atchley, R. C. (1971). The concept of old age: Changing attitudes and stereotypes. *Gerontologist 11,* 226–230.

Stern, C. S., & Henderson, B. (1993). *Performance: Texts and contexts.* New York: Longman.

Thomas, E. C., & Yamamoto, K. (1975) Attitudes toward age: An exploration in school-age children. *International Journal of Aging and Human Development, 6,* 29–40.

Waxman, B. F. (1990). *From the hearth to the open road: A feminist study of aging in contemporary literature.* New York: Greenwood.

White, L. K. (1988). Gender differences in awareness of aging among married adults ages 20 to 60. *Sociological Quarterly, 29,* 487–502.

Zipes, J. (1987). *The complete fairy tales of the brothers Grimm.* Toronto, Canada: Bantam.

11

Searching for the Fountain: Models of Aging in Contemporary Self-Help Literature

Thomas J. Darwin
The University of Memphis

Self-help literature provides a useful site for examining cultural discourses of aging because self-help literature is designed to be accessible to a wide audience. It attempts to bridge a gap between the desire of the masses to have control over their lives and the technical information necessary to give them that control. Self-help literature empowers by providing readers with a modicum of the technical knowledge held by doctors and other professionals, thereby placing them on a more equal footing with the professionals who help them. In short, self-help literature creates lay experts who have more control over their lives because they possess technical knowledge. It also provides some security in the face of life's truest inevitability by giving some technical mastery of the knowledge of aging, if not aging itself.

This chapter is based on a survey of self-help literature published since 1990 that addresses aging and longevity. The nature of the problems discussed and the assumptions made about resources available to those who use these texts suggest that they are targeted at people over the age of 50 who are reasonably comfortable. The reading level of the texts suggests an audience with at least some college education. They are targeted at both men and women, and none of the texts surveyed identified specific ethnic audiences. Based on this survey, then, this chapter articulates three different models of aging in contemporary self-help literature. The first model, the maintenance model, is present in the work of the American Geriatrics Society (1995), "Future Youth" (1987), Hayflick (1994), Kugler (1993), Pearson and Shaw (1982), and Rose (1992). It mobilizes the technical expertise of science to maintain one's body in the struggle against aging. The second model, the vital aging model, is present in the work of Coombs

(1995), Friedan (1993), McCall (1994), Silverstone and Hyman (1992), and Wiebe (1995). This model challenges the centrality of the biomedical conception of aging as decline. Instead, it offers a model of age that focuses on humans as social creatures for whom the key to aging well is in being engaged with others in one's community. It resists the negative attitude toward aging it feels is propagated by biomedicine. Finally, the mindbody model of aging, is represented in the work of Chopra (1989, 1993), Dossey (1993), Goleman and Gurin (1993), the Institute of Noetic Sciences & W. Poole (1993), and Moyers (1993). It challenges the biomedical/scientific view of aging on philosophical grounds. It argues that the mind and body are actually two aspects of a deeper unity that is timeless. It proposes that if we reconceptualize our bodies, we can find a way to overcome aging altogether.

The models described in this chapter are designed to help readers identify the sources of an individual's conception of aging. They will be useful as guides for helping someone such as a health care provider, actually hear what patients are saying when they talk about aging. The analysis in this chapter illustrates the multiplicity of meanings implied by the concept of aging and the multiplicity of practices supported by those meanings. Thus, this chapter articulates the models and then draws out the relationships and differences among them. It also pays special attention to the relationships of these models to the dominant biomedical model of aging and to each other.

CULTURE, COMMUNICATION, AND AGING

Cultural Models and Action

This chapter assumes that human behavior is directed in part by complex cultural models. Human behavior is guided by how humans make their world and experience intelligible. Their experience is made intelligible, in part, by concepts and symbols made available to them in their cultural milieu. Cultural models "frame experience, supplying interpretations of that experience and inferences about it, and goals for action"(Holland & Quinn, 1987, p. 6). These underlying models are drawn upon to perform a variety of tasks. They help set goals for action and plan how to achieve those goals. They are drawn upon to make sense of the actions and goals of others. Most importantly, from the standpoint of communication scholars, these models shape texts that direct actions as well as help interpret those actions (pp.

6–7). Another key aspect of cultural models as they guide actions is that those models must themselves be contested and negotiated (Strauss, 1992, p. 1). Humans do not necessarily arrive at one clear model with clearly defined goals as they interpret and respond to daily events. Indeed, they may find that they are operating on several models at once, even models that may conflict. As individuals make up their minds from one moment to the next, they must take into account a range of input, including "the social behavior people observe, the instructions they are given, and the constructed realities they bump up against" (p. 8). Thus, although cultural research tells us that the relationship between cultural texts and human behavior is complex, there is a relationship. Analysis of texts is essential to understanding how texts influence action and how they become cultural resources.

The idea that these texts become resources for understanding aging and acting in response to aging is consistent with a symbolic interactionist approach to aging. From the symbolic interactionist perspective, aging is but one situation in which "human beings interpret and define actions and objects based upon symbolic meaning shared with others"(Cockerham, 1991, p. 64). Symbolic representations of aging, such as those found in self-help literature, shape perceptions of aging. These perceptions, in turn, structure attitudes toward aging that influence behavior toward aging (Feezel and Hawkins, 1988, p. 82). Generally speaking, then, the analysis in this chapter is derived from the general theoretical view of aging that takes as its primary project explaining "how age itself is given meaning through discourse"(Coupland & Coupland, 1995, p. 81).

Relative to the most widely held social theories of aging, a discourse-centered approach to aging deepens broader social theories of aging. Though there are many nuances in the dominant social theories of aging, they are all *functionalist* in that they view aging as but one more function that individuals serve in society. According to the functionalist perspective, society maintains itself as long as individuals "typically behave in accordance with the norms and values common to their particular social system"(Cockerham, 1991, p. 49). According to the functionalist perspective, as people age they can serve the overall balance of society by disengaging, remaining active, though in different ways, or "accepting reduced status because of modernization" (p. 68). From whichever social theoretical view one approaches aging, analyzing the discourse of aging allows one to understand in finer detail how the aging fill these roles and how these roles are made possible and maintained through communication.

METHOD

The models articulated in this chapter are derived from rhetorical analysis of the self-help texts surveyed for this chapter. This analysis focused on descriptions of aging, itself, descriptions of the body, both explicit and implicit in description of aging, and the ways a text advocated resistance toward aging. Specifically, the analysis examined arguments made in support of a given view of aging, and how to address it, as well as metaphors used to describe the body and aging itself. From these arguments, composite arguments were constructed that represent models for aging because they tell the reader what aging is, what the body, and as result how best to address aging. For the sake of explanation, this chapter draws on specific sources which best illustrate the model in question: Pearson and Shaw (1982) and "Future Youth" (1987) for the maintenance model, Friedan (1993) for the vital aging model, and Chopra (1993) for the mindbody model. Although the models are composites distilled from analysis of various texts, the exemplars provide specifics for the model and for determining differences and similarities among the models. This chapter uses the term *resistance* to describe each model's general disposition to aging because each model invariably conceptualizes aging as involving a deep struggle. What is noteworthy is how each model diverges in how it articulates this resistance and the type of resistance it advocates. The term *resistance* also highlights the fact that each model (especially the vital aging and mindbody models) cast aging as ultimately a broader social and cultural issue.

MODELS OF AGING IN CONTEMPORARY
SELF-HELP LITERATURE

The Maintenance Model of Aging

The Body.   The body is a machine comprised of individual parts that work together to carry out various bodily processes. Because the body is a machine, its parts will wear out over time, and its processes will become increasingly inefficient. The body is a sum of its parts (e.g., eyes, kidneys, hearts, legs, muscles), the processes those parts carry out (e.g., immunity, circulation, digestion, hearing), the chemical components that nurture those processes (e.g., chemical messengers, nutrients, vitamins), toxins that threaten those processes (e.g., pollutants, cholesterol, free radicals, alcohol), and the diseases of degeneration (e.g., dysfunction of various bodily functions, cancer, heart disease, diabetes).

Aging.   Aging is a general physiological trend of decreasing efficiency, bodily organs wearing out, and diminished performance. This degeneration may be caused by two primary sources: natural decay, built into the body itself, and disease. As the body naturally becomes less efficient over time, it becomes more susceptible to disease and other disorders that further decrease its efficiency and increase its susceptibility. A slight variation on the general model of physical decline conceptualizes aging as a chemical process in which the body gradually loses a battle between nutrients and toxins.

Resistance.   Given that the body in this model is conceptualized as a machine, the model advocates two strategies for resisting aging. The first strategy is to strengthen the body against inevitable decline and, thereby, enable it to be strong and efficient for as long as possible. Through care and maintenance of the body as a physical organism, one can forestall the inevitable effects of aging. The second strategy is related to the first, except that it focuses on the chemical nature of the processes. Keying on a view of the body as a balance of chemicals, the second strategy resists aging by introducing vitamins and other nutrients to fight, ameliorate, or compensate for damage done by toxins in the body.

The Vital Aging Model

The Body.   According to the vital aging model, the fact that aging involves physical decline is true but irrelevant. The body is more than a physical, biological body. It is more importantly a social body, that is, all bodies exist in relationship to other bodies. The physical well-being of any one person (and his or her body) is as much a function of that person's relationship to other persons (and their bodies) as it is a function of physiological processes in the individual body.

Aging.   Aging is an inevitable process of physical change. As change occurs, humans are faced with choices and opportunities not available previously in their lives. The most serious problem is the change in their social relations and their feeling of being active and engaged in life. Aging is simply a process of change. Physical changes, which accompany aging, are significant but do not define it.

Resistance.   The central feature of vital aging is a constant awareness and pursuit of opportunities made possible as one changes through life. Physical processes in and of themselves are neither good nor bad. It is according to a standard that values only youth that one judges natural changes as negative. Judging these changes negatively intensifies the deleterious effects of physical changes because judging them negatively justifies the gradual decline of activity and withdrawal from others that are the truly damaging processes of aging. To resist aging, therefore, is to resist the negative evaluation of aging that is characteristic of contemporary society. Practically, people must admit the changes in the biological body but must find opportunities in them for new relationships and expressions of the social body. "Activity in society of some complexity, using cognitive ability, and involving choice, is evidently a crucial clue to longevity and vital aging"(Friedan, 1993, p. 81). Taking care of the social body is the key to successful, or vital, aging.

The Mindbody Model

The Body. The body in the mindbody paradigm is physical, but physical in a radically different way. The mindbody model conceptualizes the mind and the body as a unified entity. The physical processes of the body are seen as emanations or manifestations of underlying spiritual and mental processes. The biochemistry of the body is a product of thought and perception. Thoughts and emotions create the chemical relationships that maintain the life of each cell. Because mind and body are viewed as one entity, a "body-mind" (Pert, 1990), this model views intelligence as a quality possessed by every cell of the body. This intelligence creates the body in continually new forms from one moment to the next. As our patterns of perceptions and beliefs about the body change, the body itself changes. The body, then, is a constant accomplishment achieved by cells of the body, imbued with intelligence, constantly communicating with each other. Because the physical and the mental are two sides of the same body-mind coin, changes in the mental literally bring about changes in the physical: One changes one's physical state by altering one's mental state. In some interpretations of the mindbody paradigm, the intelligence of cells is taken to have mystical qualities that give it transcendent quality. This means that what an individual takes to be a change in the physical state of the body is ultimately a function of how the individual perceives and conceptualizes the body.

Aging. Aging in this paradigm has the same status as disease. Both are viewed ultimately as matters of interpretation and perception. It does not deny that people become ill and die. It argues that aging and disease must be viewed holistically as disruptions of the body's pervasive somatic intelligence. What most people take to be aging is actually a disruption of the body's intelligence brought about by a deep-seated (culturally conditioned) belief that the body must decay and die. Because we believe we will become older and die, we do. There may be important social reasons that we are programmed to do this, but there is no necessary reason in the nature of body-mind why we should decay.

Resistance. Ultimately, the source of resistance in the mindbody paradigm is to retrain our experience of our bodies. We must unlearn the construction of our bodies as fragmented, individualized physical machines that are destined to decay and run out of energy. If we change our perceptions, the logic goes, then we can literally change the physiological processes of aging. At the very least, the mindbody model views a healthy, vital body as one in which there is free and open communication among the body's cells. Because this communication is disrupted by various stressors, a key to resisting aging is to resist the various sources of stress in one's life. Although the focus on reducing stress and fostering peace and calmness in one's life is consistent with any of the models, what makes the mindbody perspective unique is the fact that it posits a direct physical embodiment of one's stress or calmness.

If, in fact, time is eternal, and change is but an illusion, then not only can we conquer aging, we do not really age at all. Remember that age (in the materialist sense) is predicated on a concept of time as constant and inexorable. If there is no change, then there is no aging. In the mindbody model, humans do not have to fight or resist aging. Rather, they have to resist the conception of the world that makes them think they are aging. They have to resist an illusion foisted on them by biomedical science.

ANALYSIS OF THE MODELS

Self-Help Models of Aging: Detrimental or Facilitative?

The purpose of this section is to provide a perspective on these models from the standpoint of research on communication and aging. Perhaps the dominant issue for those studying aging and communication is how communication contributes to negative attitudes and can be used to foster positive attitudes toward aging. Research shows that many negative myths and stereotypes about aging dominate American culture. Among other things, Americans believe that aging is synonymous with senility, that intelligence declines with age, that one becomes more incompetent with age, and that older people are too rigid to change (Feezel & Hawkins, 1988, p. 84). Moreover, Americans believe that pain, handicap, isolation, and preoccupation with death are also characteristic of aging (p. 86).

These negative perceptions are due in large part to the fact that biomedicine provides a dominant source of understanding aging. The *American Medical Association Encyclopedia of Medicine*, for example, offers three theories of aging: the worn template theory, the accumulated toxins theory, and the decline in the immune system theory. (Clayton, 1989, p. 78). Moreover, it explains aging with a table that lists each major body system and characterizes the natural effects of aging strictly in terms of "loss" and "decline"(Clayton). Similarly, the *American Medical Association's Family Medical Guide* (Clayton, 1994) introduces its section on aging by saying that "like all machines, a human body that has been functioning for a number of years tends to work less efficiently than when it was new" (p. 765). Finally, the *Mayo Clinic Family Health Book* (Larson, 1990) section on aging focuses on the special problems of the elderly, that include cognitive disorders, failing eyesight, impaired mobility, and loss of sexual drive.

Countering these negative views, however, are cilitative views. The motivation behind developing facilitative views is to develop healthy communication and experiences of aging by dispelling negative myths. This is not to say that one distorts reality in a positive way but that one attempts to grasp reality in a more balanced way (Feezel & Hawkins, 1988, p. 87). A facilitative view recognizes that persons are capable of growth well into older age, that they deserve respect and empathy, and that they are still vibrant, and productive members of society (p. 89). The rest of this section places each of the self-help models in a continuum between negative and facilitative, according to how much they further these respective views.

The Maintenance Model

The maintenance model exemplifies the biomedical attitude toward aging because it reduces aging to physical and chemical processes in the body. The maintenance model takes medicine's arsenal of knowledge and techniques and makes it available to the average person in the struggle against aging. In this way, self-help works that apply the maintenance model capitalize on the tremendous amount of credibility medical science has in our culture. They borrow the voice and power of science to legitimize their own programs for fighting aging. They also capitalize on the implicit promise of medical science to cure the diseases we suffer. By defining aging as the onset of disease and decay, these works equate aging with disease. Logically, then, if science can find a cure for disease, it can find a cure for aging.

People who read these works "arm" themselves against aging by using the technical knowledge of science to fight the many threats to the body that we define as aging. Resistance is predicated on the ability to unlock the secrets of those chemicals that undermine the body and to use that knowledge to fight those chemicals. Thus, if medical science bears the bad news that decline is inevitable, it also provides the means for resisting that decline. In this model, the category system and analytical imperative that drive it become the weapons in the fight against aging. By making these weapons available to the general consumer, these works enlist them in the struggle against aging.

Although this is not overtly negative, it does not directly challenge the underlying assumptions of aging as fundamentally negative, which characterize the negative view of aging. It offers hope that one can overcome aging, but even this hope may be self-defeating. If aging is still seen as something to be overcome, then it is still intrinsically negative.

The Vital Aging Model

Especially as it is articulated in the work of Friedan (1993), the vital aging model is perhaps a paradigm of the facilitative approach to aging. By focusing on consciousness and choice as the central factors in aging well, Friedan changed what is important in aging. From the standpoint of the vital aging model, however, the truly deleterious effects of aging lie in seeing aging only in physiological terms. Friedan showed how strict attention to the physical justifies and even encourages the gradual disengagement from life and loved ones that characterizes aging and perpetuates the negative view of aging. Because science tells individuals that it is inevitable that they will no longer be able to carry out their normal functions, it is reasonable and expected that as one gets older, he or she will do less and become less involved with others. Because the vital aging model defines health fundamentally as a function of our relationships with others and sense of being engaged in life, biomedicine does as much harm as good.

The vital aging model, therefore, turns the biological/social tension on its head. It models humans as social and political creatures first. Autonomy, independence, and opportunity to exercise choice and consciousness in community become the keys to successful aging. Friedan (1993) would not argue that the biomedical model does not allow choices or call for responsibility. There are choices within biomedicine, but as the maintenance model suggests, the choices are limited to biomedical techniques and treatments for undoing or forestalling the effects of aging. Responsibility amounts to the responsibility to do as one's doctor dictates.

For the vital aging model, the only true way to see aging is from a facilitative standpoint. As with this standpoint, there is no denial of the physical aspects of aging, but these physical aspects are viewed as changes to be learned from rather than purely as decline or loss of self. Moreover, similar to the facilitative view of aging, the vital aging model recognizes the power of communication to make vital aging possible. An implication of the vital aging model is that real change in aging will come about only through changes in discourse and their concomitant changes in attitudes.

The Mindbody Model

The assumption in the vital aging model that humans are fundamentally social provides the link to the next model, the mindbody model. Whereas the vital aging model assumes that sociality is a necessary link to health and aging, it is the mindbody model that offers a theoretical account of how and why this may be so, and in so doing, offers perhaps the most radical critique of biomedicine. If, as the mindbody model suggests, human physiology is an expression of a deeper intelligence, then one's body is a constant expression of one's thoughts and perceptions. Becausse thoughts and perceptions are themselves culturally mediated and constituted, it follows that human physiology is literally constituted in social and cultural situations.

By suggesting that humans are essentially spiritual and that aging is an illusion, the mindbody model opens itself to serious criticism from those who study aging scientifically or empirically. However, the mindbody model is articulated in a way that is no more unlikely or "wacky" than any other religious account of life. Indeed, the mindbody model goes farther than many religious accounts in that it offers a theoretical account of how the spiritual and the material worlds are fundamentally connected. It rhetorically bridges the gap between the physical and spiritual worlds by conceptualizing the body as information and energy. Moreover, by ultimately couching its account of aging in spiritual concepts, the mindbody model taps into that part of any reader's psyche that sustains religious faith.

Herein lies the mindbody model's challenge and resistance to materialist science. The mindbody model identifies science as the source of assumptions about the body that lead to the pain and suffering of aging. What must be overcome ultimately is not a physical process but a conceptual system that forces humans to only conceptualize their bodies (and thus the experience of aging) in purely material terms.

Thus, although the mindbody model is not as explicitly facilitative as the vital aging model, it is indirectly facilitative. This is because it offers a theoretical account of how a facilitative attitude can not only shape perceptions but also how such an attitude might actually have beneficial physical effects on the body over time. Perhaps the deepest challenge to a positive attitude that looks beyond the physical effects of aging is the view that asks one to accept reality. This reality is most often a physical reality of bodily change. It is accurate but limited. The facilitative view, however, can seem like wishful thinking against the challenges of materialist science. The mindbody model of aging attempts to meet the materialist view on its own scientific ground.

What is perhaps most important about the vital aging and mindbody models (and the facilitative view in general) is that they expand the discussion of aging to include factors beyond the purely physical aspects of aging. Even the maintenance model, which makes biomedical knowledge available for popular use, introduces the concept of responsibility. This suggests that even though biomedicine can do a great deal about aging, ultimately how an individual ages is up to that individual. The vital aging and the mindbody models illustrate the extent to which discussions of aging must inevitably draw in broader questions of political, social, and cultural values. When Friedan (1993), for example, argued that we must address aging in its social context first, this had tremendous implications for policy, both as it is made by legislators and by individuals. She implied that issues such as discrimination on the basis of age and the amount of money our society spends to ensure that older Americans have a comfortable, engaged life cannot be separated from the issue of their very health.

CONCLUSION

In the end, then, this brief picture of self-help literature has shown three strategies of resistance to aging, though each is radically different from the others. At the same time, there are points of continuity among them. The maintenance model utilizes the tools of science (both conceptual and instrumental) to fight aging by making those tools available to the average person. By studying these self-help texts, the reader presumably gains enough technical expertise to resist the physical ravages of aging by maintaining the body. Power lies in technical knowledge.

The vital aging model empowers the reader by encouraging him or her to reconsider what is ultimately most important about the experience of aging. It "reminds" the reader that life is more than physical processes. Life is the relationships and commitments humans share with each other as they are actively engaged in their communities. What must be overcome is the tendency of scientific knowledge to justify the isolation of humans from each other as they grow older. The vital aging model challenges not so much the science of medicine as the social and political implications of that science. To age well, therefore, and achieve vital aging, people must concentrate on remaining fully engaged in life. Science is not wrong. It is just that it must not be allowed to completely determine what it means to be alive and, thus, to age.

The mindbody model shares with the vital aging model the concept that humans must overcome the conceptual blinders imposed by biomedical science. The mindbody model goes farther than the vital aging model, however, because it challenges the technical and philosophical legitimacy of science's account of life. To scientific materialism, the mindbody model opposes a spiritual reconstruction of the body as timeless. It reasserts the primacy of human imagination and spirit by asserting that humans are literally the stuff of a deeper intelligence. To overcome aging, one must overcome the limitations posed by biomedical science and start with a broader set of assumptions about the body and what is possible with it.

Each of these models is about resistance and interpretation of one's experience. Although some may seem more plausible than others as accounts of aging, it is important to note two points in this regard. First, plausible or not, these models have great potential to influence the people who read them and try to apply them to their own lives and processes of aging. Second, what counts as plausibility is itself determined by one's culture and belief system. The material science that underwrites biomedicine and the maintenance model may reasonably question the mysticism and ephemeral nature of the mindbody account. At the same time, it must recognize the limits of its own account and try to recognize where alternate accounts have found truths. This point is particularly clear in the vital aging critique that argues that biomedicine is not wrong but just not the most important lens through which to view aging.

Most importantly, it is quite likely that individuals will fashion their own accounts and interpretations of aging from several models of aging available in popular culture. What research such as this chapter can provide is a starting point for understanding the different accounts that may be in play as someone copes with aging. In that light, one who is trying to determine what cultural models are motivating an individual's action in response to aging must first and foremost have respect for how that person sees the world. Because an account is not in line with that accepted view of aging is irrelevant to the person who takes that account seriously and attempts to live by it. The payoff of such respect, to borrow the words of Nussbaum and Coupland (1995), is that we come to see aging "as a process of development involving positive choices and providing new opportunities"(p. xiii).

REFERENCES

American Geriatrics Society. (1995). *The American geriatrics society book on aging.* New York: Harmony.

Chopra, D. (1989). *Quantum healing: Exploring the frontiers of mind/body medicine.* New York: Bantam.

Chopra, D. (1993). *Ageless body, timeless mind.* New York: Harmony.

Clayton, C.B. (Ed.). (1989). *The American Medical Association encyclopedia of medicine.* New York: Random House.

Clayton, C.B. (Ed.). (1994). *The American Medical Association family medical guide.* New York: Random House.

Cockerham, W.C. (1991). *This aging society.* Englewood Cliffs, NJ: Prentice-Hall.

Coombs, H. (1995). *Time happens.* San Francisco: Halo.

Coupland, N., & Coupland, J. (1995). Discourse, identity, and aging. In J. F. Nussbaum & J. Coupland (Eds.), *Handbook of communication and aging research* (pp. 79–104). Mahwah, NJ: Lawrence Erlbaum Associates.

Dossey, L. (1991). *Meaning and medicine: Lessons from a doctor's tales of breakthrough and healing.* New York: Bantam.

Feezel, J., & Hawkins, R. (1988). Myths and stereotypes: Communication breakdowns. In C. W. Carmichael, C. Botan, & R. Hawkins (Eds.), *Human communication and the aging process* (pp. 81–94). Prospect Heights, IL: Waveland Press.

Friedan, B. (1993). *The fountain of age.* New York: Simon & Schuster.

Future youth. (1987). *Prevention Magazine.* Emmaus, PA: Rodale Press.

Goleman, D., & Gurin, J. (Eds.). (1993). *Mind/body medicine: How to use your mind for better health.* Yonkers: Consumer Reports Books.

Hayflick, L. (1994). *How and why we age.* New York: Ballantine.

Holland, D., & Quinn, N. (Eds.). (1987). *Cultural models in thought and language.* New York: Cambridge University Press.

Institute of Noetic Sciences & W. Poole (1993). *The heart of healing.* Atlanta: Turner .

Kugler, H. (1993). *Life extension and memory boosters.* New York: Stein & Day.

Larson, D.E. (Ed.). (1990). *The Mayo Clinic family health book.* New York: Morrow.

McCall, E. (1994). *Sometimes we dance alone.* Thorndike, ME: Hall.

Moyers, B. (1993). *Healing and the mind.* New York: Doubleday.

Nussbaum, J.F., & Coupland, J. (Eds.). (1995). *Handbook of communication and aging research.* Mahwah, NJ: Lawrence Erlbaum Associates.

Pearson, D., & Shaw, S. (1982). *Life extension.* New York: Warner Books.

Pert, C. (1990). The Wisdom of the receptors: Neuropeptides, the emotions, and body-mind. In R. Ornstein & C. Swencionis (Eds.), *The healing brain: A scientific reader* (147–158). New York: Guilford.

Rose, J. (1992). *The youth factor.* Boulder City, NV: Winston.

Silverstone, B., & Hyman, H. (1992). *Growing old together.* New York: Pantheon.

Strauss, C. (1992). Models and motives. In R. D'Andrade & C. Strauss (Eds.), *Human motives and cultural models* (pp. 1–20). New York: Cambridge University Press.

Wiebe, K. (1995). *Border crossings: A spiritual journey.* Scottdale, PA: Herald Press.

12

Young by Day: The Older Person on Daytime Serial Drama

Mary Cassata
State University of New York at Buffalo

Barbara J. Irwin
Canisius College

The mass media in the United States—television, in particular—are considered by many to be important transmitters of social and cultural values. Hinton, Seggar, Northcott, and Fontes (1974) speculated that the social progress of African Americans in our society, for example, might be linked to the manner in which television portrays them. Several researchers have explored the relationship between television viewing and social reality (Buerkel-Rothfuss & Mayes, 1981; Perse, 1986), using the daytime serial as the context on which they based their conclusion that the soaps reflect the real world through characters and content. Recognizing that older people are the fastest growing age demographic in the United States today, many feel it is important to examine the portrayal of this age group so as to better understand how these portrayals may influence the conceptions and attitudes our society may have of them. Berry (1988) expressed concern over television's prominence as a medium of entertainment, given its potential to influence:

> Whatever else commercial television is or does, one of its primary goals is to entertain. It is a tall order, therefore, to expect television scrupulously to offer the types of portrayals that capture the multifaceted aspects of human behavior and present desirable cultural depictions. Yet, because of television's power to define social reality about viewers' own groups, as well as about people and cultural groups that are different from viewers' own groups, it is important that its cultural lessons not be distortions of reality. (p. 121)

There is a respectable body of research dealing with the subject of television's portrayal of older people, most of which focuses on prime-time.

On balance, there are substantially fewer serious studies that concern themselves with daytime television's dramatic portrayals of older people. Another body of scholarly literature deals with prime-time television's portrayal of ethnicity, an area that is also not much explored in the scholarly literature on daytime soap operas, although our literature review did manage to reveal a few such studies.

A comprehensive search of the literature combining these two strands of research, however, has failed to reveal that any studies have been done on the portrayal of older people across ethnic lines either on prime-time or daytime television. The study presented herein brings together these two disparate lines of research. It explores the portrayal of older people across ethnic lines on television soap operas and emanates from the ongoing Cultural Indicators Message Systems Analysis of Daytime Serial Drama research undertaken by *Project Daytime* at the State University of New York at Buffalo.

LITERATURE REVIEW

A number of interesting theories have been advanced as to what constitutes television viewers' perceptions of old age. Do heavy viewers place the onset of old age at a different figure from light viewers or nonviewers? Gerbner, Gross, Signorelli, and Morgan (1980) reported that heavy and light viewers alike placed the figure as being in his or her 50s. Wober (1980) reported that most of the people he sampled placed the onset of old age at 70 and concluded that the amount of television viewing had nothing whatsoever to do with that determination. Rather, attitudes of the British toward older people were said to be a function of the age of the viewer. Whether heavier viewers attribute the characteristics of television's portraits of elders to *real* older people is unanswerable at this time. Children, especially those under the age of 15, tend to think of anyone over the age of 30 as being old. Greenberg (1988) advanced the theory that it is important to have more elder characters (arbitrarily stipulated as being in their 60s and 70s) on television for two reasons; they serve as models for real people of the same age and as realistic images for younger viewers as to what being old is all about.

The preponderance of studies of the older adult on television yielded negative findings. One often cited study (Aronoff, 1974) concluded that older people were generally associated with unhappiness, failure, and evil. Other researchers have contended that the television world grossly under-represents and misrepresents the older adult (Davis & Davis, 1986; Davis

& Kubey, 1982; Gerbner, et al., 1980; Greenberg, Korzenny, & Atkin, 1980; Northcott, 1975; Powell & Williamson, 1985; Rubin, 1982; Serock, 1979).
    Gerbner et al. (1980) found that when the prime-time television world was examined according to age, it was in sharp contrast to what existed in the real world. The greatest number of people in the television world—more than 50%—fell between the ages of 25 and 45. Only 8% of the fictional population was made up of persons 18 years old and under, compared to 30% in the U.S. population (Gerbner et al., 1980). Only 2.3% of those who populated the world of television drama were over age 65, in contrast to that age group's presence of 11% of the U.S. population. The profile of older people in prime time was even more dismal when considering characterization. More older men and women were portrayed as "bad" compared to their younger counterparts, and although successful men were more likely to be found as their age increased, this pattern did not exist for women. Diverging from any other age group, there were more unsuccessful older women than successful ones. Several other studies revealed that the portrayals of older men differed from those of older women, with older women being grossly underrepresented and presented more negatively than older men (Beck, 1978; Dail, 1988; Hiemstra, Goodman, Middlemiss, Vosco, & Ziegler, 1983; Serock, 1979). The bottom line is that the portrayals of most older people in prime-time television showed them not to be held in high esteem or treated with respect.
    Peterson's (1973) content analysis of 30 half-hour prime-time programs on network television revealed 13% of the TV population under study to be 65 or older. Only 1.2% of these older characters were women. In contrast to other studies, however, the image of older people in Peterson's study was positive overall: They were shown as being active, competent, friendly, healthy, independent, nice, rich, sharp, smart, and strong. Korzenny and Neuendorf (1980) found examples of positive elder portrayals in prime time that generated positive self-concepts among elder viewers. On the debit side of the television ledger, positive portrayals aside, older people were shown as being "socially rejected" (Peterson, 1973).
    Dail (1988) found in her analysis of 193 characters in prime-time family programming that adults over age 55 were generally shown in a positive light in terms of health and physical and social behavior. Although women were portrayed more negatively and more stereotypically than men, a more positive image of elders overall emerged in television portrayals.
    Among the few studies exploring daytime television's demography, Downing (1975) determined that of all soap characters appearing, 10.5% were classified as late middle age (51–64 years old) and 3.5% were over

age 65, that there were slightly more late middle-aged men than women, and that there were twice as many male elders as female elders. Cassata, Anderson, and Skill (1983) found older people to be proportionately *over-represented* (16%) compared to their numbers in the real world. Older people were identified in this study as being 55 or older. They were shown to be influential members of the community: opinion leaders and upholders of traditional moral values. Moreover, they were highly respected, involved, and active, with a good self-image projected through a stable emotional and physical posture.

This more positive, less stereotypical view of older people was supported by Elliott (1984), who found that older serial characters (defined as age 65 and over) represented 8% of the soap opera population. They scored high marks for verbal behaviors, and their social characteristics were typical of older people in the general population. Elliott also concluded that although older characters were not the central characters of soap operas, neither were they passive.

Irwin (1990) examined soap opera characters and storylines from the perspective of those who create them. Douglas Marland, headwriter for *As The World Turns* in the 1980s, considered some of his most important work to be the creation of multigenerational storylines. Although the literature reveals that older characters on soap operas are portrayed in a positive light, their relative importance to the story is called into question, as revealed by the longest running actress on soap operas, Helen Wagner, who plays matriarch Nancy Hughes on *As The World Turns*:

> Her own character, Nancy, is a tentpole character who never really has her own storyline: other characters come to her to talk about their situations and problems, but even as such, Nancy's role has been severely cut in recent years. Storylines which involve older characters are not always developed to the extent that they otherwise might be if they involved younger characters. (Irwin, 1990, p. 98)

The second area of content analysis literature relevant to the present study deals with the ethnic make-up of the television population. Seggar, Hafen, and Hannonen-Gladden's (1981) decade-long study, which examined 18,000 character portrayals in television comedy and drama, and motion pictures between 1971 and 1980, showed that the White population grew in dominance over that period from 84% to 91% of the total entertainment population, whereas the proportion of Black men and women fluctuated from 6% to 9% and from 5% to 6%, respectively. Other ethnic characters in television and the movies decreased from 13% to 3% (men) and from 10% to only 2.5% (women).

In their study covering the years 1969 to 1978, Gerbner and Signorelli (cited in Greenberg, 1986) found that the ethnic breakdown of characters overall in prime-time television drama was as follows: Whites, 85.5%; Blacks, 8%; Hispanics, 3%; Asians, 2.5%; Native Americans, less than 1%. They reported that 8.5% of Black characters and 2.5% of Hispanic characters had major roles, paralleling their presence in prime time television programming.

Seggar et al. (1981) also explored the roles ethnic characters played in their respective programs. During the 1970s, Black men's major and supporting roles decreased by more than 50%, comprising less than 5% of all men's major or supporting roles. During the same period, Black women made up only 2% to 3% of all major or supporting women's roles.

Huston et al. (1992) cited additional research relating to television's racial and ethnic portrayals (Greenberg, 1986; Pierce, 1980; & Williams & Condry, 1989), confirming that:

> Cross-racial or cross-ethnic interactions are relatively infrequent because many shows are all white or all black. Portrayals of informal cross-ethnicity interactions occur with children and adolescents, but among adults, they tend to be more formal and distant than within-ethnicity interactions. (p. 25)

In writing soap operas, one of Agnes Nixon's goals was to bring soap operas out of "WASP valley" by introducing characters representing a variety of ethnic groups. In the 1960s, interracial marriages, romances, and even friendships were considered taboo (Irwin, 1990). More recently, such storylines have become acceptable to audiences, and the integration of characters of different ethnicities on soap operas is more commonplace. However, several content analyses examining character portrayals in soap operas revealed an overwhelmingly White daytime serial population (Downing, 1975; Gade, 1971; Greenberg, Neuendorf, Buerkel-Rothfuss, & Henderson, 1982). Other ethnic characters represented less than 3% (Greenberg, et al.,1982), 4% (Gade, 1971), and 4.7% (Downing, 1975) of all soap opera characters. These studies also confirmed nearly equal representation of men and women on soaps.

Collymore (1995a) reported that out of a total pool of 254 White and other ethnic actors on contract status appearing in soap operas on the three commercial networks, 28 were African American actors, representing 11% of all the contract players. In another article, Collymore (1995b) concluded that the answer regarding social change with regard to Black characters and storylines lies especially in Black viewer power. Although the proportion of African American viewers watching soap operas is significantly larger than that of any other racial segment of the audience ("The Numbers," 1995), these viewers are notoriously passive when it comes to expressing their views to network executives and soap opera sponsors.

In her doctoral dissertation, James (1991) classified daytime soap operas as being tokenistic, transitional, or progressive, according to their treatment of ethnic characters. On tokenistic soaps, ethnic characters had fewer than five lines of dialogue and were shown in work-related roles or functioned as "buddies" to White characters. In transitional soaps, racial ethnics were shown as being assimilated into the dominant culture. Progressive soaps took the ethnic history of their minority characters into account, anchored them in their own families, and brought to the fore the historical and ethnic realities of being minority. James did not use age as a variable in her study.

METHOD

Sample

All daytime serial drama programs currently appearing on three commercial broadcast networks (ABC, CBS, and NBC) were videotaped September 25, 1994 through September 29, 1994. This time frame represents a nonsweeps period, and was chosen deliberately to avoid holidays and summertime, during which times the soap opera storylines often reflect the interests of a significantly larger-than-usual younger audience. The sample frame included one week's worth of 10 soap operas, representing 9 hours of programming each day, for a total of 45 hours of programming.

Coding Procedure

Key Demographics. All characters who appeared during the week were identified and coded using a 137-item coding instrument. Characters were coded on a number of key demographics: gender, age, ethnicity, current marital status, religious affiliation, socioeconomic status, and occupation.

With regard to the variable of age, coders were asked to determine which age category best represented the character's age: newborn/infant toddler (1–4 years), child (5–12 years), teens (13–19 years), young adult (20–24), adult (25–34 or 35–50); older adult (51–64 years) and senior citizen (65 and over). The variable, ethnicity, included the following categories: Caucasian, African American, Asian/Pacific Islander, Hispanic, and Native American/Alaskan Native. Coders were asked to identify the character's current marital status from among these categories: single, engaged, married, separated, divorced, widowed, and living together (not married). Each character's religious affiliation was coded as Christian, Jewish, Agnostic, or Atheist. Socioeconomic status of the character was based upon observation of dress, occupational role, home, apparent wealth, and living circumstances. Given these overall assessment criteria, each character was placed into one of five categories: wealthy/upper class, middle class, low income/working class, poor/poverty, and street person. Finally, concerning each character's occupational role, the following categories were included: small business owner (e.g., boutique), large business owner (e.g., international oil company), business person, doctor, nurse, lawyer, judge, clergy/religious, teacher, scientist, service worker (e.g., restaurant employee), manager, clerical, student, unskilled laborer, skilled tradesperson, sales, human services/social work, law enforcement, government official/politician, artist/entertainer, homemaker, private household employee (e.g. maid, butler, nanny), therapist, retired, unemployed, or lawbreaker.

Character Profile. In addition, characters were also coded as to their role (major/minor), goals, success of marital/intimate relationship, fidelity, marital history, health, drug and alcohol use/abuse, personality, and activities. Coders were also asked to indicate the number of episodes in the week each character appeared.

With regard to major or minor role, major characters were considered to be those characters without whom the storyline would not be the same; minor characters, on the other hand, were not critical to the telling of a story. Coders were asked to code only those minor characters who were continuing characters in the storyline: "extras"—for example, a waitress appearing in a given scene serving others in a restaurant—would not be coded.

Additional questions asked coders to indicate which goals motivated the characters' behaviors: improved social status; financial gain; personal happiness; happiness of other(s); family happiness/well-being; establishing or ending intimate, business, or friendship relationships; revenge; justice; professional achievement; ethnic or gender equality; entrapment of others; discovering a secret; loss of social or financial status of another; or loss of happiness of another.

Coders were asked to determine whether each character's marriage or intimate relationship was primarily successful (happy, functional), outwardly successful (having the appearance of being happy, functional), or primarily troubled (unhappy, dysfunctional). Additionally, characters were coded as to fidelity of their primary relationships: faithful, unfaithful, or unfaithful with intent to end the relationship. Based upon their viewing, coders were asked to indicate all appropriate descriptors of a character's marital history according to the following scheme: never married, married once, married twice, married three times, married more than three times, separated, divorced, widowed, and living together (not married).

Coders were asked to indicate whether a character was afflicted with any of the following: a physical handicap, disability, or abnormality; a physical illness requiring treatment; a physical injury requiring treatment; a mental illness or emotional disorder; or mental retardation.

For the question relating to medication and drugs, coders were asked to indicate the highest degree of a character's use: no reference to character taking drugs, taking drugs under the care of a physician, taking drugs without a physician's care, taking prescription drugs excessively, taking illicit drugs excessively, addicted to prescription drugs, or addicted to illicit drugs. Each character's use of alcohol was also coded in terms of the most appropriate category: no reference to alcohol abuse, drinks excessively, closet alcoholic, admitted alcoholic, or recovering alcoholic.

Finally, coders were asked to indicate descriptors of a character's personality/disposition as well as the activities in which the character was engaged during the episodes viewed.

Coder Training and Intercoder Reliability. Coders underwent extensive training prior to coding. These training sessions involved an intensive, line-by-line item review of the instrument, along with practice coding of videotaped scenes from a soap opera. (In order to preclude a priming effect, the scenes used for training were extraneous to the sample soap operas.) In total, each coder underwent approximately 8 hours of training. Upon completion of the training sessions, pairs of coders were assigned one week of a particular soap opera to be coded independently.

In all cases, soap operas were coded by "expert" coders. Coding assignments were based on the coders' knowledge and viewership of particular soaps. It has been determined that expert coders are better able than "naive" coders to provide valid responses to questions relating, especially, to character and family variables (Irwin & Cassata, 1993).

Intercoder reliabilities were calculated using Holsti's formula (1969). The coefficient of reliability for these variables were as follows: gender = 1.00; age = .72; ethnicity = .98; marital status = .77; religion = .85;

socioeconomic status = .79; occupation = .69; character role (major/minor) = .80; goals = .90; marital/intimate relationship success = .85; fidelity = .81; marital history = .70; health = 1.00; drug and alcohol use = .93; personality = .77; activities = .85.

RESULTS

Across the 45 hours of soap opera programming, 328 characters were identified and coded. The majority of the characters (75%) were between the ages of 20 and 50, and 16% were over 50. More specifically, 13% of the entire daytime serial drama population were identified as "older adults" (51–64 years old), and 3% were identified as senior citizens (65 years and over). Sixty-four percent of all older characters were men.

For the entire population of soap opera characters, 85% were Caucasian, 10% were African Americans, 3% were Hispanic, and .6% were Asian/Pacific Islanders. Almost all older characters (94%) on soap operas were Caucasian. The remaining older characters— all minor—were African American (2%) and Hispanic (4%) in the 51–64 year age range. All of the senior citizen characters were Caucasian. A breakdown of the daytime serial population by age and ethnicity is included in Table 12.1.

Table 12.2 shows a breakdown of older characters by individual soap opera. Nearly one fourth of all of the characters on *The Bold and The Beautiful* were older adults, whereas only 3% of *Another World*'s characters were over age 50. *Loving* featured a higher percentage of senior citizens (9%) than any other soap opera, and four shows (*One Life to Live, The Young and The Restless, The Bold and The Beautiful,* and *Another World*) included no senior citizen characters during the week of programming analyzed.

From the results of our analysis, there seems to be some question as to the prominence of older characters. Although the appearance of characters in up to three episodes per week was relatively consistent across all age groups, the appearance of characters in more than three episodes per week was skewed toward younger characters. Even though 21% of teens and adults up to age 50 appeared in three or more episodes, less than 5% of the older adults (51–64) and only 9% of the senior citizens appeared in more than three episodes.

In all, 51% of the characters were major, and 49% were minor. Although the older characters represented 16% of the entire soap opera population, they represented only 13% of the major characters. Even though older women represented 6% of the entire population, they represented only 3%

TABLE 12.1
Age Distribution of Soap Opera Characters by Ethnicity

Ethnicity	Newborn/ Infant	1–4	5–12	13–19	20–24
	(N) %	(N) %	(N) %	(N) %	(N) %
Caucasian					
Women	(1) 50	(1) 14	(2) 29	(7) 54	(18) 38
Men	0	(3) 43	(5) 71	(4) 31	(18) 38
African American					
Women	0	0	0	(1) 8	(2) 4
Men	0	0	0	(1) 8	(5) 11
Asian/Pacific Islander					
Women	0	0	0	0	0
Men	0	0	0	0	0
Hispanic					
Women	0	(1) 14	0	0	(2) 4
Men	0	0	0	0	(2) 4
Other/Cannot Code	(1) 50	(2) 29	0	0	0

Ethnicity	25-34	35-50	51-64	65+	Total
	(N) %	(N) %	(N) %	(N) %	N = 328
Caucasian					
Women	(49) 43	(32) 38	(10) 24	(7) 64	127
Men	(48) 42	(39) 46	(29) 69	(4) 36	150
African American					
Women	(7) 6	(3) 4	(1) 2	0	14
Men	(6) 5	(6) 7	0	0	18
Asian/Pacific Islander					
Women	0	(1) 1	0	0	1
Men	(1) 1	0	0	0	1
Hispanic					
Women	(1) 1	0	(1) 2	0	5
Men	(2) 2	0	(1) 2	0	5
Other/Cannot Code	(1) 1	(3) 4	0	0	7

of the major characters. Only 1% of all major characters were over age 65 (see Table 12.3).

The analysis of socioeconomic status of soap opera characters yielded interesting results with regard to older characters. Although 41% of the

TABLE 12.2
Distribution of Older Characters by Soap Opera

Soap Opera	All Characters (n = 328) %	51–64 yrs. (n = 42) %	Over 65 yrs. (n = 11) %
Loving	7	5	18
All My Children	11	14	9
One Life to Live	10	5	0
General Hospital	11	14	18
The Young and The Restless	8	2	0
The Bold and The Beautiful	8	14	0
As The World Turns	15	19	9
Guiding Light	10	14	18
Days of Our Lives	11	10	27
Another World	9	2	0

entire soap opera population was classified as either wealthy or upper class, approximately 68% of the characters over age 50 were classified as such, and looking at the senior citizens alone, nearly 82% of these characters fit the description of wealthy or upper class. Only 4% were classified as low-income or working-class citizens, whereas this socioeconomic group represented 10% of the entire population.

The soap opera episodes in our sample did not present enough information about older characters to determine the marital status for every character. However, 57% of the characters for whom this information was

TABLE 12.3
Major and Minor Characters

Characters	All Characters (n = 319) %	51–64 yrs. (n = 40) %	Over 65 yrs. (n = 11) %
Major Characters			
Women	24	10	9
Men	27	38	9
Minor Characters			
Women	22	20	55
Men	28	33	27

available were married. The next most frequently reported marital status, widowed, accounted for 17% of these characters. Of the 21 older married characters, 76% were in marriages characterized as primarily successful (happy, functional).

With regard to marital history, all older characters for whom information was available had been married at least one time. Nearly 66% of older characters had been married only once, and 24% of the older characters had been widowed. All older characters who had been married three or more times and/or separated were men, and two thirds of the older characters who were currently divorced or had been divorced were men.

The older population on soap operas was decidedly Christian (as were the overwhelming majority of all soap characters): Ninety-four percent were classified as such. Two percent of the older women were Jewish, and the religious affiliation of 4% of the older characters was not identifiable.

A great majority of older characters on soap operas for whom occupational information was observed during the week's episodes (91%) did work outside of their homes, with only 4% (women) retired, and 6% (women) classified as homemakers. The majority of working older characters were in business or medicine, with more characters portrayed as doctors than any other occupation. Nearly half of all older characters—but nearly twice as many men as women—were actually seen engaged in their occupations. Most all older working characters were in the age range of 51 to 64 years, with very few senior citizen characters employed outside the home.

Above all, happiness of others and family happiness were identified as the goals of older characters. They were not motivated by financial gain, improvement of their social status, power, professional achievement, establishment or ending intimate or business relationships or friendships, revenge, justice, or ethnic and gender equality.

Of the 42 older adult characters, about 10% had illnesses or injuries requiring treatment, 2.4% (male) were mentally ill, and another 2.4% (male) were retarded. Of the 11 senior citizen characters, only 9.1% had any type of health problem: specifically, a physical handicap.

This study also examined the drug and alcohol use of characters on soap operas. Ninety-four percent of the 53 older characters exhibited no use or abuse of drugs (either prescription drugs, over-the-counter drugs, or illicit drugs). Less than 6% of the characters were taking drugs under the care of a physician. Moreover, there was virtually no alcohol abuse, with only 1.9% of the characters (aged 51–64) identified as "recovering alcoholic."

Our analysis also provided information relating to the characters' personality/disposition and activities. The following descriptors were relevant for the majority of older characters: fair, sociable, strong, rational, stable, happy, peaceful, independent, assertive, caring, powerful, and honest. The primary activities in which older characters engaged during the week's episodes were conversing in person, giving support to others, and visiting other characters.

CONCLUSION

Our findings support the generalization that age distribution in daytime television soap operas does not depart from age distribution in prime-time dramatic programming in that it bulges in the middle and flattens out at both ends. In other words, our study reveals that daytime soap operas are populated with characters who are neither extremely young nor extremely old. More specifically, with regard to our focus on older persons, although there are four times as many such characters in the age range of 51 to 64 years as those who are 65 or older, their total numbers comprise only 16% of the characters in the soap opera world. When the analysis is extended to the real-life population, the study reveals that although the proportion of characters aged 51 to 64 is identical to the proportion of this age group in the U.S. population—13% ("Census," 1993)—the 65 and older demographic is grossly underrepresented on daytime television. Census figures for 1990 reported that 12.6% of the U.S. population is aged 65 and over ("Census," 1993), but our study shows that only 3% of all soap opera characters are in this age group. Even more telling is our finding that in a genre in which men across all age groups typically do not seriously outnumber women, and certainly hardly approaching the extent to which this occurs in prime time, still 64% of all the older people in our study are men, feeding the notion that ours is a youth-oriented television society in which men have the power and are permitted to age more gracefully and in greater numbers than women.

When focusing on ethnicity, the percentages for older characters are even more lopsided, with only 6% of their total numbers being other than Caucasian, namely one African American and two Hispanic characters. In addition, they were neither at the oldest end of the continuum, that is 65 or older, nor were they major characters in terms of their importance in the storyline. Placing ethnicity aside, the role of the older person in today's soap operas is that of a sounding board to whom younger characters rail about their problems or recant their hopes and their dreams. Perhaps, all things considered, it is this—their intergenerational presence—that is the older characters' most important function. Their presence not only completes the picture of life as it really is but, at the least, gives older people some semblance of visibility, however clouded.

Yet, when we weigh the minor roles older soap opera characters play today against the memorableness that this age group has managed to attain in soap operas over time, we come to the realization that they are indeed the survivors who, in their younger days, played prominent roles. They are the people who have matured and grown old, each along with their respective soap operas. Who can forget, for instance, the unforgettable Alice Horton of *Days of Our Lives*; the sly and manipulative Katherine Chancellor Sterling of *The Young and The Restless*; and *Guiding Light's* lovable illustrious senior rascals, H.B. Lewis and Henry Chamberlain? *All My Children* has its Phoebe Tyler Wallingford and Palmer Cortlandt; *As The World Turns*, the McCloskeys, Nancy and Dan; and *General Hospital*, Lila and Edward Quartermaine. Even though these are some of the elders who represent the vanguard of soap operadom, next to them and also creeping up in years are the second echelon citizenry—persons in their late 50s and 60s, who, by today's standards, may not be considered old at all. We find these people in greater numbers: *All My Children's* Adam and Stuart Chandler; *Loving's* Kate Slovinski; *One Life to Live's* Asa Buchanan; and *The Young and The Restless'* John Abbott. Among older ethnic characters, only three come to mind. In the recent past, there was the dynamic, strong-willed, and opinionated Greek duo of *Guiding Light*—Eleni's grandmother Ya Ya and Uncle Stavros, and in *Guiding Light's* early years, caring Papa Bauer.

All of the aforementioned notwithstanding, were we to profile the older person in our study across the various variables examined, we would have to conclude that their portrayals are positive: specifically, all older characters, especially those at the senior citizen's level, are at the upper end of the socioeconomic scale, and most of those who are married are in successful relationships. Although there were few senior citizens employed outside the home, an impressive number in the 51 to 64 year age range were observed in active occupational roles as professionals, who, when matched with "apparent wealth," we take to mean that they are not ready to hang it up. Their goals were assessed as being altruistic rather than self-serving; their general characteristics and their personality dispositions, laudably positive; and finally, their health was shown as being in good repair and free of addictions, enabling them to engage in supportive behaviors toward their younger counterparts. All in all, this is not a bad portrait, although we argue that it is lacking in real substance and representation.

In conclusion, whereas the overall profile of the older character on soap operas is positive, it is important to note that our study revealed that a larger proportion of older characters are minor characters, that is, characters whose absence would not be detrimental to the storylines. Additionally, soap operas seriously underrepresent the over-65 population, and more particularly, they minimize the ethnic element. If one considers the role that these portrayals may play in cultivating viewer attitudes, then one would expect that viewers would have a positive impression of older people but, at the same time, might question their significance in our lives. One must also consider that the negative messages of prime time with regard to the older person may override the positive messages of daytime. It appears to us that although daytime soap operas have consistently presented a more positive and equitable portrait of older people compared to prime time dramatic programs, still the gap between this age group and their younger counterparts needs to be addressed within the genre itself if a more socially responsible portrait of old age is to be communicated.

REFERENCES

Aronoff, C. (1974). Old age in prime time. *Journal of Communication, 24*(1), 86–87.

Beck, K. (1978). Television and the older woman. *Television Quarterly, 15*, 47–49.

Berry, G. L. (1988). Multicultural role portrayals on television as a social psychological issue. In S. Oskamp (Ed.), *Television as a social issue* (pp. 118–127). Newbury Park, CA: Sage.

Buerkel-Rothfus, N., & Mayes, S. (1981). Soap opera viewing: The cultivation effect. *Journal of Communication, 31*(3), 108–115.

Cassata, M., Anderson, P., & Skill, T. (1983). Images of old age on daytime. In M. Cassata & T. Skill, (Eds.), *Life on daytime television: Tuning-in American serial drama* (pp. 37–44). Norwood, NJ: Ablex.

Census of population and housing, 1990: Summary tape 3 U.S. (1993). [Machine-readable files]. Washington, D.C.: The Bureau of the Census.

Collymore, T. (1995a, February 14). Black-Lash. *Soap Opera Digest, 20*(4), 36–42.

Collymore, T. (1995b, July 18). Black-Lash. *Soap Opera Digest, 20*(15), 42-46.

Dail, P. W. (1988). Prime-time television's portrayals of older adults in the context of family life. *The Gerontologist, 28*, 700–706.

Davis, R.H., & Davis, J.A. (1986). *TV's image of the elderly*. Lexington, MA: Lexington.

Davis, R.H., & Kubey, R.W. (1982). Growing old on television and with television. In D. Pearl, et al. (Eds.), *Television and behavior: Ten years of scientific progress and implications for the eighties* (Vol. 2, pp. 201–208). Technical Reports, Washington, D.C.: U.S. Department of Health and Human Services.

Downing, M. (1975). *The world of daytime serial drama.* Unpublished doctoral dissertation, Annenberg School of Communication, University of Pennsylvania, Philadelphia.

Elliott, J. C. (1984). The daytime television drama portrayal of older adults. *The Gerontologist, 24*, 628–633.

Gade, E. (1971). Representation of the world of work in daytime television serials. *Journal of Employment Counseling*, 37–42.

Gerbner, G., Gross, L., Signorelli, N., & Morgan, M. (1980). Aging with television: Images on television drama and conceptions of social reality. *Journal of Communication, 30*(1), 37–47.

Greenberg, B. (1986). Minorities and the mass media. In J. Bryant & D. Zillman (Eds.), *Perspectives on media effects* (pp. 165–188). Hillsdale, NJ: Lawrence Erlbaum Associates.

Greenberg, B. (1988). Some uncommon television images and the drench hypothesis. In S. Oskamp (Ed.), *Television as a social issue* (pp. 89–102). Newbury Park, CA: Sage.

Greenberg, B., Korzenny, F., & Atkin, C. (1980). Trends in the portrayal of the elderly. In B. Greenberg (Ed.), *Life on television* (pp. 23–33). Norwood, NJ: Ablex.

Greenberg, B., Neuendorf, K., Buerkel-Rothfuss, N., & Henderson, L. (1982). The soaps: What's on and who cares? *Journal of Broadcasting, 26*(2), 519–535.

Hiemstra, R., Goodman, M., Middlemiss, M. A., Vosco, R., & Ziegler, N. (1983). How older persons are portrayed in television advertising: Implications for educators. *Educational Gerontology, 9*, 111–122.

Hinton, J. L., Seggar, J. F., Northcott, H. C., & Fontes, B. F. (1974). Tokenism and improving imagery of blacks in TV drama and comedy: 1973. *Journal of Broadcasting, 18*(4), 423–432.

Holsti, O. (1969). *Content analysis for the social sciences and humanities.* Reading, MA: Addison-Wesley.

Huston, A. C., Donnerstein, E., Fairchild, H., Feshbach, N. D., Katz, P. A., Murray, J. P., Rubinstein, E. A., Wilcox, B. L., & Zuckerman, D. (1992). *Big world, small screen.* Lincoln, NE: University of Nebraska Press.

Irwin, B. (1990). *An Oral history of a piece of Americana: The soap opera experience.* Unpublished doctoral dissertation, State University of New York at Buffalo.

Irwin, B., & Cassata, M. (1993, November). *Families on daytime television: The cultural indicators perspective.* Paper presented at the annual meeting of the Speech Communication Association, Miami, FL.

James, C. L. (1991). *Soap opera mythology and racial-ethnic social change: An Analysis of African American, Asian/Pacific American, and Mexican/Hispanic American story lines during the 1980s.* Unpublished doctoral dissertation, University of California at San Diego.

Korzenny, F., & Neuendorf, K. (1980). Television viewing and self-concept of the elderly. *Journal of Communication, 30*(1), 71–80.

Northcott, H. C. (1975). Too young, too old—Age in the world of television. *The Gerontologist, 15*, 184–186.

The Numbers speak for themselves. (1995, February 14). *Soap Opera Digest, 20*(4), 42.

Perse, E. M. (1986). Soap opera viewing patterns of college students and cultivation. *Journal of Broadcasting and Electronic Media, 30*(2), 175–193.

Peterson, M. (1973). The visibility and image of old people on television. *Journalism Quarterly, 50*, 569–573.

Pierce, C. M. (1980). Social trace contaminants: Subtle indicators of racism in TV. In S. B. Withey & R. P. Abeles (Eds.), *Television and social behavior: Beyond violence toward children.* Hillsdale, NJ: Lawrence Erlbaum Associates.

Powell, L., & Williamson, J. (1985). The mass media and the aged. *Social Policy, 16*, 38–49.

Rubin, A. M. (1982). Directions in television and aging research. *Journal of Broadcasting, 26*(2), 537–551.

Seggar, J. F, Hafen, J., & Hannonen-Gladden, H. (1981). Television's portrayals of minorities and women in drama and comedy drama, 1971–1980. *Journal of Broadcasting, 25*(3), 277–288.

Serock, K. E. (1979). *An analysis of the portrayal of the elderly in television commercials viewed by children.* Unpublished doctoral dissertation, University of Maryland.

Williams, M., & Condry, J. (1989, April). *Living color: Minority portrayals and cross-racial interactions on television.* Paper presented at the meeting of the Society for Research in Child Development, Kansas City, MO.

Wober, M. (1980). *Television and old people: Viewing TV and perceptions of old people in real life and on television.* London: Independent Broadcasting Authority.

13

The Image of Aging
in Television Commercials:
An Update for the 1990s

Wendy J. Hajjar
University of New Orleans

By coincidence, the first day of programming videotaped for this study was the 50th anniversary of VE Day, the day that the Allied forces declared victory over the Axis powers in Europe on May 8, 1945, marking the beginning of the end of World War II. CBS News covered President Clinton's appearance at a veterans' celebration live from Arlington Cemetery, Virginia, suspending regular programming for about an hour. The celebrants included thousands of World War II veterans and their families. As the camera panned the crowd, it revealed for television an unprecedented vision of the nation's elders. To place this study in perspective, even a year of television advertisements would not yield numbers nearing the size of the crowd appearing live before those cameras, but like the military that indoctrinated so many soldiers into its ranks some 50 years ago, television commercials continue to present a uniform cultural vision of aging, a vision that is largely White, predominately male, void of ethnic distinction, and not especially old.

The three American television networks, ABC, NBC, and CBS, have been criticized for avoiding portrayals of aging and for promoting negative stereotypes in the few older characters that do appear, but two changes warrant reexamination of the image of aging in the 1990s. First, the population is significantly older than it was even a decade ago. Because society has been steadily aging and life expectancy has more than trebled in the last century,[1] there are more older television viewers than ever before. Second, with the growth in other media channels and the waning influence

---

[1] Americans over 65 were 4% of the population in 1900. By the year 2000, this population will exceed 12%, climbing toward 20% by the end of the next century (United States, 1989).

of the three television networks, younger and wealthier audiences are exploring a wider range of program options in satellite, cable television, video rental and other media. As a result, smaller, more specialized audiences of various constituencies are increasingly attractive to advertisers. Thus, there is reason to hope that the portrayal of aging might improve as advertisers seek out an older market. According to Jones (1991), 42% of NBC's prime-time audience is currently over 50 years old, giving today's elders more clout than any previous generation of older consumers. This is especially true in the niche market media such as local broadcast television that rely more on older consumer dollars. Minkler (1989) contended that the elder consumer now has greater power, especially the middle-aged to young-old known as the gray market.

Responding to the interest in gray-market dollars, some modest improvements have been demonstrated in network programs with strong, likable older characters in programs such as *Murder She Wrote*, *Matlock*, and *The Golden Girls*. Whether this new recognition has translated into improved characterizations in television commercials has yet to be demonstrated. Advertisements are ideally suited to signify a change in cultural perception of aging because they are highly controlled messages represented in purchased time when the promotion of particular images is motivated by sales goals. At the very least, the advertiser will wish not to offend the potential customer. However, if elder consumers are seen as a primary target market, advertisers may strategically employ positive images of aging. Thus, the purpose of this study is to assess the portrayal of aging in daytime television commercials to determine whether recognition of the gray market has visibly improved the treatment of aging.

More specifically, four research questions frame this study:

1. What percentage of daytime television commercials characters are older?
2. How are older characters distributed by sex and ethnicity?
3. How do older characters in commercials in the 1990s compare with the target market population?
4. What types of advertisers are the sources that produce positive and negative images of aging in television commercials?

A review of pertinent literature establishes a framework for a content analysis of the cultural image of aging in commercials.

LITERATURE REVIEW

In 20 years of research, scholars have consistently found unfavorable images of aging in advertising. Invisibility is almost universally cited as the primary problem, particularly invisibility of the oldest old and elders of ethnic backgrounds (Dail, 1988; Harris & Feinberg, 1977; Northcott, 1975). Excluding the occasional prominent obituary, research indicates that the media rarely features anyone over the age of 70. Thus, conclusions about the improvement or decline in the quality of their portrayal over time are difficult to determine, yet the qualitative portrait of aging that emerges from the research reveals several notable trends: a bias toward youth, a bias favoring males, and a White ethnic bias.

A youth bias is evident in studies that show that when older actors do appear in commercials, they tend to exhibit markedly negative characteristics such as weakness, dependency on younger characters, failure, and unattractiveness. For example, Harris and Feinberg (1977) described the older characters in television commercials as unflattering, unhealthy, and unstylish, and Hess (1974) contended that invisibility is inevitable. The elderly make "poor copy," reminding us of role loss, deprivations, and ultimate demise (p.80). Hess argued that these qualities are not commercially helpful product associations.

Northcott (1975) found that older men suffered more than their average share of problems, contrasted with attractively portrayed young men on whom they relied on. However, older men seem to fare better than the women in television commercials, resulting in a male bias. Aronoff (1974) found higher failure associated with aging for females whereas Harris and Feinberg (1977) found that authority and esteem increased with age for men but not for women. They concluded that advertisers still preferred young women to sell their products, but that age represented more of an asset for men. Francher (1973) noted that age seemed

> to be more flexible in the case of the male character, reflecting the inclination of American society of holding the woman more accountable for physically aging than the man. Men as seen in advertising copy are permitted graying temples and a certain cragginess of face so long as the image of virility and sexual appeal are maintained. (p. 248)

The research indicates an ethnic bias as well. Most characters in commercials are White (Bush, Solomon & Hair, 1977; Weigel, Loomis & Soja, 1980), but few studies have looked at both age and ethnicity together. Ethnic characters so rarely appear in samples of television commercials that drawing conclusions about their improvement is difficult from an examination of the data alone (Greenberg & Brand, 1994). This is particularly true for older characters that are neither White nor Black. Because they are rarely featured, they are less likely to be studied. However, a comprehensive sample taken from a 3-year study by Gerbner, Gross, Signorelli, & Morgan (1980) indicated that one in five commercials contains Black characters. Hispanic characters appear in nearly 2% of prime-time commercials. However, they argue that ethnicity is most conspicuously absent among the oldest portrayals, who tend to be White, male, and not especially old.

Furthermore, these studies suggest there may be a trend toward certain production styles characteristic of the image of aging in commercials. Role prominence, for example, which has been used to distinguish between major and minor portrayals, indicates that aging characters tend to appear in minor, often nonspeaking roles (Greenberg, Korzenn,y & Atkin, 1979; Northcott, 1975). Prominence alone does not account for range and variability of character types. Aging has also been associated with patently negative qualities such as lack of authority and physical weakness (Harris & Feinberg, 1977), useful primarily because they identify the recurrent stereotypes of aging. Together, these studies show how aging characterizations are employed in commercials. Tending not to occupy lead or protagonist roles, negative characteristics result from the appearance of age as subordinate to youth. Aging actors are most frequently cast as dramatic foil or mere scenic backdrop. Most important for this study, the research suggests that insight can be derived from the identification of the narrative conventions that preclude character depth (Seiter, 1986).

Studies of the portrayal of ethnic minority groups (Poindexter & Stroman, 1981; Weigel, Loomis, & Soja, 1980), and women (Simonton, 1995) suggest the relevance of additional attributes. Cross-race interaction, for example, has been used to identify ethnic character subordination, but it also can indicate whether age and ethnic integration are enacted or merely simulated through juxtaposition of images. Taken together, these studies suggest that the image of aging in television commercials is largely a function of the way various character traits are encoded in each portrayal. The methodological goal, then, is to determine how best to decode commercial character portrayals.

METHOD

Sample Selection

The sample is selected from daytime television commercials in an urban area (New Orleans) with an ethnically diverse local population. Three procedures used here intentionally bias the sample to ensure the most favorable universe for the representation of aging. First, daytime television is chosen to maximize the importance of older consumers to advertisers. Although prime time television has higher overall numbers of older (and younger) viewers, the daytime demographic is proportionately older than any other day part. Second, a higher proportion of the daytime audience is female in all age groups (Schreiber & Boyd, 1980). Because older women have tended to be poorly represented in previous image research, care is taken to enhance the possibility of a stronger feminine representation. Third, the sample is restricted to those channels available through Cox Communications, the New Orleans cable delivery system, that has the highest ratings among older viewers (Nielsen, 1993). Changes in the distribution of audiences suggest the need to study cable channels to provide a more valid accounting than studies based on samples of network television alone. Furthermore, the sample is taken in a high density Black Area (Nielsen, 1993), with a significant level of Hispanic and Asian population (6%) as well. This increases the likelihood that local advertisers would make an overt attempt to target multicultural audiences with correspondingly diverse imagery.

Gathered from 11 days of daytime television, excluding weekends, the coded sample represents 61½ hours of programming videotaped in 6-hour segments, from 9:00 a.m. to 3:00 p.m. cdt, Monday through Friday. The sampling strategy sought 72 total hours of programming in order to have at least 60 commercial television hours[2] for coding. A 60-hour target sample is somewhat arbitrarily chosen as a number larger than previous published studies have used. Among researchers conducting content studies of elder images, no consensus determines the required number of characterizations for inferences, but most look at fewer than 100 characters in samples of less than 30 hours. The numbers of elder characters studied range from 7 (Northcott, 1975), to approximately 180 (one third of a 3-year sample, Gerbner, et al., 1980). However, as a general rule, a large sample bears less risk of being atypical of the whole. Additionally, for measurement purposes, a large sample drawn from consecutive weekdays at any period produces comparable results to a sample drawn randomly throughout the year (Wimmer & Dominick, 1994).

Videotapes used for the study are labeled 1 through 15,[3] corresponding to the list of television networks with the most appeal to an older audience.

---

[2]Five and one-half hours of taped programming were eliminated from the coding process; 2 hours of religious programming aired without commercials, and 3½ hours of children's cartoons.

[3]Television stations in the coded sample are WVUE (ABC, New Orleans), WWL (CBS, New Orleans), WDSU (NBC, New Orleans), WTBS, A & E, TNT, USA, LIFE, BET, FAM, and WNOL (FOX, New Orleans).

Then, videotape selection is ordered using a random number table to designate the sequence of recording dates and a replacement. The local cable system failed twice during the sample weeks, resulting in an initial loss of 6 hours. Taping continued on successive weekdays from May 8 until May 24, 1995, when adequate replacement hours were achieved.

Content Categories

In a content analysis, characterizations need to be aggregated into meaningful units to permit description. In this study, commercials are indexed by television station, time, target audience, and product, and characters are nominally coded in three demographic categories: age, ethnicity, and sex. Characters are assigned a code representing the category of production style used in the commercial. Production styles coded are montage, testimonial, dramatic scenario, celebrity endorsement, noncelebrity endorsement, business owner/spokesperson, and multivoice testimonial. Coders then evaluate the portrayal using a list of adjectives. Portrayals are rated as positive, negative, or neutral, based on the perception of the coder regarding the characterization. The coding categories are explained further on.

Arbitration between age coders who might disagree on age assignment is often resolved by relying solely on visual cues such as gray hair, wrinkles, or the stereotypes of aging that they are attempting to evaluate. These are subjective criteria that can lead to circular conclusions, identifying stereotypical images through establishing coding stereotypes that compromise validity (Harris & Feinberg, 1977). Perhaps this is due to overreliance on student coders, who are likely to apply strictly visual cues, but even with the most rigorous coding procedures, coding for age becomes increasingly subjective as the age of the coded participants increases.

Because coding for age is the object of this study, a system had to be devised that was both flexible enough to be functional and rigid enough to apply with consistency. Precise age categorization is not possible based on visual cues alone, so additional information must be used to estimate age. For purposes of this study, coders are instructed to use five indicators in making age attributions: a. known or overtly stated age over 60 years, (b) physical attributes such as gray hair, balding, or wrinkles, (c) activities such as retirement or nursing home care and artifacts such as historical clothing or popular culture references, (d) stereotyped characteristics such as exaggerated clothing and props (shawls, canes, ear trumpets, or rocking chairs), and (e) relational characteristics[4] such as the presence of adult children and grandchildren.

---

[4]Age of offspring can be used to extrapolate the age of the parent. Commercials remain rigid generationally, illustrating age appropriateness for marriage, childbearing and grandparenting, among other life events.

Coding for sex is less ambiguous than age, requiring only a distinction between male and female characterizations. However, coding ethnicity is complicated by standard coding practices that only distinguish between common racial categories, such as White and Black, based solely on physical appearance codes.[5] Obviously, a binary (Black/White) coding system cannot reflect cultural diversity even if past studies indicate that not much ethnic variance is expected. So, in addition to the Black/White coding distinction, the category of Other is used. However, to accurately depict the ethnic portrait, coding is augmented with a verbal description of all overt cultural references to give the best chance of identifying ethnicity in the elders portrayed.

The production style category is established to determine whether distinctions in the treatment of aging might be a reflection of the generic distinctions between commercials of different production styles. Because this distinction has not been made in prior image studies, the subcategories established here are somewhat tentatively offered. Stylistic distinctions first observed are montage, testimonial, dramatic scenario, and celebrity endorsement. After testing the coding procedures on a small pilot sample, the testimonial category is expanded to account for attributes not clearly represented in the first coding: noncelebrity endorsement, business owner/spokesperson, and multivoice testimonial. Seven production styles are coded in all: montage, testimonial, dramatic scenario, celebrity endorsement, noncelebrity endorsement, business owner/spokesperson, and multivoice testimonial. Each of these is explained in the following section.

A montage is a commercial constructed from a series of still or nearly still images used more to evoke mood than to tell a story. A montage might contain multiple character images, depending on the length of each camera shot and the number of people in each frame. A testimonial is a statement about the virtues of an advertised product, constructed to appear as though solicited from a consumer. The dramatic scenario contains multiple features common to narrative presentations, such as character, scene, costuming, and plot. A celebrity endorsement lends the celebrity's image to the commercial product. A noncelebrity spokesperson uses an unknown to represent the product. A noncelebrity may also be a business owner who serves as spokesperson for his or her own company or product. The final stylistic category is the multivoice testimonial comprised of remarks made by more

---

[5]Ethnic coding schemes based on census categories tend to make only overt distinctions. Thus 85% of the U.S. population claims to be White. Italian and White or Nigerian and Black violate category exclusivity other ethnic designations such as Hispanic and Mideastern, obscure with assimilation. Multiethnic actors and cosmetics further obscure ethnicity. Coding requires additional information such as a language, accent, name, or clothing cue.

than one person. Each character is coded with the primary style illustrated in the commercial.

Finally, the category of positive and negative character attributes is evaluated using a list of adjectives culled from previous studies of aging on television. The positive attributes are successful, good, friendly, credible, worthy of respect, active, attractive, independent, and stylish. Negative attributes are unsuccessful, evil, unfriendly, not credible, inactive, unattractive, dependent, and unstylish. One additional negative attribute was added to the list after the sample coding procedure when two coders independently suggested that "irritating" or "annoying" ought to be included. Coders rate each character favorable or unfavorable, based on the presence of one or more of the character attributes. Characters not clearly positive or negative are coded neutral.

The Coding Process

After a brief instruction and practice session on the definition and use of the coding categories, two coders were given one page of verbal coding instructions, a set of videotapes, and blank coding sheets on which to record responses. Coders used a remote control device to stop and review tape as necessary. In all, 4,617 commercial characters were evaluated by two independent coders. Reliability estimates were calculated using approximately 5% of the total sample. Intercoder agreement was 82%.

RESULTS

The number of characterizations derived from each of the eleven television stations and distinguished by age, sex and ethnicity is displayed in Table 13.1. There are 355 characters over age 60, 8% of the 4,617 total sample. Male dominance and White ethnic dominance are both pronounced in the older age bracket. The over-60 characterizations are 70% male and 30% female; 84% White, 14% Black, and 2% Other.

When characterizations are distinguished by production style, ethnicity and sex, other patterns are evident. Most striking is the absence of ethnic characters in several categories, as the data in Table 13.2 indicate. Where Black and Other ethnic groups are represented, they tend to be clustered in the montage or multivoice testimonials, rarely as primary spokesperson for a product. Dramatic scenarios account for the majority of observations of White characterizations, but the Other ethnic groups are not represented in

TABLE 13.1
Characters from Each TV Station by Age, Sex, and Ethnicity

TV	Characters Char	Age 60+	Sex M	F	Ethnicity W	B	O
FOX	391	29	17	12	11	18	0
LIFE	441	36	22	14	35	1	0
TNT	297	26	17	9	23	3	0
CBS	491	38	27	11	37	1	0
FAM	458	31	24	7	31	0	0
A&E	422	28	21	7	25	2	1
BET	385	31	27	4	13	16	2
WTBS	235	37	27	10	33	3	1
ABC	540	23	14	9	22	1	0
USA	415	32	23	9	28	2	2
NBC	542	44	29	15	40	2	2
Total	4617	355	248	107	298	49	8

Note. M = Male, F = Female, W = White, B = Black, O = Other.

TABLE 13.2
Older Characterizations by Ethnicity, Sex and Production Style

Production Style	White N	%	Black N	%	Other N	%
			Ethnicity With Males			
Montage	49	14	28	8	1	0
Multivoice Testimony	13	4	2	1	7	1
Dramatic Scenario	68	19	0	—	0	—
Celebrity Endorsement	12	3	0	—	0	—
Owner Spokesman	47	13	5	1	0	—
Non Celebrity	13	4	3	1	0	—
			Ethnicity With Females			
Montage	34	10	8	2	0	—
Multivoice Testimony	9	3	0	—	0	—
Dramatic Scenario	32	9	0	—	0	—
Celebrity Endorsement	13	4	0	—	0	—
Owner Spokesman	0	—	0	—	0	—
Non Celebrity	8	2	3	1	0	—

Note. N = 355

that category, nor are older ethnic characters represented in celebrity endorsements. Black males fare better than Black females and Other ethnic groups of both sexes, with 1% of the sample product spokesperson in the area of business owner.

The favorability ratings in Table 13.3 show that when characters are distinguished by product and production style, other trends are evident. More positive than negative attributes were found. Table 13.3 indicates that 48% of older characters are evaluated as favorable, and 8% are evaluated as unfavorable.[6] In addition, more than half of the favorable characterizations are clustered in the two product categories of food and beverage, and financial and insurance. The unfavorable characterizations are largely clustered in the area of medical and pharmaceutical products. In terms of the production styles, the dramatic scenario accounts for the majority of both favorable and unfavorable portrayals. With 35 observations, the owner spokesperson category supplies 20% of the favorable characterizations.

CONCLUSION

Most studies declare areas of underrepresentation based on the demographic portrait of the sample, but although Blacks comprise about 12% of the national population, the ethnic proportion varies widely by locality.[7] For a medium such as television, with strong national and local representation, there is no single appropriate comparative. In this sample, drawn liberally to ensure inclusion, older Blacks represent 14% of the over-60 sample, which underrepresents the local Black population but would be considered comparative overrepresentation nationally. Other ethnic groups are distinctly underrepresented locally, comprising 2% of the sample. However, census data indicate 2% is in line with the national population. Males are represented disproportionately relative to females, reversing the population trend where 60% of the over 65 population in society is female in all ethnic groups (Bureau of the Census, 1989).

In addition, the discrepancies between male and female portrayals attributed to male bias tend to collapse two dimensions: male dominance and male preference. Male dominance is established quantitatively in the relative frequency of male and female portrayals, but male preference is established in some measure of valence, the positive and negative dimensions that indicate more favorable treatment for male characters.

---

[6]Neutral characterizations (157) equal 44% of the sample.

[7]According to U. S. Census, 30% of the state of Louisiana and 60% of the city of New Orleans are Black. Hispanics and Asians comprise about 6% (United States, 1989).

TABLE 13.3
Favorability Ratings by Product Type and Production Style

			Production Style				
Product	Drama	Mont.	Owner	Celeb	Nceleb	Multi	Total
			Favorable Characterizations				
Food/Bev.	27	12	2	2	2	16	61
Fin./Ins.	18	1	12	2	0	0	33
Med./Phar.	1	0	3	1	4	0	9
Leis./Ent.	0	6	6	4	1	0	17
Clean/Repair	5	0	4	4	2	2	17
Furn./Trans.	0	0	8	7	3	0	18
Telecomm.	4	2	0	0	1	0	7
Pers./Cosm.	0	1	0	2	6	0	9
Total	55	22	35	22	19	18	171
			Unfavorable Characterizations				
Food/Bev.	3	0	0	0	0	0	3
Fin./Ins.	0	0	0	0	0	0	0
Med./Phar.	9	2	0	0	5	0	16
Leis./Ent.	1	0	0	0	0	0	1
Clean/Repair	3	0	0	0	2	0	5
Furn./Trans.	0	0	0	0	1	0	1
Telecomm.	0	0	0	0	0	0	0
Pers./Cosm.	1	0	0	0	0	0	1
Total	17	2	0	0	8	0	27

Note. Production styles are: Dramatic Scenario, Montage, Owner/Spokesperson, Celebrity Testimonial, Noncelebrity Testimonial, Multivoice Testimonial. Product Categories are: Food/Beverage, Financial/Insurance, Medical/Pharmaceutical, Leisure/Entertainment, Household Cleaning/Repair, Home Furnishings/Transportation, Telecommunications, and Personal Care/ Cosmetics.

Conclusions about the valence of the portrayal of severely underrepresented groups are suspect from the examination of data alone. Even comparatively large samples (e.g., Gerbner, et al., 1980) find such low cell sizes, particularly regarding older ethnic females, that any further manipulations are problematic. That is true of this sample as well. However, the finding that production style affects characterization offers a means to examine the origin of both favorable and unfavorable attributes. The images represented here demonstrate distinct regularities identifiable in the ways aging is encoded by advertisers. The style of the production determines, among other attributes, the degree of prominence of the elder portrayal and the degree of realism in the portrayal.

Not as clear from the tables is the tendency to feature Black characters largely in the role of entertainers. The ethnic distribution of characterizations shows 15 of the 17 favorable observations in the category leisure and entertainment category and 12 in the same product category rated neutral are Black. In addition, 10 of the favorable observations in the food and beverage montages are Black entertainers, accounting for 37 of the total 49 older Black characters. Of these, 13 Black characters have speaking roles. The only ads using cross-ethnic interaction are in the business owner/spokesperson category. Otherwise, integration is simulated with the montage and multivoice testimonials.

Commercial imagery has not kept pace with the clear trend of aging in the population. Aging in commercials bears little resemblance to the increasingly older and healthier population it represents, and it may never do so. Other populations might use the metaphor of a mirror to explain the reflection of their culture, however distorted the resulting image, but age is marginalized to a degree that it is not reflective of real world aging at all.

As Gerbner et al. (1980) noted some years ago, the demographics of the television world reflected the spending curve more than the population curve, largely male and White. These relations still hold. Because the overall number of elder characters remains comparatively low, the appearance of one or two regular recurring images or characterizations has a significant effect on the sample. Thus, a single commercial shown multiple times can create the statistical appearance of age and diversity, yet little diversity is truly evident in this sample. More than 60 hours of programming yielded no images of older female characters who were not White or Black.

The most realistic are testimonials and a few dramatic scenarios. For male images, the business owners/spokesperson for their companies create the most colorful and prominent advertising characters. Most importantly, because they own the businesses they promote, they stay in control of their own image portrayals. Virtually all other characters are at the mercy of those who determine how images are employed. Even celebrities risk compromising their images with negative associations from elder products such as denture adhesives or incontinence aids.

The dramatic scenarios here feature Italian families in order to sell cheese and detergent. In these dramas, the family is a plausible reflection of reality. Without concealing the signs of aging, elders are used because the family configuration they represent creates helpful product associations such as tradition and stability. However, the majority of commercials use young, nuclear families. Multigenerational ethnic families seem abnormal by contrast. The symbolic relationship of elders to their families is peripheral and needy, inherently problematic to the nuclear families who continually reject them. Elders are routinely entreated to buy pharmaceuticals, invest in financial plans, and purchase home security systems, all in order to maintain independence from the young.

Chosen for their symbolic characteristics, the older images are more iconic than realistic, symbolizing values such as tradition, simplicity, intrusiveness or dependency. Portrayed in montage or in dramatic scenarios, positive portrayals tend to reside outside families. Elder images are meant to unify the audience in a shared, sanitized vision of cultural assimilation that belies real aging families with diverse roots in class and culture.

Commercials aimed at older audiences do create a more positive view of maturity, but there are too few here to impact the sample. This is the paradox in the relationship between advertisers and the elder market today. Even though the oldest consumers have built the longest loyalties with advertisers they are courted with little effort from advertisers who still commit greater resources to young consumers. As the baby boomers born after World War II continue to age, greater concern is being devoted to aging, but it is largely in anticipation of the market potential of this soon-to-be-older population.

Finally, media and the advertised products they supports are the most lucrative exports from the United States in this global economy, accounting for some 20% percent of domestic revenues. These messages promote not only products but also the western values they symbolize, values that ultimately affect the treatment of a society's elders. But literature that argues for the elimination of stereotypes of aging to remedy imbalance may be focused on perfecting a single, idealized image of aging when perhaps higher visibility and cultural diversity are the more important goals. The idealized image is too easily co-opted. Creating a world populated by only a few vigorous, important elders, television imagery continues to distort the presence of the old in society, further disempowering and alienating the misrepresented group, that is largely female and still invisible.

REFERENCES

Aronoff, C. (1974). Old age in prime time. *Journal of Communication, 24*, 86–87.

Bush, R. F., Solomon, P. J., & Hair, J. F. (1977). There are more blacks in TV commercials. *Journal of Advertising Research, 17*, 21–25.

Dail, P. W. (1988). Prime-time television portrayals of

older adults in the context of family life. *The Gerontologist, 28,* 700–706.

Francher, J. S. (1973). "It's the Pepsi Generation. ...": Accelerated aging and the television commercial. *International Journal of Aging and Human Development, 4,* 245–255.

Gerbner, G., Gross, L., Signorelli, N., & Morgan, M. (1980).Aging with television: Images in television drama and concepts of social reality. *Journal of Communication, 30,* 37–41.

Greenberg, B. S., & Brand, J. E. (1994). Minorities in the mass media: 1970s to 1980s. In J. Bryant & D. Zillman (Eds.) *Media effects: Advances in theory and research* (pp. 273–314). Hillsdale, NJ: Lawrence Erlbaum Associates.

Greenberg, B. S., Korzenny, F., & Atkin, C. (1979). The portrayal of the aging: Trends on commercial television. *Research on Aging, 1,* 319–334.

Harris, A. J., & Feinberg, J. F. (1977). Television and aging: Is what you see what you get? *The Gerontologist, 17,* 464–468.

Hess, B. B. (1974). Stereotypes of the aged. *Journal of Communication, 24,* 76–85.

Jones, R. (1991, October 21). Are viewers getting older at NBC? *Mediaweek, 5.*

Minkler, M. (1989). Gold in gray: Reflections on business' discovery of the elderly market. *The Gerontologist, 29,* 17–23.

Nielsen, A. C. (1993). *Nielsen television index.* Northbrook, Il: Nielsen.

Northcott, H. C. (1975). Too young, too old: Aging in the world of television. *The Gerontologist, 15,* 184–186.

Poindexter, P. M., & Stroman, C. A. (1981). Blacks and television: A review of the research literature. *Journal of Broadcasting, 25,* 103–122.

Seiter, E. (1986). Stereotypes and the media: A reevaluation. *Journal of Communication, 36,* 14–26.

Schreiber, E., & Boyd, D. (1980). How the elderly perceive television commercials. *Journal of Communication, 30,* 61–70.

Simonton, A. (1995). Women for sale. In C. M. Lont (Ed.) *Women and media: Content, careers and criticism* (pp. 143-164). Albany, NY: Wadsworth.

U.S. Department of Commerce, Bureau of the Census (1989). Current Population Reports. *Statistical Abstracts.* Washington, DC: U. S. Government Printing Office.

Weigel, R. H., Loomis, J. W., & Soja, M. J. (1980). Race relations on prime time television. *Journal of Personality and Social Psychology, 39,* 884–893.

Wimmer, R. D., & Dominick, J. R. (1994). *Mass media research: An introduction* (4th ed.). Belmont, CA: Wadsworth.

EPILOGUE

Hana S. Noor Al-Deen
University of North Carolina at Wilmington

Generally speaking, the societal contributions of elders have helped younger generations to enjoy better lives. Because of such contributions, many societies around the globe, particularly traditional ones, view their elders as the pillars of their societies. As reciprocity, younger generations tend to make sure that their elders spend their autumn years with dignity and respect. Still, youth-oriented societies, such as the United States, are inclined to overlook the contributions of their elders and instead focus on qualities that younger people usually enjoy, such as attractiveness, vitality, strength, and so on, when dealing with old age. Both of these stances, traditional and youth oriented, are certainly rooted in nations' cultures. Hall and Hall (1990) explained in their book *Understanding Cultural Differences* that "culture...guide[s] the actions and responses of human beings in every walk of life" (p. 3). Samovar and Porter (1995) added in their book *Communication Between Cultures* that "the content of our repertory of communicative behaviors depends largely on the culture in which we have been raised" (p. 44).

All too often, this culture overlooks the neglect, abuse, and ridicule of elders, and such attitudes are nonchalantly passed on to our younger generations. It is even more disturbing to observe that the hardships that our elders face have been portrayed as amusing and entertaining. An example drawn from a popular television show serves as a good case in point. Each week, millions of television viewers tune in to a successful youth-oriented comedy entitled, "The Wayans Brothers." The show begins its nightly humor by featuring an elder woman being tossed through the air after being hit by a bus. Apparently, the regard for our elders has dwindled to such a low point that they are now worthy of being used as the vehicular cannon fodder to garner "yuk yuks" from youths in the audience.

Considering the upcoming, massive generation of elders—baby boomers—it is essential that we rethink our perspectives about elders and aging. Then, we, citizens and researchers alike, can truly realize that the current state-of-affairs under which our senior citizens live is in need of some profound changes as we prepare to embark on the next millennium. Research such as contained in this volume, which has dealt with issues ranging from technology to popular culture, may serve to increase the awareness about the plight of our elders, which, in turn, may hopefully improve their status. After all, older people in the United States certainly deserve the dignity and respect that is extended to their peers in many other nations.

REFERENCES

Hall, E. T., & Hall, M. R. (1990). *Understanding cultural differences.* Yarmouth, ME: Intercultural Press.
Samovar, L. A., & Porter, R. E. (1995). *Communication between cultures* (2nd ed.). Belmont, CA: Wadsworth.

Author Index

Subject Index

A

Acculturation, 85, 88
Acrolect, 71, 75
Across generations, 65, 97
Adaptation, 17, 18, 25, 83, 128
Advice, 24, 87, 90, 91, 100, 109, 111, 119, 140, 152, 190
African Americans, 15, 167, 219, 220, 223, 224
Aged Men, 193, 195, 196
Ageism, 24, 133, 150, 186
Agency, 45–47
Age-related identity, 13
Aging, 205, 206
Aging concerns, 27, 184
Alabama Information Age Task Force, 45
All My Children, 225, 228
Alzheimer Web, 50
American organizations, 123, 125, 126, 128, 129, 139, 140
Analytic induction, 104
Another World, 223, 225
Anxiety reduction, 18
Arab Americans, 65, 83
Argue, 87, 90, 92
Artificial intelligence, 53
As The World Turns, 218, 225, 228
Asian Americans, 15
Asian/Pacific Islander, 220, 223, 224
Assumption of flexibility, 18
Attitudinal change, 149
Authority, 85, 127, 137, 187

B

Basilect, 71
Biomedicine, 202, 208–211
Body, 204–206
Brothers Grimm, 183, 187

C

Care, 87, 90, 92
Caregiver thrust, 152
Caregivers, 145–150, 152–154, 156
Caregiving, 25, 29, 149, 153
Caretakers, 187, 192
Caucasian, 220, 223, 224
Celebrity endorsement, 236, 239, 240
Centrality of people, 17
Character profile, 221
Cherokee, 161, 167
Children, 106, 107, 111, 119
Church of Jesus Christ of Latter-Day Saints, 101
Church's Influence, 104, 113
Closer, 87, 90, 91
Cocooning, 47
Co-culture, 12–15, 28, 65, 145, 147, 150, *See also* Subculture
Cognitive schema, 14
Communicate, 73, 87, 90, 91
Computer
    confidence, 54
    literacy, 54
Confounding symbolism, 144, 145
Confronting stereotypes, 144, 145
Contemporary society, 165, 185, 206
Continuity theory, 30, 70
Cost, 84
Cross-cultural
    communication, 3, 5, 43, 123, 143, *See also* Intercultural communication
Cross-generational
    communication, 63, 67, 70, 72, 81, 83
    continuity, 65, 67, 72, 75
Cultural
    approach, 11, 13, 17
    beliefs, 125, 130
    continuity, 72, 73, 77
    differences, 245
    identity, 69

253